THE PRIVATE PRESSES

THE PRIVATE PRESSES

Colin Franklin

Dufour

To Helen Bentwich
who started these pleasures in
the old Caledonian Market
about thirty-five years ago

© Colin Franklin 1969

Published in the United States of America 1969 by Dufour Editions, Inc.,
Chester Springs, Pennsylvania 19425
Library of Congress Catalog Card Number: 69–18426

Designed by John Lewis
Set in 12 point Van Dijck
Printed in the Netherlands
by The Hooiberg Printing Co. Ltd, Epe

CONTENTS

LIST OF ILLUSTRATIONS

PLATES

ILLUSTRATIONS IN THE TEXT

6

ACKNOWLEDGMENTS

I am most grateful to Mr John Lewis for his care in criticizing and designing; to Dr Alan Fern, Mr John Dreyfus and Miss Elizabeth De Haas for help of various kinds on the way; to Mr David Lincoln for preparing the Bibliography and to Mr Christopher Sandford for generously allowing us to use his notes towards a final volume of Golden Cockerel bibliography; to Mr Peter Fischer for most expertly photographing pages from my books without giving me heart failure; to my children for enjoying or tolerating the comings and goings, and to my wife Charlotte who by sharing the fun has doubled it.

NOTE ON THE ILLUSTRATIONS

The private press books both in their letterpress and illustrations depended not only on the quality of the composition and the abilities of their artists, but also on fine presswork and fine paper. These latter qualities cannot possibly be shown by reproduction, so the illustrations in this book are no more than a reminder of the general *mise-en-page* and the character of these pages.

A Daniel Press title page

From a Daniel Press 'minor piece', done at Frome when the printer was fifteen years old.

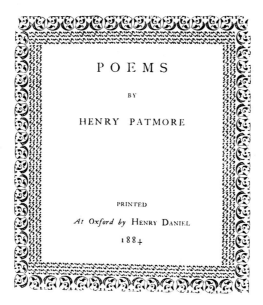

POEMS

BY

HENRY PATMORE

PRINTED

At Oxford by HENRY DANIEL

1884

A CHRISTMAS TALE

OF THE

OLDEN TIMES.

What is Love?   If earthly only,
  Like a meteor of the night :
Shining but to leave more lonely
  Hearts that hailed its transient light.

But when calm, refined and tender,
  Purified from passion's stain ;
Like the moon, in gentle splendour,
  Ruling o'er the peaceful main.

Colloquy with myself.

Kelmscott Press, *The Wood Beyond the World*, 1894. Double page opening, with a wood engraving after Burne-Jones.

THE WOOD BEYOND THE WORLD

Chapter I. Of Golden Walter and his father ✿ ✿

A WHILE AGO THERE WAS A YOUNG MAN DWELLING IN A GREAT AND goodly city by the sea which had to name Langton on Holm. He was but of five and twenty winters, a fair-faced man, yellow-haired, tall and strong; rather wiser than foolisher than young men are mostly wont; a valiant youth, & a kind; not of many words but courteous of speech; no roisterer, nought masterful, but peaceable and knowing how to forbear: in a fray a perilous foe, & a trusty war-fellow. His father, with whom he was dwelling when this tale begins, was a great merchant, richer than a baron of the land, a head-man of the greatest of the Lineages of Langton, and a captain of the Porte; he was of the Lineage of the Goldings, therefore was he called

Before the Holy One of Israel.
The singers also praised him with their voices;
With great variety of sounds was there made sweet melody.

Now bless ye the God of all,
Which everywhere doeth great things,
Which exalteth man from the womb,
And dealeth with him according to his will.
May he grant you wisdom,
And may there be peace among you.

With two nations is my soul vexed,
And the third is no nation:
The inhabitants of Samaria and Philistia,
And that foolish people that dwelleth in Sichem.

Compiler's Colophon.
Jesus, the son of Sirach of Jerusalem,
Hath written in this book wise instruction & apt proverbs,
Which he declared in the explanation of his heart,
And which he poured forth with understanding.
Blessed is he that shall be exercised in these things;
And he that layeth them up in his heart shall become wise.
For if he do them, he shall be strong to all things:
For the light of the Lord leadeth him.

From *Ecclesiasticus*, Ashendene Press, 1932. Initials in red, blue and green were drawn by Graily Hewitt and his two assistants. Subiaco type.

INTRODUCTION

The activity of the modern presses forms a circumscribed movement, its history clearly visible. There are always people who enjoy printing at home and doing it themselves; but several special qualities have placed this area outside the ordinary record of printing work. Dates are not satisfactory, but the recognizable start of it was in 1891 when William Morris printed his first book, his own *Story of the Glittering Plain*, at the Kelmscott Press. And one might say reasonably that it ended with the Second World War. Plenty of work is produced from private presses at the present day, experimental and traditional; but there is fair argument, beyond the convenience of this history, for saying that the *movement* ended with 1939. Kelmscott had caused an excitement and shown a way. After, others would follow and vary it and apply its example. Forms of the conventional book were tried and used to the limits of splendour and ability. Now, such materials are too expensive and nobody has so much time. The paper, ink, vellum and skill are missing; and so is the impulse, for renaissance means new birth and the newly born grow up.

The development is most easily followed in landmarks. The Daniel Press at Oxford started before Morris, as the private pleasure of Henry Daniel who became Provost of Worcester College and died just before his eighty-third birthday in 1919. His wife and daughters helped sometimes with the printing and Mrs Daniel used to draw initial letters and occasionally bind special copies of the books. The Daniel Press might have rested in the older and more ordinary history of private printing, had Daniel not shown such taste in the proportions of a page and used a type face which has its place in the revival of printing. There was also a peculiar interest and affection in the books printed, for the manner of them and for the circle of Daniel's friends – among them a young poet living on Boars Hill, Robert Bridges, much of whose early work first appeared in these small editions from Oxford.

The years of the Kelmscott Press were startlingly few considering the energy of its achievement – 1891 to 1898. Morris died in 1896 and the few books in preparation at that time were completed and issued by the Trustees. So it was the last burst of energy from a most diverse and effective life, and perhaps the finest. His own part in it is apparent everywhere, in its standards and qualities, techniques and materials and literary choice; but most visibly in his decorations. The pages of Kelmscott books are decorated with frames, borders, corners and initials from his hand, showing his affection for old German printing and for the patterns of flower and leaf which he loved to design. What Morris wrote of Gothic architecture was true of his Kelmscott Press: 'The cant of the beauty of simplicity (i.e. barrenness) did not afflict it.' We are always told that Emery Walker played a great part in the work of the Kelmscott Press; but since the pages of his own Doves Press were perfectly simple and unadorned, the constant advice he gave to Morris must have concerned composition, presswork, and other technical aspects of printing.

The next figure of importance was Charles Ricketts, whose Vale Press began to print books in 1896; but Ricketts had interested himself in type design and book reform for ten years before that. It was not so much that Morris thought up an idea which others followed, but that he, beginning to interest himself in the subject, being 'a giant among men', took charge of it. Ricketts and Shannon at the Vale Press produced a sort of transitional book, less grand and more commonsense than Kelmscott, easy to recognize in the Vale type which Ricketts designed with occasional and very beautiful ornamental borders. His initial letters are especially fine and the books are generally quite slender and modest in scope. Ricketts had theories about designing for metal, rather than pretending that letters in books could still be formed by pens in the way of calligraphy. His press closed with the issue of a bibliography in 1908 and it was the only one among them all to have managed a complete edition of Shakespeare's work. Three other important presses date from the nineties – Eragny, Essex House and Ashendene. Lucien Pissarro and his wife ran the Eragny Press, and its early books seem similar in style to Ricketts' – partly because they worked in close association, using the same type face and the same printing press. But his style was very different, especially in his taste for coloured illustration; and there is a homely, French, almost nursery quality in Eragny books, always on a small scale, which makes them a thoroughly endearing collection.

The Essex House Press was one of several activities of the Guild of Handicraft founded and led by C. R. Ashbee, first in the Mile End Road, later at Campden in Gloucestershire. The books and bindings were often excellent, experimental, generally small, but among them was the ambitious *Treatise on Metal Work* by Cellini and a folio *Prayer Book of King Edward the Seventh* for which Ashbee designed an original fount of type. The Press began in 1898, consciously to carry on the traditions of William Morris, and continued to issue books almost until the Great War; but the whole enterprise is perhaps most interesting in the context of Guild Socialism and the application of ideas which had been preached by Ruskin and Morris.

The Ashendene Press was different again from all these, the enterprise entirely of St John Hornby, a director of W. H. Smith. It followed a peaceful and splendid course for nearly the whole of the period of this history – beginning in 1896, continuing with a short break for the war, until the folio bibliography was issued in 1935. It is the most removed, untroubled and classical of them all, the most finished achievement.

And to complete the list of important English presses before the Great War there is the Doves Press, often considered the finest of all, partly through a very successful letter designed by Emery Walker for its use, and partly from its *magnum opus*, the Doves Bible in five tall volumes bound in white vellum. The Doves Press, with its austere and correct typography, its simple action accompanied by Cobden-Sanderson's high-flying spirit and aspiration, became a clear influence on twentieth-century book design. Its period was from 1901 to 1926 when the bibliography appeared.

Between the wars in England the work of three presses stands out, private and semi-private: the Gregynog Press in Wales, Shakespeare Head at Stratford and Oxford, and the Golden Cockerel at Waltham St Lawrence. The work of the Nonesuch Press is only briefly described in this book, because it may be regarded as the extension and practical application to commercial publishing of ideas which had developed from work in the private presses. There is no doubt about the importance and beauty of Nonesuch Press books.

11

These few comments trace the general development and leave out the entertaining historical details of private presses. They also leave out America and Germany, though something will be said about German and American presses. On the whole this can be recognized as an English or British movement, which inspired imitation and revivals of printing elsewhere. In its first stages at least, developments in America were imitative. When Thomas Mosher of Portland, Maine, produced his edition of *Empedocles on Etna*, it was advertised as 'an example of Kelmscott Press work similar in idea to Mr Mosher's last year's reprint of *Hand and Soul*. To this end what has seemed to us one of the choicest of the Kelmscott books – *Coleridge's Poems* – has been firmly drawn upon for borders, initials and format. The result, we believe, is a very charming approximation to the work accomplished by Morris, especially so as the paper used is the same as made for him.'

The Roycrofters in East Aurora, Erie County, New York, ran a kind of craft guild and printed attractive books of a pseudo-Morris sort. They advertised a Roycroft Inn at two dollars a day and among its pleasures were 'Specially Furnished De Luxe Rooms with private bath, namely, "Ruskin", "Morris" and "Emerson", four dollars a day for each person.' But, of course, there were such fine and original designers as Theodore Low De Vinne, Bruce Rogers and D. B. Updike. American presses have made their attractive and independent contribution.

The German presses are chiefly interesting for their influence in forming taste which German designers have most successfully absorbed into the work of commercial publishing – and that is outside the scope of these chapters; but the Bremer Press and the Cranach Press were sometimes close to the English movement, taking practical advice from Emery Walker and his associates. The most startling instance was in printing the Cranach Press *Hamlet*, which represents a kind of ministry of all the talents brought over from England to share in the work of type design, composing, illustration and scholarship.

The whole movement can be seen as an amateur rebellion. No two people agree about definitions of private presses – whether the work

12

was the chief thing, or its privacy. This argument can be by-passed, however, for a wider view of the movement as a shift from commerce to art. It was one of the facets of common revolt in the nineteenth century against mechanical standards and mass production, routine, acceptance, inherited values. Rebellions in art come from time to time and this was among them. Sometimes this is manifest in a desire to clean off the varnish from old pictures and see what lies beneath; that was much of the Pre-Raphaelite idea when the Brotherhood formed in 1848. Morris had something similar in mind through his knowledge of incunabula, which were strangely different and disconnected from work he saw in production.

The other half of the root lay in the fascination of minor arts, which rose in respect with ideas about the dignity of manual labour, pleasure in work and the soulless character of machines. To take people away from appalling industrial boredom, and educate them in tasks where pride was possible, was the first intention of Ruskin at his Guild of St George and Ashbee in his Guild of Handicraft. The arts and crafts movement gathered force and talent, held exhibitions, gained influence. Morris had always enjoyed working with his hands, learning how to do it himself rather than merely designing and instructing.

The physical book was excellent ground for this sort of cultivation, half-way between art and craft. Some printers had an established tradition of care and skill in the books they issued, but the field had not yet been entered by artists who took the whole process into their own hands: designing, printing, thinking it out again from the first ordering of materials to the design of new type faces. So the revival of printing was less a retreat from bad prevailing work, than a dicovery of new scope for the arts and crafts movement. The establishment of arts and crafts standards in books makes this a valid subject with its wider effect on book-production in publishing offices to the present day. And those ideals were described by Ricketts in his volume of Vale Press bibliography:

'The aim of the revival of fine printing is, I repeat, merely due to a wish to give a permanent and beautiful form to that portion of our literature which is secure of permanence. By a permanent form I do not mean merely sound as to paper and ink, etc.; I mean permanent in the sense that the work reflects that conscious aim towards beauty and order which are ever interesting elements in themselves.'

The subject is nicely limited and deserves attention. There was common agreement in the eighteen-nineties that the Kelmscott Press, and the edition of Chaucer as its masterpiece, represented the most splendid book production since printing began. That view has carried through seventy years, and now we can add another, which looks ahead and decides simply that we shall not see its like again. We shall have superb printing, but new techniques are likely to be found for it. Forms of plastic will be discovered, with the qualities of vellum. Miracles will happen, but this particular burst of skill in the old craft of book printing seems likely to have been the last of its kind. Between 1891 and 1940, a period played itself out and expressed itself thoroughly. Its influence has carried into the production of trade books. From flourish to simplicity, private designs to commonly available book faces, home press to guild endeavour, hand illumination to machine printing, it was all attempted and worked over. Kinds of paper, ink, vellum, binding – each facet of a book had experiment and improvement. It was the last cry from a time when handicraft could be practised without overtones of archaism and absurdity. They thought they were making new orders of society, not retreating or clinging to the irrecoverable.

Perhaps the making of superb books needs some defence – though the first effort might be to see again the spirit in which they were made and to banish the false overlay of modern saleroom prices. They were produced for joy and with delight, and sold for quite modest prices. A few would commonly be printed on vellum and sold expensively, for collectors and anybody with taste and cash for them – as it had been usual, earlier, to produce small numbers of 'large paper' copies for those who liked their books limited and numbered. Otherwise, nothing that came from the Kelmscott Press was unapproachably rare or extravagant. The published price of the Keats, for instance, was thirty shillings. The Chaucer folio was issued at twenty guineas, but always stood by itself apart.

So if we see these as simple examples of work from people who aimed higher in book production, we can read and see them in the right way. One can often envy the paperback mind – the commonsense argument, all that matters about a book is to read what the author wrote. It suggests strong powers of concentration and blindness to conditions which exist outside the reading brain. But reading habits often contradict that feeling, even among the paperbackers. Most of us like a book in pleasant surroundings – sitting at an open window, by a river or on the rocks. A fact of life is that the mind likes to wander and absorb, even beyond the author's meaning. And if some persistent absorbent is there – the sea, a summer breeze – we like it, are comforted and it seems to help with the reading. Now, the argument for finely made books extends easily from there: the mind which needs absorption beyond the meaning of the printed page, will find it in the beauty and good sense of the overtones of the page. The river's function, the wind's job, is performed by the fitness of margin, the texture of paper. A fine binding is as good as a fine view. The whole slack of reading experience is taken up by the book.

Of course, for clever dons this is a lot of nonsense. They can clamour for their Wittgenstein in paperback and be all brain. For the rest who like peace and a slow pace in reading, this subject is valid.

Historical perspectives in movements of this sort go oddly wrong. By praising the new, the merits in whatever it replaced are misjudged. In 1859 Morris and Philip Webb plotted the building of a brick villa at Abbey Wood near Bexley Heath, which they called Red House because it ignored current fashions in plaster stucco. The books about it suggest that this was a revolution, leaving the red brick exposed like that; and they ignore the streets of red brick and the hundreds of red brick country vicarages which Morris and Webb and anyone else could see in each day of their lives. When Morris wanted to furnish his rooms he looked round and, as everyone knows, decided no good furniture was being made, so he designed his own. His admirers pay highly now for the treasures he refused to have in his home. So also with the books. We are very glad to have and to handle what Morris was rejecting. It would be senseless for us to start by an assumption that standards were as poor as he thought. Several roots nourished the Kelmscott Press – ideas from the arts and crafts movement, Walker's scholarship, Morris's affection for the fif-

teenth century and his youthful gaiety about mastering a method –
in the same way as some people enjoy pulling their cars to pieces.
And above these, or uniting them, was a thought he pleasantly expressed in his introduction to Ruskin's chapter on the Nature of
Gothic when he printed it at the Kelmscott Press; that 'the hallow-
ing of labour by art is the one aim for us at the present day'.

In the quality and character of the printing, its taste and merit,
nobody can lay down the law. Whether the use of a hand press was
aesthetically important, or mere employment of an available tool;
whether the type faces were sensibly designed and which had its
influence on future work; whether ornament was used successfully;
whether the whole affair expressed socialist ideals or, in Morris's
phrase in another context, 'the swinish luxury of the rich' – all these
can be debated. Mr Sean Jennett wrote in a letter to me:

'Even those books widely acclaimed as masterpieces of the hand press
are not usually examples of surpassing technique. What is appreciated
in these works is not, I hope, the method or the perfection of printing, for these are really immaterial, but the personality, the genius,
the force of the man behind the design and nature of the printed
work.'

Anyone can feel, for instance, the affection which went into a Daniel
Press book. The ghosts they carry, the affection and care, are their
endearing qualities apart from skill in printing. The rest can be discussed later and in its chapter.

THE PRIVATE PRESSES

THE DANIEL PRESS AND NINETEENTH-CENTURY OXFORD

The Daniel Press forms a pleasant bridge across from one to another kind of private printing. Through all the five centuries of printing there have been private presses, run by independent spirits who for different reasons chose to make their own books rather than go through usual channels. The motive might be pleasure, secrecy, propaganda or art, and perhaps profit too. The core of it, in ideas or design, was generally self-expression and one's own taste. The private press is for private taste. It had a dilettante quality. At the end of the nineteenth century all the bias went towards art in the design and production of these books.

Daniel joined two moods, belonging to each. One earlier tradition, from the hundred years before him, came from the antiquaries and country gentlemen. Walpole had enjoyed showing his press to visitors at Strawberry Hill. He employed professional printers and had no severe notions about craftsmanship, but books from his press have an agreeably private character and were very adequately produced in the standard of his day. The first among them, two of Grey's odes, printed for Dodsley, seems not much unlike the Foulis press edition of Grey issued at the same time in Glasgow. Caslon type was the rule at Strawberry Hill, Wilson's types held sway in Glasgow, but both books take the same formal attitude, tall and slender quartos with large well-spaced letters. His third production, very much a private affair from the pleasures of a sound library was Walpole's *Catalogue of the Royal and Noble Authors of England*, with lists of their Works; a curiously snobbish and futile form of reference book, but enjoyable for the author to put together. The title page bears an engraving of his Gothic house. The setting and design are sound and professional, the paper and press work less than adequate – but so were most books in his time. Strawberry Hill did not rise above them. The date, 1758, marks Baskerville's great period of Milton and the Cambridge Bible. Walpole's press never achieved wonders in skilful printing, preferring 'all the delightful negligence of a gentleman'. Yet he received a happy compliment

19

from Italy. His novel *The Castle of Otranto* was printed by the Bodoni Press at Parma in 1796; and rather ungraciously he wrote to a friend, 'I am glad you did not get a Parmesan *Otranto*. A copy is come so full of faults that it is not fit to be sold here.'

Then there was Sir Thomas Phillips with his chaotic Middle Hill press, recording and circulating some minor discoveries and manuscript pieces which formed part of his library; more bibliographical curiosity than printing art. Later again, at the end of the Napoleonic Wars, Sir Egerton Brydges ran an interesting press at Lee Priory, his house in Kent. It appears that Brydges, an unsuccessful poet, chose this way to enter the book world; but pleasant editions of other poets came from his press and his daughter married a soldier called Edward Quillinan who had in common with his father-in-law this quality of writing poor verses. There are many ways up Parnassus and his walk took a different route; for after the death of his first wife he married Wordsworth's daughter Dorothy.

The Lee Priory Press, more than Strawberry Hill, marks a conscious endeavour towards fine printing. In 1820, near the end of its time, Brydges and his printer had the happy idea of gathering into one volume all the wood engravings which had been used in seven active years – of making, indeed, a kind of bibliography of engravings employed at Lee Priory. But instead of pages of mere pictures with no literary setting, they asked for poems to illustrate the illustrations. As Quillinan wrote in his apologetic Preface – set in a vigorous and large Scotch Roman – 'The embellishments in most books are secondary to the printed composition: in this, with very few exceptions, the reverse is the fact.' But he did quite well and the *Woodcuts and Verses* printed in one hundred copies in 1820 make a thoroughly endearing book. The house looks most peaceful and splendid in several excellent wood engravings and Quillinan wrote his affectionate *Farewell to Lee Priory:*

> Adieu, the pensive still retreat,
> The woodland paths, the classic dome,
> Where float the mental visions sweet,
> And Fancy finds her genial home.

20

The Wanderer oft, where'er he roves,
Dear cherished scene, shall think on thee,
In Memory's glass review thy groves,
Thy green luxuriant pastures see.

The two printers at Lee Priory were John Warwick and John Johnson, but in 1818 Johnson had left to spend the days preparing his learned and delightful printing manual and history which he called *Typographia*. Skill and knowledge of a rare sort went into the books from Lee Priory.

The pleasure Daniel gave was akin to this, though he did most of the work himself and in married life his family shared it. In himself he combined Egerton Brydges and John Johnson; the combination of taste in books with ability to print them. Though he was about the same age as William Morris, as a printer he linked the earlier and later periods fairly evenly; for if we are to take his childhood hobby half as seriously as Falconer Madan did, he became a printer in 1845 at the age of nine. He died as Provost of Worcester College in 1919.

And we can agree with Madan, because Daniel seems to have been a fortunate child in finding his proper enthusiasm very young. There is true taste, of the kind we connect with his mature printing, in the little pieces from early years at his father's vicarage in Frome. The title page from a Christmas poem by his uncle Cruttwell, printed at Frome in 1851 when the printer was fifteen, shows a fastidious design, the condensed capitals for CHRISTMAS well leaded and the subtitle in black letters; a classical urn stands for colophon, above the serious phrase 'Imprinted at the private press of H. Daniel'. The same is true of the next year's offering, by another Cruttwell uncle, *Sir Richard's Daughter: A Christmas Tale of the Olden Time*. Here the title in three lines is varied with deliberate care, with the middle line in black letters; and at the bottom in three lines, 'Excudebat H. Daniel: Trinity Parsonage, Frome, 1852'. This is a pleasant little book, quite recognizably in Daniel's style: small, square, discreet, with large margins, the typographical focus rather low and central than high up the page in the orthodox way. It has blue paper wrappers, as most of the later books did, and its appearance as a small Christmas offering is also in sympathy with the character of his press at Oxford. Typographically, there was from the start a Tudor taste about Daniel's printing, as Herbert Warren of Magdalen wrote in his poem:

> For you enrich the poet-shrining shelf
>   With daintiest treasures old and new, and give,
>   In many a nice and justly-ordered page,
>   Back to mechanic days of haste and pelf
>   The tasteful Tudor touch.

A page from a Tudor book, Jaggard's edition of *The Passionate Pilgrim*, 1599, is remarkably similar to Daniel's manner; the sonnet in small type on its small page, with thick bands of type flowers above and below – more flowers than Daniel would have chosen, but the influence is there. And this shows independence from Morris who kept his admiration for German and Italian typography of the fifteenth century. It was the difference between the bias of a designer and a scholar, for both he and Morris shared the two qualities; but design possessed Morris and a taste for Elizabethan poetry remained in Daniel.
It is almost impertinent to write about the Daniel Press, because Madan did so very well – but that was nearly fifty years ago. His remains a flawless bibliography, with some charming essays and poems by friends of the printer. Madan, Bodley's librarian, was a faintly fussy bibliographer, noting the qualities of his own book in Addenda issued later. He says it seems to have six unusual features, and lists seven. All is seen in bibliographical terms – the book has a rambling poem in tribute from Masefield, and Madan observes 'the *editio princeps* of a poem by John Masefield has been noted'. Daniel did a Greek exercise in 1857 at Frome, and this is welcomed as 'the only separate edition of the Epistles to the Seven Churches in Greek'! But it is an entirely enjoyable bibliography, printed in the Bodleian on Daniel's press in the spirit of Daniel's books. All the little ephemera from Frome and Oxford are faithfully described, and about them he writes with humorous affection:
'Unfortunately there seems to be no dignified and yet suitable term

for these waifs and strays, here termed Minor Pieces. One thinks of λείψανα, Reliquiae, Quisquiliae, Minima, Fragments, Notices, Papers, Scraps, Remanents, Fly-sheets, Broadsides, Fugitive Pieces: but the right word is as elusive as the corresponding one for Magic Lantern. They are what remain when the majestic Car of the professional Cataloguer has passed by and left them strewn on the wayside. The occupant of the Car calls them succinctly and comprehensively Trash.'

We see the Daniel Press a little differently now, if only because part of its charm rests with his friends, including Madan, who were writing this book, and with their work, and Oxford of 1880 to 1900. It carves off Oxford, which itself was carved out from other English life, and displays one civilized small community there. Of course the fast trains ran to London all through Daniel's Oxford period, but the great changes in mood had not come. North Oxford was built already, lodging houses spread along the Iffley Road then as now, Fellows of Colleges married, religious orthodoxy staggered about – but enough of the old life survived. Some quality from that earlier Oxford is in the poems, essays and reminiscences which appeared from the Daniel press.

The other quality, giving Daniel some right to be honoured as a pioneer in the revival of printing, was his use of Fell type. This is a slightly complex story and should be looked at carefully. The facts are set out clearly in Appendix A of Madan's book.

But one can overstate the connection between a printer's reputation and his use of type face. Pickering is partly remembered for the revival of Caslon types in the books he published after 1844 – but his earlier books, with a little transitional letter, are equally delightful and the same neat taste is present there. Hornby was a fine printer without the Subiaco type, and Daniel without Fell. But, of course, the discovery delighted him and gave new excitement to the idea of his printing in Oxford; it suited his manner and helped to form his style. The pleasure of the Elizabethan and seventeenth-century type ornaments dived straight into his literary taste and provided printing tools with which he felt at ease.

Most successful reforms in book making are returns rather than revolutions. That was true of Charlemagne's reform of calligraphy, Jenson's roman letter, Caslon's return to good Dutch letter-shapes, Pickering's return to Caslon, Daniel's return to Fell, Morris's to Ratdolt or Jenson. The interesting ambiguity at Oxford is that nobody seems to know who fished out the Fell matrices from the Clarendon Press archives; and those who provided them seemed happy to leave the trials to Daniel and let him experiment, rather than risk a dashing innovation in their own books.

There was nothing grand about the Daniel Press. Nothing could be further from, say, the Kelmscott Chaucer. And probably this was not from lack of resources, because that might one way or another have been managed. If the word had gone round that Daniel wanted to print a bible, there could well have been support and adequate sub-scription. But there is no hint that he ever wished for such gestures, or wrestled with these ambitions. The scope and taste of all the books is quiet, a little off the main road, as his college was. But we do find harmony of design with subject, sympathy between author and printer. It is this apt and happy union which still makes an impression.

His books have to be held and read. Sometimes there is no obvious art in the typography – as with *Our Memories*, the fruit of an enjoyable idea from the eighteen-eighties. Daniel, settled then as a Fellow of Worcester, had the notion that some of his elderly Oxford friends might be persuaded to write short recollections of Oxford as they remembered it fifty and sixty years before; and as they would be recalling famous old characters of that epoch, the essays would recall ways and people of Oxford in the late eighteenth century. He invited, they accepted; and people who might in those diffident days have feared to write publicly at length on such personal themes, were quite happy to set some hours aside for the pleasure of a small group. Daniel printed these pieces from time to time as they came to him, and sent them out to friends. They were not printed for sale. Twenty issues appeared in this way between 1888 and 1893, and two more in 1895 to start a second series which went no further. Sensible readers kept this pleasant gift, and bound it as a book when the time came, but it is hard to find now. No great typographical grace is evident,

24

but an abundance of good tales makes up for that. As Madan puts it, they were 'not ordinary authors, least of all journalists, but Heads of Houses, Canons of Christ Church, and the like, and men who do not write much'. Two examples may show the character of this collection – stories agreeable rather than riotous, of habits in the old Oxford. Several of the pieces have memories of Mo Griffiths, a peculiar Fellow of Merton obviously much prized for eccentricity in his own day. G. C. Brodrick recalled an incident one evening in 1842:

'In the Long Vacation of 1842, Dr Wootten, then in the forefront of Oxford medical practice, came to dine with us in the Common room. Dr W. was a man wholly devoted to his practice, and knowing nothing of the pleasures of the table. Mr G. had ordered a most ample dinner, and according to the only code of hospitality known to his generation, he felt bound to urge his guest to eat five times more than his wont. The generous host was vexed by the guest's frequent refusals. He broke out: "You have made a most admirable fast, Dr Wootten." "Oh, Mr G., I am bound to practise what I preach." "And pray, sir, what do you preach?" "I preach, Mr G., *Eat and leave off hungry*." "*Eat and leave off hungry*, Dr W.? Only to think that I should have lived so far into this 19th century, before I learnt that the object of eating was to leave off hungry! But," he added in a changed voice, "Dr W., why not wash and leave off dirty?" '

And Edmund Ffoulkes remembered Ward of Balliol. 'His rooms in Balliol latterly faced Broad Street on the ground floor, and in summer he always slept with his windows open. A Balliol man and old school-fellow of mine, half a wag and half a rake, never went in by the lodge when Ward thus slept. He would come in at any hour of the night or morning, vault in at the window and pass through only to hear how loud Ward snored. Sometimes if he had nothing on hand to keep him out he would vault out at Ward's window and then in at the Porter's lodge, and see how many times he could do this without eliciting any remark from the Porter. At last the Porter would rub his eyes and say "Why, Sir, I think I let you in once before." "Oh, my dear fellow, you are dreaming," he would reply: and then went off to bed laughing boisterously all the way.'

Most of the Daniel books were planned with immense care. Within their scope one looks for small type, flower ornaments, and Mrs Daniel's decorations most delicately executed in red ink on the black page. These might be lightly sketched initial letters, with tendrils curling into the type below, or white letters on a red background, or in Margaret Woods' lyrics, a beautiful miniated initial letter showing a meadow and the Oxford skyline. These are pleasures which cannot be repeated over very long runs and one hundred or a hundred and twenty-five formed the average Daniel Press edition.

Mrs Daniel was also an accomplished binder, learning the craft under Katharine Adams. Her embroidery bindings were remembered, and suit the books well – as for a copy of the little Blake *Songs of Innocence*, embroidered linen between slender decorated borders of crimson calf which include the title; or a vellum binding of Binyon's poems in the Katharine Adams manner, a regular pattern of fleurs de lys over the covers and spine.

As the Daniel books generally appeared in a peculiarly awkward kind of paper cover jutting out beyond the printed page, there was often a chance for imaginative binding. Purists and the pious liked to preserve this outer paper, but that was never easy. In a bookshelf the lower edge is crushed if the book stands up, and that tends to happen in a box too. Binders could treat the covers reverently and bind too large for the book itself; or, more commonly – and according to common sense – the overlap would be cropped and these covers treated like half titles in the bound book. In any case, it is not rare to find very attractive bindings for Daniel books and those who decline them are irrational snobs among bibliophiles. Bindings by 'Morley of Oxford' are easily recognizable; well designed and thoroughly sound, with beautiful marbled end-papers. 'Maltby, Oxford' is another familiar signature. It is clear that these little books were treasured in the eighteen-nineties by those who knew them. Major Abbey possessed two of them most sumptuously and excessively bound by the Club Bindery in Chicago for Robert Hoe. After penetrating the splendid package there is really very little book. I have also seen several of these books bound quite simply by Katharine Adams.

The bindings by Morley of Oxford are perhaps most appropriate and successful, apart from the obvious aptness of Mrs Daniel's own work. And for a volume bringing together the various qualities of this press, I would choose among all the Daniel books I have seen, a copy of *Poems* by Henry Patmore, issued in 1884 and bound by Morley. The varied use of flower ornaments is particularly happy. Mrs Daniel rubricated the first initial letter with delicate care. The small pica roman fount of the Fell type, still early days for its use, appears very well with wide margins on the white Whatman paper; Madan calls this size 'the favourite type'. The introductory pages are in small pica italic. And apart from all this, just equally important in a Daniel book, there is poignancy in this slender collection of poems by Coventry Patmore's son who had died of tuberculosis a year before, aged twenty-three. The father wrote for the book a moving little note which ends:

'Once when I had been commending his verses, he laughed and said that I should perhaps be known to future times as "the Father of Patmore". Had he lived his jest would probably have become prophecy.' The sorrow of the time is communicated by the printer, merely through the special affection and variation of his work. The invalid poems are deceptively slight. One is called *On a Tree in a 'Wilderness'*.

> From where I sit I often see
> A certain tall, misshapen tree,
> And, when the wind moans from the West,
> It rocks much more than do the rest;
> It tosses its unhappy head
> Now this way, now that way instead,
> Now tries to catch a passing cloud,
> Now almost breaks with being bowed;
> And all the others bow and nod,
> And seem to think it wild and odd.
> That ugly indecorous tree
> I like, because it seems like me.

The double pica Fell italic was a fine large letter, used only twice

27

apart from incidental pieces – once quite appropriately in the *Peace Ode* by Bridges, though that was a poor poem which reads embarrassingly now, and, its first appearance, in a pamphlet which brought new year greetings to the printer's daughters from the President of Magdalen at the end of 1895.

> Mistress Rachel, Mistress Ruth,
> Dancing down the ways of youth

could feel happy that this unimportant piece is one of the best examples of their father's printing, and it is a pity we do not have other poems in this splendid italic. But Daniel preferred intimacy and this, apart from the irony of its first outing, might have been a little formal or monumental for his ordinary choice.

A family quality remains in these books time and again. This aspect of the private press is more true here than in any other. May Morris helped a little at Kelmscott, Esther and Lucien Pissarro worked together, but Mrs Daniel and the two girls share in the work or give a purpose to the books. The best known book from the press had a family inspiration: *Garland of Rachel*. It took the happy form of a greeting to Rachel on her first birthday, eighteen poems as an offering from friends of her parents. The friends included Austin Dobson, Andrew Lang, John Addington Symonds, Robert Bridges, Lewis Carroll, Edmund Gosse, F. W. Bourdillon and W. E. Henley – so it becomes a pleasant volume from its content and printing equally; and as only thirty-six were printed, one would be lucky to find a copy. The old Frome press was still in use, and this is the first complex instance of the use of Fell type. Madan has a special word here for Mrs Daniel's skill in rubrication: 'the capital letters in red which she supplies at the beginning of each poem are decked with tendrils which in some cases stray at will into and among the words, with beautiful effect.'

But in future years some of the most attractive little books would be set and printed entirely by Mrs Daniel and the children. They tended to use one or other of the small founts – small pica italic as for the *Royal Guest* at Christmas 1900, or brevier roman in the successful

MISTRESS Rachel, Mistreß Ruth,

Dancing down the ways of youth

By the dancing rills of truth,

Fairy muſic lead your meaſure,

Bring you to the hidden treaſure

And the oracles of ſooth,

Bid all ſprites of evil vaniſh,

Gnome and Kobold ban and baniſh,

Charm each dragon head uncouth !

Daniel Press, from Herbert Warren's New Year Poem, to the printer's daughters. This was his first use of the large Fell italic.

little edition of *Ode on the Morning of Christ's Nativity*, set up and printed by Mrs Daniel for Christmas 1894. It was quite common since Daniel's boyhood for a book to be prepared at Christmas time, or for a charitable occasion such as a sale of work. Then the early arrivals would be delighted to find copies of a new book from Daniel's press, and the late would regret they had all been sold.

Two Herrick examples show this charitable and intimate side of the press very nicely. In 1891 a little book of Herrick's poems was prepared for sale on behalf of St Thomas's Orphanage at Oxford. The sale appears to have been on 19 November, and a short doggerel was set up in the formal black letter of the Fell type as a kind of prospectus, presumably to advertise the book among early arrivals – handed out to them as they came in at the gate:

> Stay /buy my flowers
> > While yet you may/
> A few short hours/
> > They pass away/
>
> Buy caps and Shawls/
> > And shoes & socks/
> Buy bags and balls/
> > Buy dolls & frocks/
>
> To make an end/
> > Buy Herricks page/
> And so be-friend
> > The Orphanage/
>
> You must lay down/
> > To fill our till/
> A good Half-crown/
> > Or more at will/

And a proof of this leaflet exists, with one extra verse

> You munch
> > Your lunch/
> We work
> > Like Turk.

Madan says these words were 'made up by Mr Daniel as he composed.' It seems to me more likely that the daughters set that verse, and left it for their father to pull the proofs.

The other little Herrick book, companion to this, appeared next month at Christmas time. It took the form of a Christmas greeting from Rachel and Ruth to thirty-six of their friends, whose names are printed over three pages and include Elizabeth Bridges, Frank Madan, Nigel Stebbing. Sixty copies were issued, and numbered. A poem, presumably by Daniel, precedes the title page:

> Who then are these, with smooth round face,
>   With merry eyes undimmed by tears,
>   Long locks unbleached by tedious years,
> With limbs so free, so full of grace?
>
> Children are we, on tiptoe stand,
>   Forerunners of a world to come;
>   Curious we gaze from out our home,
> And sport upon an unknown strand.
>
> Ah children! riddles not yet read,
>   In you is hid our future fate,
>   The Masters of our coming state; –
> May God pour wisdom on your head!

It is easier to let Daniel himself represent an older Oxford, than see him in an everyday context over that period. Bits and pieces from tributes in the bibliography come nearest. In 1881 when he hoped to become Provost, news came that the election had gone against him. 'I am not to be Provost,' he said to his wife when the telegram came from London in 1881; 'I think I should like a pipe,' and he said no more. We are told that at the end of his ten years as Proctor, 'he made an epoch in the little academic world as the first to dare to give gaiety to a dull and dead convention by the novelty and humour of his Latin oration, a very echo in wit and Latinity of Erasmus himself'. The academic world would be smaller now, and gaiety less. Another friend recalled 'the vision of a tall fair man mounted on a tall horse and followed by a big dog, riding rapidly up Beaumont Street and round the corner of the Taylor Building, a proceeding less hazardous in those days than it would be now'. He was writing in 1920. Margaret Woods, whose poems were twice printed at the press, remembered affectionately the vacation suppers looking over Worcester Garden from the Provost's lodge which kept something of the character of a country house; and peaceful summer expeditions in his houseboat far above Oxford.

There is no doubt that in 1969 some of the poets, and the kind of poem, printed by Daniel are under-valued. It was the period of Beardsley and *The Yellow Book*, but Daniel and his friends were not likely to befriend and encourage nineties' decadence. The poetry of Binyon, of Richard Watson Dixon and Robert Bridges is due to be heard again. Minor poets of the press – Sara Coleridge, Herbert Warren, F. W. Bourdillon – deserve to be remembered. Dixon's lyrics are absurdly neglected. Here is a short poem by Sara Coleridge, from her collection called *Fancy's Following*, printed in 1896.

> The clouds had made a crimson crown
> Above the mountains high.
> The stormy sun was going down
> In a stormy sky.
>
> Why did you let your eyes so rest on me,
> And hold your breath between?
> In all the ages this can never be
> As if it had not been.

These were young poets of that day, not conservative and established voices. Among them all, Bridges was nearest to Daniel and nine of his books were issued by the press – counting four sections of *Shorter Poems*, issued at different times, as one book; from his play *Prometheus the Firegiver* in 1883, to the *Peace Ode* written on the conclusion of the Three Years' War in 1903. This included work of great beauty, especially in the three volumes of *Poems* (1884), *The Growth of Love* (1889 and 1890) and *Shorter Poems* (1893–4). The reprint of *The Growth of Love* and the volume of *Shorter Poems* were both in the Fell black letter, slightly difficult to read and defended by Madan for an in-

32

teresting reason: 'the black letter giving just the check to hasty reading which thoughtful and elaborate poems need'. Those poems are not too complex, but some moving sonnets from *The Growth of Love* are both difficult and concise:

> They that in play can do the thing they would
> Having an instinct throned in reason's place
> – And every perfect action hath the grace
> Of indolence or thoughtless hardihood –
> These are the best: yet be there workmen good
> Who lose in earnestness control of face
> Or reckon means and rapt in effort base
> Reach to their ends by steps well understood.
>
> Me whom thou sawst of late strive with the pains
> Of one who spends his strength to rule his nerve –
> Even as a painter breathlessly who strains
> His scarcely moving hand lest it should swerve –
> Behold me now free from the care that stains
> And master of the art I choose to serve.

The poem was of Bridges and his love. It might have applied to Daniel and his printing.

Daniel remains an independent figure, outside fashionable taste and movements, beyond the current influences in his printing. His manner was not touched by the common faults for which enterprising printers in his time were criticized; medievalism, escape from the present, or mere scholarship. Sir Basil Blackwell, who made a splendid contribution to private press work, has referred in conversation to 'manufactured rarities'. Daniel Press books are all rare, some of them excessively so, but never for a device in collecting or selling; they are rare for us, because they were made for his friends. Some outsiders treasured these books, and after 1884 he printed for sale; no reason why the thing should not pay for itself; but nothing was offered expensively or for glory. The published price of Binyon's poems, to take one at random, was ten shillings. *Garland of Rachel* was not sold.

33

There is an indefinable affection in the Daniel Press, which might fail if one looked too carefully or tried hard to analyse. A favourite book from the press is a small collection of carols, *Christmas 1897*, sold in aid of St Thomas's Orphanage, the printing by Mrs Daniel who said she 'found them very difficult to do'. I found this in New York one autumn day, opened it in my room high above Gramercy Park and the distant noises of traffic. The carols were beautifully bound by Morley. I started to read, Christmas not far off:

> Midnight scarcely passed and over,
> Drawing to this holy morn,
> Very early, very early Christ was born.

And I was hearing not hooters far below from the New York rush hour, but voices in Worcester College Chapel sixty-eight years before. That is the magic of the Daniel Press.

THE KELMSCOTT PRESS AND WILLIAM MORRIS

The Kelmscott Press, in any obvious way of type and decoration, had slender influence upon the twentieth-century book but it was far and away the most splendid of all private presses; not a pioneer, as scholars eagerly point out, not the greatest influence, but quite without peer. It is a paradox.

This matter of influence can be stressed beyond sense. Morris never meant to make models for others; the joy of a private press is indifference to public demand. Below the surface his printing had profound importance, but those who copied it in the decade after his death produced inadequate or ugly books, and escape into a simpler manner was wise. The influence of such new standards as the Kelmscott Press discovered, even if economically they cannot be imitated, remains with us.

To look at the books now, comparing them with our own, serves nobody. The style of a Doves Press book lies closer to us, we can be at once more at ease with it – as it is also nearer to what went before. Visually, there is no more distance between a Pickering book and the Doves Press, than between that and Nonesuch or the Folio Society. Morris, in his books and ways, looked more notably different.

But the position of the Kelmscott Press is such that our view of it does not much matter. Criticism of those books now has no more lasting effect than Morris's hard words about St Pauls Cathedral. The response of his contemporaries weighs more heavily, and from the start the press was received into the place it has held ever since in spite of commonsense criticism.

Collectors are supposed to be contemptible people who keep public treasures in private hands – but no fine book is familiarly passed about in the way which might be sensible for pictures or china. It ought to be kept clean. Museums are the worst, for then nobody sees them. Libraries, like book shops, keep their best stuff hidden away and the librarian is no less possessive than a private collector. On the whole, no better place exists for them. Books cannot be in display cases, open, without suffering damage. Collectors look at their things with love, preserve them worthily and show them to those who can appreciate. Luckily, most of the Kelmscott books are likely now to be in the hands of collectors. A foolish legend grows from this about their futility through staying untouchable. That is of course no fault of Morris or his press, which produced such work that it is treasured and preserved now. Fourteenth-century illuminated psalters would not now be used for the common work of prayer.

Worse still, they were so much admired that binders used all their skill and then hid it in protective boxes. Morris had no special interest in bindings, though earlier he had designed a couple for Fairfax Murray. He might have come round to them. His design for the Chaucer bindings executed by the Doves Bindery suggests that his style might then have led back towards a taste for early German work. One can very well imagine it, and our shelves might have a few awkward treasures with silver clasps and elaborate keys. But he died too soon. Doves bindings upon Kelmscott books have particular attraction from the joy which appears when the artist knows a job deserves his best. Cobden-Sanderson used to complain about the poor books his clients often asked him to bind splendidly. Kelmscott books suited his designs wonderfully well. As Douglas Cockerell and McLeish both worked for him, their bindings also are highly appropriate for the press. Private and commercial binders of that renaissance were glad to receive a Kelmscott book – Sarah Prideaux, the Guild of Women Binders, Cedric Chivers, Zaehnsdorf, Rivière. The propriety of it may be doubtful, the rich results are manifest.

If we look to the purposes of the Kelmscott Press it is easy to see why it stood alone. Morris's eye was always upon the first years of printing, the second half of the fifteenth century; not for queer antiquarian reasons, but because he knew, and few deny, that the finest printed books were also the earliest. And instead of looking back wistfully, which would have been the sentimental attitude, regretting that nothing of that sort could be done in his decadent day, he set about showing that the thing could be managed; that if type and paper, ink and the art of it were built from foundations again the printed book could become as fine as ever before. It suggests a faith in his present moment, not helpless admiration for the irrecoverable past.

36

And this attitude lifted him clear of others who might have slightly similar ambitions. The phrase 'private press' carries simpler and modest overtones – doing what one likes, perhaps with art, as an amateur. But only he had the grand notion, for which 'revival of printing' is an inadequate phrase, because 'I have always been a great admirer of the calligraphy of the Middle Ages, and of the earlier printing which took its place'. The general and practical research into the right materials, a typical Morris operation, was his entirely and the other printers benefited from his results. His efforts with Batchelor to find the right paper, and struggles with the English ink makers to discover the appropriate ink – they showed no interest, and he had to use ink from Jaenecke of Hanover at last, who was prepared to make what he wanted – are part of the familiar Kelmscott story. Returning in imagination to the late eighteen-eighties, the grand idea of starting from foundations must have looked impossibly difficult or arrogant. It showed startling energy and originality. To find the old ways of stained glass or carpet-making made sense; but breaking into the thoroughly efficient and expert printing industry must have seemed a little ridiculous.

As with furniture, his objections need to be understood. He would have agreed – his disciple Sparling, secretary of the Press, agrees anyway – that fine books had been produced during the nineteenth century by the publisher Pickering and his printer Charles Whittingham. In his own time, with Jacobi who had taken over the Whittinghams' press at Chiswick, Morris had made several experiments in book production and design – careful editions of the *House of the Wolfings* and the *Roots of the Mountains* in the eighties, and a cranky reversion to a Caxton type in setting a few copies of his *Story of Gunnlaug the Worm-Tongue*.

But the wider climate which brought Morris into printing was the Arts and Crafts Exhibition Society, with emphasis upon the level merit of each part of an object – not merely the high skill of one quality in a book – and this, he could see, is where the grand Victorian books went astray. The examples offered by historians now, as showing the way to the Kelmscott Press, do nothing of the sort; they italicize the urgency which Morris felt to do something different.

Such grand works of illustration as Owen Jones's *Grammar of Ornament*, or the books which Henry Shaw illuminated with his flair for medieval letters and ornament, are interesting instances of a scholarly Victorian concern with the medieval. They form a link with Pre-Raphaelite taste but have nothing to do with Morris's view of what a book should be. No special care shows itself in the ink or paper of books which Owen Jones decorated. Pickering never gave a thought to the whole control of a book in all its details, which had been a workshop condition of early printed books.

Morris was generally blind to the merits of the eighteenth century. Bulmer and Bensley cared deeply and publicly about 'fine printing' and showed most of Morris's symptoms in the subject – impatience for new type faces, special paper, carefully balanced illustration. In two notable examples, Bewick worked for Bulmer in the same spirit as Burne-Jones for Morris. He had no regard either for Baskerville, and positively despised Bodoni. These are strange judgments, the prejudice of genius. When he says his *Roots of the Mountains* is finer than anything printed since the seventeenth century – we reach for our Bulmers.

His progress from first practical notion to printing of the first book was startlingly fast; for no tradition of a private press existed to guide him. Daniel's enterprise at Oxford had followed more expected ways. Emery Walker's lecture in November 1888 had shown old letter-forms on the screen, and given the thought that new ones could be designed with photographic help – blowing up small drawings by photography, correcting, reducing, and so again. Type design started in the next year, and the last punches of Golden type were cut in December 1890. A trial page of the first Kelmscott book was pulled in January 1891. An example of it exists among Emery Walker's books at 7 Hammersmith Terrace, in London, with the happy pencilled phrase in William Morris's hand, 'William Morris fuit hic.' That expresses the excitement of it – the man himself was there, in the type.

The two books studied especially in making this type, as Cockerell has explained, were 'a copy of Leonard of Arezzo's *History of Florence*, printed at Venice by Jacobus Rubens in 1476, in a roman type very similar to that of Nicolas Jenson. Parts of this book and of Jenson's *Pliny* of 1476 were enlarged by photography in order to bring out more clearly the characteristics of the various letters; and having mastered both their virtues and their defects, Morris proceeded to design the fount of type which, in the list of December 1892, he named the Golden type, from *The Golden Legend*, which was to have been the first book printed with it'.

Morris described how after a while he felt the need for a gothic type, 'and herein the task I set myself was to redeem the gothic character from the charge of unreadableness which is commonly brought against it. And I felt that this charge could not be reasonably brought against the types of the first two decades of printing; that Schoeffer at Mainz, Mentelin at Strasburg, and Gunther Zainer at Augsberg, avoided the spiky ends and undue compression which lay some of the later printers open to the above charge.' The result is known as Troy type, because its first proper use was in *The Recuyell of the Historyes of Troye*, a Caxton reprint issued in two volumes, large quarto, in 1893. The type first appears in a little paragraph announcing this book, at the end of the list of May 1892.

When the first experimental page was set up for the Chaucer, it became clear that something smaller than this Troy face would be needed; and Chaucer type is simply a smaller version of it, used quite commonly in Kelmscott books, of which *The Order of Chivalry*, 1893, came first.

Morris also went some way towards designing a semi-gothic type based upon the three books printed by Sweynheim and Pannartz during their stay at Subiaco near Rome in the fourteen-sixties. He never completed it; but it is easy to see why Walker and Cockerell persuaded St John Hornby to let them design a type in the manner of those books, and the result was the beautiful Subiaco fount which is known in connection with the Ashendene Press.

Morris worked in this to please himself. His own choice led to gothic type – nobody else in England had been doing it. No tendency in public tastes was consulted, he managed without market research. Twenty copies of *The Glittering Plain* were to have been printed for distribution among Morris's personal friends. There was as yet no

KELMSCOTT PRESS, UPPER
MALL, HAMMERSMITH.

July 1st, 1895.

Note. This is the Golden type.
This is the Troy type.
This is the Chaucer type.

Secretary:
S. C. Cockerell, Kelmscott Press, Upper Mall,
Hammersmith, London, W., to whom all
letters should be addressed.

Front of a Kelmscott Press book list, showing the different
founts of type.

thought of offering any for sale, Sparling tells us. If his prose romances
were a kind of wandering in worlds which worked in the way he
wished, his adventure in printing might be viewed similarly. Strength
characterized it, the honest force of his work-table which Philip
Webb had designed. In printing language it meant a heavy letter
well inked, in contrast to the light and often elegant faces commonly
available to printers; and this came best with the hand press upon

40

which each sheet could receive, with skilled pressure and the right pause for effect, a firm blackness which in just the same way had been achieved by Gutenberg in the fifteenth century. No machine, he felt, could have done it. 'He found that his letter would have to be thinned, his paper softened and his ink diluted,' Sparling tells us, 'thereby destroying the beauty of his book, were he to submit himself to the limitations thought by ordinary printers to be imposed by the machine.' He made a sensible deduction, even if others have quarrelled with it since. The finest printing had been upon hand presses, and with the machine age came serious decline. A return to fifteenth-century quality might be helped by the use of fifteenth-century method, in this as in the other arts he had investigated.

It is said sometimes that the books are unreadable, expensive and, even if readable, too precious to be used. 'It is doubtful,' Paul Thompson writes, 'whether anyone possessing a Kelmscott book would take it down to be read.'

The eye gets used to gothic type quickly, and there is no difficulty in reading the beautiful Kelmscott letter forms. A word has been said already about the published price of these books. If they became expensive through recognition, that was no fault in the printer. Fifteen were published at two guineas, fifteen at thirty shillings – including *Poems of Keats*. Three cost fifteen shillings, four ten shillings. Two were six guineas, and Chaucer, an island of grandeur, twenty pounds. Those are not high prices, and never stood beyond the reach of many who might have appreciated them. And if they are used carefully now, they should give the same pleasure as seventy years ago. Nothing will be damaged.

The design of the books varied – some decorated and illustrated, others plain; some little pocket books, others folio. No one book-case easily holds them. For the long Caxton reprints, and Morris's long stories, gothic type in large quarto seems right. If his gothic letter had been designed at the time, it would perhaps have been used for the *Golden Legend*. The editions of modern poets – Shelley, Keats, Herrick, Coleridge, Rossetti – were quite simply set in the roman letter, with very little ornament except the decorated initials. Swinburne's poem, *Atalanta in Calydon*, was by mutual sympathy a candidate for the more ornate style, and it remains among the best of them all, a large quarto set in Troy type. One of the more elaborate books, in decorative attention but without illustration, is the crusader chronicle of Godfrey of Boulogne, first king of the Latin Kingdom of Jerusalem. Each small chapter has its ornamental border, and it is an admirable work to read from cover to cover in the Kelmscott edition. Decoratively, the two which show three printings – red, blue and black – were successful pieces of work; even if most of us get no nearer than the pleasure of a well-set page in our admiration for *Laudes Beatae Mariae Virginis*, and not much closer than that in our appreciation for *Love Is Enough*. If that title suggests affection for the typography, it can stand accurately.

As much care went into the little books of the Press – the stories Morris translated from Old French, his tale of *Child Christopher*, the essay on *Gothic Architecture*, and (in Golden type) Rossetti's story from *The Germ, Hand and Soul*. And of all the smaller books, perhaps the old metrical version of the penitential psalms, with its Latin title *Psalmi Penitentiales*, showed the most delicate taste and judgment.

Morris designed all the initial letters – three hundred and eighty four of them. These were printed from metal. Many of them he had himself engraved on wood in the first instance. The titlepages were printed straight from the wood. The illustrations went through a more complex progress, and Sparling assures us we are very lucky to have had such an harmonious team as Burne-Jones, Catterson-Smith and Hooper. Burne-Jones made a drawing, Catterson-Smith reduced it to technically proper form and Hooper engraved it on wood. To us it is strange that Morris never expected his friend to interest himself a little in the necessary skills. It cast no shadow. 'Until the accidents of time and life have once more united such a team as was found in Morris and Burne-Jones, with Catterson-Smith and Hooper to aid them, we are unlikely to be lucky enough to fall in again for so rich a heritage of enduring beauty.' Burne-Jones had adjusted himself to cartoons for stained glass, but seems to have kept clear of the printing.

It is interesting to isolate the Kelmscott illustrations, and look at them without their ornamental setting. We see then what they owe to Morris's part in the page. After the days of the Kelmscott Press, Hooper engraved some drawings Burne-Jones had made for an illustrated Kelmscott edition which never appeared, of Mackail's bible stories. They look very bare on the page, lacking their leafy borders. The same thing happened with *Eros and Psyche*, Bridges' poem printed at Gregynog many years after. Isolated, they lack force. It was also true of Gere's engravings for the Ashendene Press *Le Morte Darthur* – weak results, needing Morris's decoration. Together, they formed memorably rich pages which characterize the Chaucer.

Apart from the drawings from Burne-Jones, one book had illustrations by Walter Crane and another by A. J. Gaskin. Walter Crane's engravings for the second Kelmscott version of Morris's *Story of the Glittering Plain* are not very successful. He must have been more conscious than anyone (for he could write fluently about it) of the need to balance type with decoration; but his designs turn out too heavy and dark, lacking definition. Gaskin's drawings for each month of the *Shephearde's Calender* are perhaps the happiest of all Kelmscott illustrations, bringing a strictness of form and composition none of the others provided, and looking forward to similar merits in the work of Eric Ravilious. It is disappointing that Gaskin did so little book illustration.

The Kelmscott Chaucer should not stand alone above the other books. The page was bigger, it had far more illustrations than all the others and a heavier paper; but there is nothing except scale to divide it from the little essay on Gothic architecture which sold for half a crown. One received no more care than the other. There was no inferior or superior. Type and impression were the same in each. Yet from first appearance, the Chaucer gained a name as the finest book since Gutenberg. It has held its place near the head of the polls ever since. Booksellers take its current price for an index of the state of the nation. The terms which critics used in the eighteen-nineties to welcome it simply show us what an impression Morris's printing made upon late Victorian bookmen.

Morris's choice of books comes from his heart. He and Cobden-Sanderson were the best examples of this. Several Kelmscott books had been commissioned by publishers – Rossetti's poems, *Maud*,

Book of Wisdom and Lies, Blunt's *Poems*, *Hand and Soul* – but all were within his taste. He would never have printed a book unwillingly. Apart from the editions of poets, and an immense historical novel translated from the German by Oscar Wilde's mother, most of the books were his own work or Caxton reprints. One may wish for a wider choice, but that is how it was. Several great works were planned, but got no further than that – especially Froissart, which went so far that after Morris's death a double page of the folio book was printed and issued, to show rather wistfully what might have been. It is unfortunate that nobody these days reads his long prose romances. There most of them are, in superb editions with beautiful titles – *The Story of the Glittering Plain, Well at the World's End, The Wood Beyond the World, Water of the Wondrous Isles*. All in impossible odd language which once seemed acceptably fresh though personal to him. 'The book is to be read,' H. G. Wells wrote of one of them, 'not simply for pleasure. To those who write, its pages will be a purification; it is full of clean strong sentences and sweet old words.' 'The interest,' Swinburne wrote, 'for those who bring with them to the reading of a work of imagination any auxiliary or sympathetic imagination of their own, is deeper and more vivid as well as more various: but the crowning test and triumph of the author's genius will be recognized in the all but unique power of touching with natural pathos the alien element of natural or supernatural fiction.' So presumably our descendants will come back to it again, discovering Morris's language and imagination as we have unearthed other aspects of the Gothic revival. They may turn with relief, in a period when wit is less compulsive, to humourless day-dreams.

And one other group of the books, much in Morris's country, can be read happily now – the small books of medieval poems: *Syr Ysambrace, Syre Degrevaunt, Syr Percevalle of Gales;* fit for their subject, finely set and illustrated, showing all the merits of the Kelmscott Press.

The plain Kelmscott page has been safely admired, and the ornament much criticized. Apart from their other distinctions extravagant decoration is the call note of the Press and a stamp of their maker's character everywhere. 'The actual drawing with the brush,' Lethaby wrote, 'was an agreeable sensation to him; the forms were led along and bent over and rounded at the edges with definite pleasure; they were *stroked* into place, as it were, with a sensation like that of smoothing a cat . . . thus he kept alive every part of his work by growing the pattern, as I have said, bit by bit, solving the turns and twists as he came to them. It was to express this sensuous pleasure that he used to say that all good designing was felt in the stomach.'

This was an absolute originality of the Press, because the early examples which influenced him show nothing like his power or ease in ornament. The first page of Ratdolt's Appian, 1477, has a border very similar to Morris's title border for the first Kelmscott book, though the flowers are less natural; and Morris withdrew from this style of border, finding it rather too black. The *De Mysterio Missae*, printed by John Zainer at Ulm, had light foliated ornament reminiscent of Morris's work, but not with his vigour. On the whole, unless it happens to irritate, this wealth of decoration may be accepted as the great gift of a master hand and the best visual quality of these books. 'It was only natural that I, a decorator by profession, should attempt to ornament my books suitably; about this matter I will only say that I have always tried to keep in mind the necessity for making my decoration a part of the page of type.' He designed fifty-seven whole borders for the press, and one hundred and eight half-borders or margin ornaments.

His old affection for Latin manuscripts of the fifteenth century, and his own occasional illuminated manuscript, helped towards making the manner of ornament in the books; but it is interesting that the marginal ornaments he designed for a grand edition of *The Earthly Paradise* which had been planned in 1866, many years before the Kelmscott Press, are near to the close work of manuscript decoration and, if printed at the side of a type page, would have shown a dense texture to distract and spoil the balance. They were like reduced strips from his wallpaper patterns.

Title pages of books of poems could be a nonsense of decoration at the expense of all meaning, a designer's enjoyment with no inhibition. The double opening of the Kelmscott Keats is a fair example – a solid block of capitals in its thick border, no concessions to sense or line division. Coleridge is the same. It was a minor and splendid

affectation. As these embroidered title openings are commonly reproduced, or exposed in museum cases, the whole book is sometimes
assumed to be of that kind. When Geoffrey Grigson refers to 'the
absurd over-filling of a Kelmscott page' he can only be thinking of a
title page.

Morris had always intended that a few copies of his books should be
printed as grand examples and sold more expensively, but not in the
customary way as 'large paper copies'. The logic of this was clear
– a just margin is not improved by extension; there should be no
tampering with the proportions of margin, or with the position of
type. As with one or two other of Morris's minor aesthetic theories,
this seems now to be untrue and the large paper copies do give
pleasure from a sense of space and of careful printing. That had been
so from time to time in the history of books. The booksellers are always glad to have large paper copies, tall copies, uncut copies.
Ackermann's illustrated books gain in grandeur from wider white
margins, and so do little editions of the poets, the *Muses Library*,
published by Bullen just before the Kelmscott Press. It was never a
fault. Whistler and George Allen took the margins beyond good sense,
but the eye does not generally object.

Yet Morris was right, and our coarser eyes probably wrong. He
made the time-honoured choice instead, of special editions on vellum,
an extremely expensive matter and always a problem for the printer.
The old manuscripts Morris knew were written on vellum. For the
same reason, Gutenberg had printed a few copies of his works on
vellum – because he was trying to reproduce the splendour of manuscript. But it must have been an anachronism, a confusion of mind,
from the start; because these sheets shaved from the skins of month-old
calves could never be supplied in large numbers for the purpose of printing, which was to make large editions widely available. Printing looked
forward to mass education, vellum back to the private manuscript.
And having dutifully said that, vellum can be looked at in another
way – as a fine material for printing, in spite of its difficulties and
uncertainties. A successful page on vellum stands out, stares and
half-dazzles with its pure black. Paper texture, rougher and erratic,
could never give back such a strong form. Against that, paper takes

46

an impression and vellum keeps its hard flat surface, losing in that way one characteristic masculine feature of paper books. There is less sign of the work. And where vellum is less than perfectly printed, there may be excess of ink and irritating show-through. This uncertainty is quite interesting in itself – and one can be sure that every vellum copy had the printer's particular care, for it was meant to be the best.

Morris was not a sudden pioneer in this revival, for there had been vellum printing in a few copies from time to time. When Haslewood's edition of Painter's *Palace of Pleasure* appeared in 1813, a long work, seven copies were printed on vellum and sold for seventy pounds a set. One copy of Ackermann's *Oxford* and *Cambridge* exists on vellum. At the time of writing, a Sotheby catalogue lists *Barker's Delight, or the Art of Angling* by Thomas Barker, second edition 1820, 'printed on vellum, only one copy so issued'. These are random examples. It was not a very rare habit, but they must always be rare copies.

Five copies of the *Historyes of Troye* were printed on vellum, five of *Maud*, six copies of *Godefrey of Bologne*, six of the *Life of Wolsey*, eight of *Beowulf*, ten of *News From Nowhere*, thirteen of *Chaucer*. Such numbers were dictated by the expense and difficulty, and the problem of supply. It is at least an interesting oddity of printing and the other presses followed this habit. Vellum is a strong material, which binders sometimes use for the first and last sections of a book for safety and permanence. In 1891 Morris still possessed some of the Roman vellum he had used for writing his manuscripts – enough for six copies of *The Glittering Plain*, and one or two copies of *Poems By The Way*. It is finer, more delicate and better prepared, than the skins made for him after that by Bland in Brentford. The Vatican needed its own vellum, and could not supply skins for a few copies of *The Golden Legend* – so none of that book appeared on vellum. Morris thought it tiresome of the Pope, as these stories of saints should have interested him. Only five of the editions issued from the Press were entirely in paper. According to the bibliography *The Sundering Flood* appeared only in paper, but vellum copies are known. The price of the two volumes of *Troye* on vellum was eighty guineas. One of those five was kept by Morris, one went to Ellis the editor, one to Fairfax Murray – and two

47

to Quaritch. Those were presumably the only copies sold on the open market, so price hardly mattered. They must have cost as much to produce.

The bits and pieces, ephemera, of the Kelmscott press form an attractive small subject. They range from trial pages, such as Cockerell loved to hoard, on paper or vellum, to a beautiful four-page leaflet with pieces from Tennyson and Ruskin for the Ancoats Brotherhood in 1895, an invitation to the unveiling of an American memorial to Keats in Hampstead parish church, and menus for annual jaunts of the Kelmscott staff. These last are entertaining, because we are told that Morris had nothing to do with the typography – and that is manifest. They show what an enjoyable Victorian jumble could be made from Kelmscott Press equipment, and nobody else has been allowed to play about with it like that. The third annual dinner, at the Dumb Bell Hotel, Taplow, has a grand mixture of red and black, a laying on of ornament and muddle of type. The 'firm's outing' dinner has not changed much down the years, from 'All Vegetables in Season' to the fruit tarts, blancmanges, wine jellies, compote of fruit, queen's pudding and Swiss pastry which they were about to receive at Taplow on the last day of that August. But opposite the food, instead of wine, we have a list of songs and their singers. Apart from two toasts there were seven songs, and Binning the Father of the Chapel (a compositor from Morris's *Commonweal* days) gave a recitation, Cassius instigating Brutus. May Morris sang, described here for perhaps the only time as Mrs Sparling.

A history of the press can be traced through the Lists occasionally issued, announcing new books and recording the old – apart from smaller prospectuses which went out with order forms. In these lists we can see when the Chaucer was first announced, and how it grew in scope; we find the early ambitious mention of Froissart and of the *Vitas Patrum* which never went further than a specimen page, and the change in style when Cockerell took over from Sparling as Secretary of the Press. In the earlier lists each book is described in the type which was used for the printed work. They are the shortest way to become acquainted with the three types faces of the Press. At the end of the last list, dated 22 November 1897, after an announcement of the bibliography, we read:

'This will be the last book printed at the Kelmscott Press, which will close early in the New Year. The type will remain in the hands of the trustees for future use, but all the special ornament will be discontinued, and the woodblocks deposited in the British Museum.'

Apart from this early appearance of that unpleasant word 'discontinued', this was better than throwing them in the Thames. They are now in the little printing museum at the University Press in Cambridge. It is amusing to guess how the types and ornaments might have been used, if others had had the same chances as in the menu at Taplow. Sparling obviously had nightmares about it. 'If a certain letter, for example, came to be familiarly associated with alarm clocks or underclothing, it must necessarily be less effective when employed upon a noble poem or one of the stories or plays which count among the enduring glories of the world.' He was not imagining the day when splendid plays might be written about such things.

Going back to an earlier time, to one who could look at Kelmscott books critically but without foolish respect, and without the awe of the sale room, it is pleasant to end by quoting the very sane verdict of Alfred Pollard from his Introduction to a published catalogue of the Library of William Andrews Clark, printed in San Francisco in 1921: 'Morris did not print books as so many testimonials to the respect or reverence in which he regarded them or their authors. He printed long books, many of them story books which he loved reading himself and which he wanted other people to have the pleasure of reading in jolly editions. The fifty-three books he printed, or planned to print, are all eminently readable. There are still some of them I have not read, but I look forward to a leisure time in which I shall make good my omissions, though it is possible I shall find myself wishing that Mr F. S. Ellis had been content with a single volume of the best of Shelley (instead of three volumes of all his poems), as he was content with single volumes of Herrick and Coleridge. But, with this one exception, to anyone who cares at all for poetry or romance the Kelmscott books are extraordinarily attractive, and the beautiful types, while they inspire a subconscious pleasure, do not divert my attention from the text.'

49

ASHENDENE AND THE QUALITIES
OF A GENTLEMAN

A mixture of influences, by friendship and training, brought St John Hornby to enjoy printing. As a young man he joined W. H. Smith and spent his long professional life as a director. Part of his apprenticeship was in the company's printing works, and that is all the formal training he received. Nobody taught him in a close working relationship, though there were influences and friends; as anyone may tend to meet others who practise his craft. The point has to be made, that Hornby was a craftsman in his own right. The little early books from the summer-house show it well. Later, in his grand days, the work of the press became especially identified with a beautiful type face designed for it by Emery Walker and Sidney Cockerell; but fine type with indifferent printing would be nothing to remember.

An important printing friend in the early years was Horace Hart of Oxford, printer to the University. Hart, ten years before Hornby thought of printing, had helped Daniel by lending the Clarendon Press Fell type. After the first three Ashendene books, Fell type was used in one form or another until Walker and Cockerell had perfected their new designs in 1902. Hornby continued to employ Fell for pamphlets, short stories, orders of service, Christmas cards and headlines, and the style he formed in the use of it was always present in his printing.

So, apart from a memorable meeting with Morris at the Kelmscott Press in 1895, the early influence upon Hornby was rather from the Daniel Press at Oxford – and from Hart, who in these first years seems to have guided them both in the way that Emery Walker helped Morris and his successors. The dates of these presses are important in the story. Henry Daniel and his brothers began to print as children in their father's vicarage at Frome in the eighteen-forties – but the first Daniel Press book of any importance appeared in 1876. Emery Walker's lecture came in 1888, and the Kelmscott Press issued its first book three years later. Another four years, and Hornby's first small book was printed at Ashendene.

In 1896 Morris died, and the trustees closed his Press two years later.

Ricketts had printed his first Vale Press book (not so called at that time) in 1894. So there was a continuity, but Hornby straddles them by his constant progress and activity after 1895.

One quality of a private press is the printer's own choice without reference to any public, and this characterizes the whole story of the Ashendene Press which printed steadily, except for a wartime break, from 1895 to 1935. St John Hornby had no concern with profit from his books, though from sheer merit and beauty they were bought and collected from early days, and looking back over its long history he was able to say that the press had just about paid for itself. As costs had never restricted him, that was an eloquent result.

The Ashendene Press had a quiet history. The work itself was not always calm, and Hornby tells us that in early experiments – his apprenticeship to printing – he and his few helpers went through all sorts of trouble and failure, from the wrong damping of paper to a simple shortage of leisure which meant dividing a single task between one Sunday morning and the next. But the summer-house in the garden of his father's home at Ashendene in Hertfordshire, where it all began, looks charming in Charles Gere's woodcut above the printer's Foreword in Hornby's fine volume of bibliography. There must have been peace in 'the little garden-house of happy memory' on Sunday mornings of the eighteen-nineties, in the 'small inner room about 10 feet by 5 feet' where he printed the first few books of the Press before moving to his own house and more space in London. Ten small books were made between 1894 and 1899, in very modest numbers for the joy of it, mostly as gifts to friends, and from then until 1935 the home of the press was Shelley House in Chelsea. They are rare now and there is special pleasure in a volume printed at Ashendene in those years. The history of the Ashendene Press is from that friendly beginning to some of the most stately folios in the revival of printing.

Hornby's approach was not from the wide-angled idealism of Cobden-Sanderson, or aesthetic sensibility of Ricketts, or the reforming range and mastery of Morris. He says this clearly himself:

'In the choice of books to print I have been influenced partly by my own personal taste in literature and partly by the suitability of a

51

book from a purely typographical standpoint – or perhaps it would be more true to say by a combination of these two factors. My choice has therefore fallen in the majority of cases upon books which gave scope for a certain gaiety of treatment in the use of coloured initials and chapter-headings; or, as in the case of *Utopia* and *Thucydides*, marginal notes in colour. Such books present a more interesting problem to the printer, and as I have worked for my own pleasure and amusement without having to keep too strict an eye upon the cost, personal indulgence in this respect has been easy.'

So this is one far point from average publishing. No publisher is likely to sit at a table and defend his recommendation upon the ground that it gives 'scope for a certain gaiety of treatment in the use of coloured initials and chapter-headings'. There would be black looks and tapping of foreheads if he did. We must recognize this attitude to a book privately printed, and accept it or reject the whole subject, for that was its root.

Hornby brought educated English qualities to his work, and this is the most gentlemanly of the private presses. Morris printed Caxton's work and his own, Cobden-Sanderson brought Ruskin and Emerson into it and also Milton on freedom of speech. Hornby's thought turned to Horace, Vergil and Lucretius, to the Italian of Dante and Boccaccio, and Jowett's translation of Thucydides. His choice of English books is not startlingly original, in early days or late. The range was from Malory to Spenser, Milton, Sir Thomas More, Chaucer's *Prologue*, the Bible, *Omar Khayyam*. He moved within the common circle of private press taste, except for an educated interest in Latin and Italian. Morris had followed a taste of his own towards medieval English. Hornby made no contribution of this sort, and his choice came rather from school, background and friends.

It is mildly surprising, from first to last, that there was such a following and repetition in choosing works to be printed. In early days Hornby set up his *Omar Khayyam* when everybody else was doing just that. They seem to be children following the one who leads. When it came to English literature, was their reading so very limited that they worked upon obvious first thoughts? 'Never a man's thought in the world keeps the roadway better than thine,' one feels. Why should the Ashendene Press go to all the time and design of printing Ralph Robinson's translation of More's *Utopia*, when the Kelmscott Press had done it very well a few years before? Would it not have been more attractive to make a fresh choice and expression? These men were either ill-read and limited, or the second and fifth treatment of the same work was deliberately undertaken, almost for purposes of comparison. That was what he made of it, now see how mine looks. It could have been a form of criticism, a demonstration. And nobody needed to worry about flooding the market with copies. Morris printed three hundred and eight copies of his *Utopia*, Hornby one hundred and twenty. They might exist together in a few private libraries of people who followed this renaissance. Each book was partly a technical performance, an act among friends.

It is worth looking at the notices, subscription forms, announcements of presses. Hornby issued his first notice to subscribers in 1901 from Shelley House, Chelsea. He had just moved there, setting up on a more ambitious scale than in the summer-house of his father's garden. It is in the form of a letter, inviting subscriptions for 'a small edition of Tyndale's Translation of *The Revelacion of Sanct Ihon the Devine*. It is being printed with an old fount of Black Letter, in double column, in black and red. The size is small quarto, about eight and a half by six and a quarter inches. The issue is limited to 54 copies, of which not more than 30 will be for sale. The price is £2.2.0. Subscriptions may be sent to me at the above address, and should be on the accompanying Form. As my spare time is limited, I cannot promise the book by any fixed date, but it will probably be ready by October. Payment need not be made until receipt of book.'

Not many could have gone out, as he only had thirty to sell. He goes on to announce that 'I am proposing shortly to begin printing *The Inferno* of Dante Alighieri (the Italian text), for which I am having cut a new fount of type, modelled closely upon an old 15th-century fount, a very noble type.' Page three is an order form for both books, and on the back he prints the charming woodblock with Jost Amman's drawing, the first emblem of the press.

That was at a crucial point in the story. What impresses now is the beauty of this small piece of printing, close set in the roman letter of

53

his Fell type, perfectly placed on the page with the quiet three-line heading in text capitals taken out to the left of the type area. It is the sort of page which Bernard Newdigate designed in his years at the Arden Press, and no doubt Hornby was an influence upon him.

This was a good moment for work to begin with his 'very noble type', and to come under the care of Walker and Cockerell – as Morris had been worthy of Walker's tuition eleven years before.

And in this prospectus he announces something else. 'I am thinking of having the initial letter of each Canto illumined by hand, and probably there will be several woodcut illustrations after the old manner, in the text' he says, in describing the edition of Dante. 'I propose to print no more than 125 copies on paper, and possibly 5 or 10 copies on vellum. The price will depend upon the cost of the type, paper, initials, illustrations, etc. It will probably be about £3.3.0 for the paper copies, and £10.10.0 for those on vellum, but I cannot say anything definite at present. In any case the whole amount received in subscriptions will be spent upon the book.'

Morris, Ricketts and Pissarro, more and less, had decorated their books with woodblock borders. Morris had designed borders and initials almost as a woman knits and talks. Hornby possessed no talent of that sort, but at the turn of the century Edward Johnston and his pupil Graily Hewitt were beginning to be known for their revival of early calligraphy, a movement parallel to the interest in old printing.

Here is another link with Daniel's press at Oxford – Emily Daniel and Mary Bridges were both involved. For one of the Daniel books, Mrs Bridges had beautifully copied twenty-three lines for reproduction by collotype.

Graily Hewitt's initials were quite different from Mrs Daniel's – they derived from the Roman lettering which is often traced back to inscriptions on Trajan's arch. This has become associated especially with the stone carving of Eric Gill, and the Perpetua type which he designed. There is stately grace in the red, blue and green initials which Johnston and Hewitt drew for the Doves and Ashendene presses.

This brightness accords with Hornby's taste for 'a certain gaiety of

54

treatment in the use of coloured initials and chapter-headings.' None of his books after this time is quite without it, and his taste was shaped by the later private presses – in the more cheerful work from Gregynog, the Golden Cockerel and the Shakespeare Head. Morris had printed two books in three colours, but he found more pleasure in design than colour. The simplicity of an Ashendene page, with splendour of coloured initials, gave character to the later phases of that press.

The art of Hornby's friends contributed happily to his work: Walker and Cockerell in type design; Florence Kingsford (Cockerell's wife) in painting illustrations on vellum for editions of the *Songs of Solomon* and the *Book of Songs and Poems from the Old Testament and the Apocrypha*; and Douglas Cockerell and Katharine Adams in fine bindings. Cockerell's work is sometimes hidden in the trade name of W. H. Smith on bindings of Ashendene books. He was in charge of Smith's bindery for many years, and designed for them. It is accepted that Ashendene books bound by W. H. Smith are indeed Cockerell bindings. Hornby commissioned some for his own library, and the copies printed on vellum were generally issued in W. H. Smith bindings. The strict tradition, until the Gregynog Press appeared and changed it, was to assume that the page of type mattered and the printer would end his responsibility at that point, merely arranging for its issue in paper boards or white vellum. It was assumed that an owner would often want to commission his own binding, and could look after himself in that respect. Hornby mentions and illustrates some of Katharine Adams's elaborate designs. In 1903 she bound very austerely in dark green morocco the twenty-five vellum copies of *Fysshinge with an Angle*, crowding the first word of the title into the first panel of the spine, and allowing more place and space for the full title in two lines across the front. No rods or lines and fish, or little medieval men. Once her work was welcomed rather casually, and Sydney Cockerell used to wonder whether this book or that had been 'Katied' yet.

The Ashendene Press is often identified with the Subiaco type which was made for it. After the sack of Mainz in 1462, two printers, Sweynheim and Pannartz, wandered south to Italy, and settled in the little town of Subiaco north of Rome. They produced three books, among them an edition of Cicero's *De Oratore* in a type face which lay appropriately half-way between the northern Gothic and southern Roman. It was, in strict description, a black letter – showed black and thick on the page, but had such skill in form that the shapes of letters never lost their definition or gave an impression of too much ink. It was a finely chiselled black letter. This was the type which Walker and Cockerell followed in designing their own for Hornby. And they followed it closely, for a page from the Subiaco *Cicero* seems at first sight to belong to an Ashendene book.

It is a type which needed good margins, close setting, a sound solid body of printed area and no nonsense. A poorly inked page in the Subiaco type would fail – it demanded formal skill. One might think on other lines in, for instance, Daniel's use of Fell type. That had innocence, affection – but not perfection. Hornby was reaching high in using this instrument.

The page could be played with in various ways – initial letters, chapter heads in colour, woodcuts, red shoulder notes; but the body of type stayed solid and flawless. Hornby had an eye for the placing, and skill in use. His friends decorated enjoyably but with strict discretion. His books are always simple. Anything of art nouveau or Beardsley's influence might have put them badly wrong. One has the impression from this type face that a statement is there unalterably. Twenty-five years later another fount of type was designed for the press by Walker. For this he took as model a book printed at Ulm in 1482, the *Geographia* of Ptolemaeus. It is known as Ptolemy type, and Hornby used it for four of the late productions of the Press before it closed in 1935: the two tall folio volumes of *Don Quixote*, Jowett's translation of Thucydides with the beautiful start of each chapter designed by Graily Hewitt and printed in red, and the red shoulder notes in Blado italic – a stately book – the *Amours Pastorales de Daphnis et Chloe*, and his *Bibliography*. This is a much lighter, more elegant letter than the earlier fount; less mannered for modern use, and very easily acceptable, one would guess, if ever the Monotype Corporation were tempted to prepare it for normal book work. It has beauty of form, and lightness of touch. For pleasure in the look of a page, the openings of each Book in the *Thucydides* are the happiest climax of Ashendene printing. And with the use of this less dictatorial type face, the printer could cast away a little of his restraint in planning whatever lay outside it. So in *Don Quixote* we find at last an alphabet of open and freely drawn, decorative initial letters, designed by Louise Powell and shadowing something of Kelmscott Press taste from years before. 'Ornamental letters are taboo in the work of this press,' Ransom wrote. But that was before he had seen a full page of Ptolemy type in the Ashendene *Don Quixote*.

Nobody can declare that one or another book was a printer's best, with the variety of Ashendene books issued and the changes over four decades. Hornby had particular pride in the major works, the most ambitious efforts. 'I am glad that you like *Morte Darthur*', he wrote to a friend, 'I find it very difficult to say which of my books I consider the "chef d'oeuvre" of the Press. Public opinion seems to have fixed on the folio *Dante*, possibly because it is the most difficult to get. On the whole I think I like *Faerie Queene* and *Morte Darthur* best. *Il Decameron di Boccaccio* is also a great favourite of mine. It can be bought more cheaply than the other folios. I don't know why.' His folio Dante was said to stand beside the Doves Bible and Kelmscott Chaucer as one of the monuments of private presses. Hornby liked his large books best. It is easy to see why the two tall volumes of Spenser ranked high for him. He enjoyed the problem of a vast page, initials in blue and red, the just spacing of stanzas in Subiaco type. Somebody who wants to read the *Faerie Queene* might be discouraged by the sheer area of verses to cover between one turn of the page and the next. In that way it is at a disadvantage compared with eight volumes of Spenser from the Shakespeare Head Press under Newdigate. In Hornby's Spenser there seems more splendour than poetry. Of his grand works, *Don Quixote* in two folio volumes may be preferred; easier to read and turn pages of prose, and very fine in his later type with Louise Powell's initials. The paper copies were issued in patterned paper boards and holland back, or in strong green morocco. Paper board is appropriate to the book's design, but cannot be expected to last for ever.

Morte Darthur is a splendid Ashendene folio but long lines of prose in

57

the Subiaco type tend to dazzle. There are woodcuts by Charles and Margaret Gere, in the manner of Walter Crane but making no fresh style of their own. Illustration in the Ashendene books is not particularly memorable, except for Gwen Raverat's wood engravings for the *Amours Pastorales de Daphnis et Chloe*.

His edition of Boccaccio is a tall folio in Subiaco type unadorned, and may well be a pleasure to those who read Boccaccio in Italian. Here the page is set in two columns, so there is less dazzle to worry about. The most successful folio is Jowett's *Thucydides*, less tall than the others, handsome and sound to handle, lecterns not needed. Ptolemy type is light to read and carries one happily over the pages. Shoulder notes in red are a feature of this work, beautifully arranged and printed. Graily Hewitt's lines of drawn lettering recall the opening of Genesis in the Doves Bible. Vellum copies were bound by Douglas Cockerell strongly and simply, with light geometrical design and the name of the press, in brown calf. The title page is flawless, much of it in quiet text capitals with no second colour.

No other press produced such variety in scale and mood. Any father finds that children check a tendency to be solemn, and so it was with Hornby's printing. One of his delightful small books was *The Young King and Other Tales* by Oscar Wilde, produced for the tenth birthday of his daughter Rosamund in 1924. Subiaco type is used with appropriate margins on a small page, and Graily Hewitt designed four initials for printing alternately in red and blue. This book has headlines to each page – an unusual feature in these presses, because an early custom from Kelmscott declared that headlines were a sort of bourgeois decadence and all should return to early German habits of pure text; and they are pleasantly printed between rules, in Fell italic. There is a typically austere Ashendene title page, and the little book is bound in a gay patterned paper board. Rosamund aged ten was rather fortunate to have this, and a blue poem from her father at the start of it. This is indeed private printing, and seventy-two copies were made for her and her friends. One feels it should not be bartered in bookshops and auction rooms, but this is respected as one of the treasures of the press. Copies are likely to be inscribed from the printer and, in a child's hand, his daughter.

Several other books and pamphlets in a small scale were printed for friends or family, and not for sale; as for example, the *Story Without an End*, translated from the German by Sarah Austin. This too had marked a family birthday, and only thirty copies were printed – a little book on Japanese vellum, with initials drawn and coloured by Graily Hewitt. On several occasions short pieces were printed in Fell type as pamphlets, bound in blue paper, and sent to friends. When Hornby married in 1898 he printed the form of service; and he printed it also for his son's wedding thirty years later. These, and a few carefully designed notices and announcements, are the minor pieces of the press. Spenser, *Don Quixote*, Malory, Dante, Boccaccio, Thucydides – and the *Bibliography* – were the major works. Half-way between the two, in physical size, were several productions which in scope and skill have as much appeal as any Ashendene books. In Latin, there is Vergil and Lucretius; in English More's *Utopia*, an Elizabethan translation of the *Golden Asse* of Apuleius, and a composite translation of *The Wisdom of Jesus Son of Sirach, Commonly Called Ecclesiasticus.*

Eric Gill designed initial letters for the *Utopia*. One hundred copies were printed on paper, bound simply in blue paper boards and holland back; and the merit of this was always that it opened easily. A double page with its handsome red intitials and shoulder notes, and fine proportions of white space, looks as well as any Ashendene book; and though Hornby says he chose it partly for the technical exercise, there is a special aptness in the book itself for anyone alive to the ideals behind the arts and crafts movement of those years. Hornby worked effectively with his hands. 'But yf all those that be nowe busied about unprofitable occupations, with all the whole flocke of them that lyve ydellye and slouthfullye, whiche consume and waste everye one of them more of these thinges that come by other mens laboure, then ij of the workemen themselfes doo: yf all these (I saye) were sette to profytable occupatyons: you easelye perceave howe lytle tyme would be enoughe, yea and to muche to stoore us with all things that maye be requisite either for necessitie, or for commoditye, yea or for pleasure, so that the same pleasure be trewe and natural.'

The Booke of the Golden Asse, printed in 1924, is physically a similar

59

production. This time the initial letters, designed by Graily Hewitt, are rather more elaborate and printed in blue and red.

Booksellers continually declare the Ashendene *Ecclesiasticus* to be the finest book from the private presses. These are the people who handle the books and know them better than anyone else, and there is good ground for this opinion. Hornby announced it without emotion in his prospectus: 'It is a volume of 184 pages measuring about eleven and a quarter by seven and a half inches, printed in red and black, with numerous small initials in blue and green filled in by hand by Graily Hewitt and his assistants.' The verse lines of varying length look particularly well in his formal black type on the tall page. There is a sense of relaxation in this last original work from the press, suggested by the many small and larger initial letters brightly drawn in red, blue and green, and by the orange vellum binding. Green, blue and red often appear on the same page. Struck by the beauty of his version of *Ecclesiasticus* written out and illuminated on vellum, A. D. Power 'happened to tell me that he thought of having the version printed, as many of his friends wished to possess it. The temptation to add yet one more book to my list was too strong for me to resist and I there and then offered to print a small edition. I have never regretted having done so, as in my humble opinion it is one of the most satis-factory of the books of the Press.'

Several of the smaller books should be described, but accounts of books can be tedious to read. The *Fioretti del Glorioso Pove Rello di Cristo S. Francesco di Assisi*, which Hornby printed in 1922, is a modest book bound in the Kelmscott manner in vellum with green silk ties. He printed one other comparable book in Italian, the *Vita di Santa Chiara Vergine*. In both, the red and blue Graily Hewitt initials are splendid and the pages laid out with gay confidence. These are the good middle-period, middle-level works he did. Hornby had printed part of the *Fioretti* in 1904 in a slim folio volume. Gere made designs to illustrate both books, but I find these woodcuts reach the standard of a jolly but inaccurate school text-book of the period. Typogra-phers might say that they fit well with the page of type, but they do not compare with, for instance, Gaskin's designs for the Kelmscott Press *Shephearde's Calender*.

Songs and Poems from the Old Testament, 1904, is one of the most charming works of a modest sort that the Press produced. Graily Hewitt as usual drew and coloured the blue initials at the start of each poem. There is red and black Subiaco type, happily mixed in the *Song of the Three Holy Children* at the end, where a double page dazzles with the recurring line 'Praise and exalt Him above all for ever' printed each time in red. This book might be seen together with the *Ecclesiasticus*, for it is somewhat like a diminutive version of it. Viewed with other superb copies of Ashendene books in Major Abbey's sale at Sothebys, this, in its dark green Cockerell binding, the long title crowded in panels up the spine, seemed possibly the most attractive of them all. A slim volume of poems printed at the start of the war, the last book until the Press opened again in 1920 with the grand Boccaccio folio, was *Poems Written in the Year MCMXIII* by Robert Bridges Poet Laureate. Bridges was peculiarly the poet of the private presses, another link with Henry Daniel. The book itself is perfectly printed in the Subiaco type with red and blue initials by Graily Hewitt. There is some poignancy in it, this last from the old world. Hornby says, 'This book printed during the first few months of the Great War was done for private circulation only, 50 copies going to the Poet Laureate and the remainder being distributed by myself. When the book was finished the Press was closed down until the beginning of 1920.' Paper left over from the original 'making' of his Kelmscott stock from 1896 was used. There are eleven short poems, and twenty pages. 'A mood for writing came on me last Autumn,' Bridges wrote to the author; and later in the same letter, 'There is to me a great charm in a few choice pages.' Between them, that is what they provided.

> But this late day of golden fall
>   is still as a picture upon a wall
>   or a poem in a book lying open unread:
>   Or whatever else is shrined
>   When the Virgin hath vanished:
>   Footsteps of eternal Mind
>   on the path of the dead.

Hornby was aware that book collectors took an interest in his work, but of course he printed to please himself and a few friends, and not for them. A pleasant example of the books printed briefly for friends is *Three Poems* of John Milton, the fourth book from the press, issued in 1896. They were bound in mauve cloth by Zaehnsdorf with the first colophon of the press on the back. The poems (*L'Allegro, Il Penseroso, Lycidas*) are nobly printed in a large size of the roman Fell type, and there is a bold border to the first page of the first two poems – the second time bravely in red, with an initial H from the same hand (his future sister-in-law, Cassandra Barclay). This gay opening was for the poem beginning:

> Hence, vain deluding Joys,
> The brood of Folly without father bred!...
> But hail, thou goddess, sage and holy,
> Hail, divinest Melancholy!

And *Lycidas* has a sixteenth-century border and initial copied from Ratdolt. This book is private as can be. Opposite the Contents page (headed 'This Book Containeth') the printer has put a notice in italic: 'This Book, of which there are 50 copies and no more, was imprinted by me, St John Hornby, upon my private Press at Ashendene in the County of Hertford, with types cast from matrices given to the University of Oxford by Bishop Fell in or about the year 1670, and kindly supplied to me, in this year of Grace 1896, by Horace Hart, Controller of the University Press. Printed for my Friends, whom God preserve, and not for sale by myself or any other Bookseller. This copy is Number   and belongs to   .'
This archaic flamboyance was common at the signing-off before the colophon in Ashendene books, even in the later and more public books. 'Here ends the *History of the Peloponnesian War* by Thucydides the Athenian,' we read, 'Translated out of the Greek into the English tongue by Benjamin Jowett, sometime Master of Balliol College, and now newly imprinted by me, St John Hornby, at my Press at Chelsea by the kind permission of the Delegates of the Oxford University Press. The printing was begun in the month of October of the year

1928 and finished in the month of August of the year 1930. Laus Deo.'
Then comes the grand colophon in red, designed by somebody in
Emery Walker's office.

There are other excellent Ashendene books – in Latin and Italian, the
absurd minute Queen's-Dolls'-House book of Horace which was
printed in three copies, Marcus Aurelius, *Aucassin and Nicolette*. Hornby
printed for his pleasure – not for reform; though Morris, Cobden-
Sanderson and Crane might have denied that craftsmanship and socialism could ever be divided. 'Thus endyth the Boke of the Revelacion of Sanct Jhon the Devine, the whych is ryght utile and profytable
unto all Christian men, translated and drawen oute of Greke into oure
Englysshe tonge by William Tyndale, and emprynted by me St John
Hornby on my Presse at Shelley House, Chelsea, in the County of
London, the same havynge bene begun in the moneth of October
mdcccc, while oure gracious soverayn Ladye Queen Victoria yet
raygned over us, and fynysshed in the moneth of July in the fyrste
yere of the raygne of Kynge Edwarde the Seventhe, whom God
preserve, the yere of our Lorde one thousande nine hundred and
one.'

Each moment some new birth
hasten'd to deck the earth
in the gay sunbeams.
Between their kisses dreams:
And dream and kiss were rife
with laughter of mortal life.

A verse from *Poems Written in the Year* MCMXIII, by Robert Bridges. Ashendene Press,
1914. Subiaco type.

The Essex House Press came from the heart of the arts and crafts movement. The history of that movement should be written; full of good intention and achievement, a protest for man-as-artist against the assumptions of industrial society but suffering sudden changes in reputation from oddity to idolatry. The overtones are of sandals and scandals, hand-weaving, smocks and country dancing. In its time it represented vigorous socialism and a struggle to live with pleasure in the new order. What these people produced – the silver, books, furniture – is prized now and sold at Sothebys, but that is the turn of fashion. A pioneer in the movement was C. R. Ashbee, who started his Guild of Handicraft in the Mile End Road in 1886, running it there and at Chipping Campden with varying fortunes for twenty years. Reviewing the seventh exhibition of the Arts and Crafts Exhibition Society, in 1903 when the Guild was at Campden and in all its vigour, Arthur Symons wrote wearily that his 'eye was shocked and dazzled by a mingling of what was tawdry with what was trivial. Colour blazed, writhing dragons of form clawed at me on all sides; nothing allured or persuaded or stood aloof, content to be alone; the voices of rival eccentricities cried down each other, in a hubbub of self-praise. I felt as if I had found my way into some monstrous market, in which the fruits and vegetables were all of gold and fiery stones, and the stalls asked to be admired, and the nails that fastened plank to plank said: Look at us, we too are Art. Everything was dead, and had a dull glitter, like the scales of a dead fish.'

But its aim had been alive, practical and charitable. Symons admired Georgian terraces and simple silver. Ashbee, Morris and Walter Crane had felt the power of Ruskin's writings about Gothic art, emphasizing each man's happiness and independence at his work. They searched for the quality of joy in making, to replace the wasted days of thoughtless tasks performed merely for a living wage. There is sense behind the mockery about nails which said 'Look at us, we too are Art'. The point was that somebody had made and knocked them home with pride, had promoted the nails to a position of respect and seen their place in the planks' structure.

64

PSALME XVI.

CONSERVA ME DOMINE.

THE BADGE OR ARMES OF DAVID.

RESERVE ME, O GOD, FOR IN THEE have I put my trust. O my soule thou hast sayd unto the Lorde: thou arte my God, my goodes are no~ thing unto the. All my delyte is upon the saynctes that are in the erth, and upon soch as ex~ cell in vertue. But they that runne after another God, shall have greate trouble. Their drinckoffrynges of bloude will not I offre, nether make men~ cion of their names within my lyppes. The Lord hym selfe is the porcion of myne enheritaunce: and of my cup: thou shalt maynteyne my lot. The lot is fallen unto me in a fayre ground, yee, I have a goodly heritage. I wyll thanke the Lorde for gevynge me warn~ ynge: my reynes also chasten me in the nyght season. I have set God al~ wayes before me, for he is on my right hande, therfore I shall not fall. Wherfore my hert was glad, & my glory rejoysed, My ffessh also shall rest in hope. For why? thou shalt not leave my soule in hell, nether shalt thou suffre thy holy one to se corrupcion. Thou shalt shewe me the path of lyfe: in thy presence is the fulnesse of joye, and at thy ryght hande ther is pleasure for ev~ ermore.

From Archbishop Cranmer's translation of the book of Psalms. Essex House Press. Endeavour type.

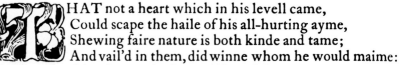

THAT not a heart which in his levell came,
Could scape the haile of his all-hurting ayme,
Shewing faire nature is both kinde and tame;
And vail'd in them, did winne whom he would maime:
Against the thing he sought, he would exclaime;
When he most burnt in hart-wisht luxurie,
He preacht pure maide, and prais'd cold chastitie.

THUS meerely with the garment of a Grace,
The naked and concealed feind he cover'd,
That th'unexperient gave the tempter place,
Which, like a cherubin, above them hover'd.
Who, young and simple, would not be so lover'd?
Aye me! I fell; and yet do question make
What I should doe againe for such a sake.

THAT infected moysture of his eye,
O, that false fire which in his cheeke so glow'd,
O, that forc'd thunder from his heart did flye,
O, that sad breath his spungie lungs bestowed,
O, all that borrowed motion, seeming owed,
Would yet againe betray the fore-betrayed,
And new pervert a reconciled maide!

The revival of printing, in the form it happened to take among private presses, very well represents the arts and crafts ideal. Good materials, sound work, the equal importance of all arts and refusal to accept a notion of 'minor arts', pleasure in labour, a concern for the whole work rather than production in parts by different hands – all this came into the concept of good printing. 'Business consultants' in our time could learn from the intelligence of this cooperative approach. It was very far from the executive who gives orders and goes out to lunch. These were men who loved to do the job themselves and knew it technically – like sailors in their small boats. All these private printers belonged to the arts and crafts movement, but none quite so thoroughly as the Essex House Press. So it is worth looking at its background and Ashbee's ideas in the history of the Guild. He published a number of books and wrote well, so we may turn to them and let him tell its history.

The Essex House Press issued its first book in 1898 and the volume of bibliography in 1909. Three more books appeared in 1910, under the care of Coomaraswamy, who had been associated with the press since 1906. In the eleven years before the bibliography eighty-three books are listed – an energetic achievement. Perhaps the most useful in tracing the Guild's history is not among these, though it was 'published by the Essex House Press'. Ashbee's collection of essays called *Craftsmanship in Competitive Industry* appeared in 1908, 'printed for the Author by Messrs. Grant & Co. Ltd.' This was a time when the Guild ran short of cash, and probably Ashbee felt his own book should not be a charge on Guild funds. It would have been typical of his generosity to think so. He describes there quite clearly the purpose of his life.

'The Arts and Crafts movement began with the object of making useful things, of making them well and of making them beautiful; goodness and beauty were to the leaders of the movement synonymous terms.'

From *Poems of Shakespeare*, Essex House Press, 1899. Caslon type with Ashbee's woodcut initials.

65

His theme was that fragmentary and theoretical knowledge taught in Polytechnics, away from the workshop, would not do. The worker needed to learn in the context of his own craft, to understand its needs and follow the teaching of his master according to the way of medieval guilds. This was the meaning of a phrase he often used, 'workshop reconstruction'. This was the practical intention he worked for. So he founded the two aspects of working life at once – workshops, and classes for apprentices who could learn about design from men who practised it in a working environment. 'To those who were acquainted with the beginning of the Guild,' he writes in one of his essays, 'the various educational undertakings connected with it between the years 1888 and 1894, the first workshop on the top of a warehouse in Commercial Street, and the classes for the study of design and the reading of Ruskin, carried on by me at Toynbee Hall in the years 1886 and 1887, it will be known that the Guild as originally conceived was the productive side of an undertaking that was also educational.' And again, '... the notion was that a School should be carried on in connection with a workshop; that the men in this workshop should be the teachers in the school, and that the pupils in the school should be drafted into the workshop as it grew in strength and certainty.' A few years later he was able to write with pride:

'It may seem paradoxical and also presumptuous to say – and yet it is not altogether untrue – that we at Essex House have for the last twelve years or so been engaged in the making of things that we consider the public ought to want, provided meanwhile that the man that makes them is the happier in their making.'

The purpose was well defined, too, in a book of rules printed by members at their own cost, in 1899:

'The Guild of Handicraft is a body of men of different trades, crafts and occupations, united together on such a basis as shall better promote both the goodness of the work produced and the standard of life of the producer. To this end it seeks to apply to the collective work of its members whatever is wisest and best in the principles of Co-operation, of Trade Unionism or of the modern revival of Art and Craft, and to apply these in such manner as changing circumstances permit or as shall be most helpful to its individual members.'

The astonishing thing, with all this talk and idealism and statement of principles, is that it worked for twenty-one years, starting at Toynbee Hall and the Commercial Road, establishing itself at Essex House in the Mile End Road for fifteen years and settling in peace at Chipping Campden though that happy move killed it at last. In this time remarkable work was produced in furniture, jewelry, silver and books, as well as all the devotion to teaching many subjects and aspects of life. It was the civilization of a small community.

One could say that it still lives. Campden is a quiet place to visit, with few obvious traces of the Guild of Handicraft. A Tudor altar-cloth in the church was copied by the Morris company and given by the King as a present to Westminster Abbey at the wedding of his daughter. The antique shops have nothing from that time, and their owners look blank if asked about it. The umbrella stand in a coffee-shop was obviously made by the Guild – 'Yes, that's very old,' the lady said when I mentioned it. But two hundred yards from the High Street and in a little lane is the old mill house which formed the Guild workshops; and two floors up Mr George Hart is making silver chalices and bowls as he did more than sixty years ago. He works with his son and grandson, and 'my first apprentice' who was just then pottering about in fawn overalls and a beret, making tea. Mr Hart joined the Guild soon after coming home from the South African war, and is not an old man. He uses the tools of those years, and says that the work 'gives me just the same kick as it did then'. It is a long wide room with low wooden ceiling and beams, a large photograph of Ashbee on the wall. The years of the Guild seem very close. 'A funny thing about Mr Ashbee, quite useless with his hands.' Why did the Guild break up? 'It really got too big, too much organization. People were there to tell you what to do, and then they had to keep up the shop in London.'

He looked in a shelf of files and gave me a catalogue from sixty years ago, of what could be ordered from the 'Workers in Applied Art Silversmiths and Jewellers'. They had an impressive list of patrons, among them Lady Hornby, the Macintosh of Macintosh and the Grand Duke of Hesse. Most of the objects look attractive, except for an odd lapse at the end – 'Statue of St Benedict – Carved in Wood,

Jessoed and Coloured in the manner of the 14th-Century Ecclesiastical Work.' To the top of his crozier he was five feet nine inches, and his price only came on application.

By the stairs there hangs a faded plaque of beaten copper from the Mile End Road days obviously, to the memory of a young worker at the Guild who died on a day in June when the white pinks came into flower. Those pinks are the symbol of the Essex House Press, and appear in all its work.

One recalls the fact of this Guild and its life at Campden. Next door to the silver shop the books were bound. In the evenings at Campden some members used to gather and sing, with help especially from Mrs Ashbee and Mrs New the wife of the artist whose woodcuts are familiar in books from the press. Mr Hart says he enjoyed the singing more than anything, and Ashbee wrote about the book they put together from printed sheets of these songs, the *Essex House Song Book*. It was his favourite book of all they printed. He searched to express the Guild Idea, and, 'To me, perhaps, its completed expression in the life of the Guild is to be found in its Song Book, printed and published by the Essex House Press in 1905, and entirely ignored by the General Public.'

Though nobody should have blamed the public, which was not split up in little guilds through the land.

The governing idea through this activity was that all art had equal claim to respect – no priorities and superiorities were accepted. Spreading paint for framing on walls seemed no higher than shaping the handle of a knife or strengthening the back of a book. Three aphorisms from Ashbee, who wrote forcibly, express the attitude: 'That under modern conditions of Art, picture painting is forced into an artificial prominence and the constructional and decorative arts, the real backbone, have, as yet, no right recognition among us.

'That the problems of machine production will have by degrees to be solved from within the workshop. That a sharp distinction will have to be drawn between what is produced by machinery and the direct work of man's hands, and that the standard of artistic excellence must depend ultimately upon the pleasure given, not to the consumer, but to the producer.

68

'That at the present day the social problem has prior claim to the artistic'.

Ashbee had the hard task of going forward from ideal principles and testing them in the practical world of 1890. He could not repeat the large resentments about machinery, but needed to discover where his hopes for workshop 'reconstruction' could be tried. He saw that the guild idea could only be useful in certain forms of industry, and would not be worth attempting in others. 'What I seek to show is that this Arts and Crafts movement, which began with the earnestness of the Pre-Raphaelite painters, the prophetic enthusiasm of Ruskin and the titanic energy of Morris, is not what the public has thought it to be, or is seeking to make it: a nursery for luxuries, a hothouse for the production of mere trivialities and useless things for the rich. It is a movement for the stamping out of such things by sound production on the one hand, and the inevitable regulation of machine production and cheap labour on the other.'

In a way the phrase Arts and Crafts was not what he wanted, because in his view crafts were arts.

No trace survives from other similar experiments, but Campden shows itself. Nearly next door to the workshops is the yard of Pyment the builder; and Mr Pyment's father taught wood-carving at the Guild. Building and wood-carving are not far apart. The little book of Guild rules from 1909 is in front of me now, marked 'Mr J. W. Pyment's copy'. Mr George Hart's brother has a house in the High Street, crammed to the roof with truly splendid furniture and bric-a-brac which Morris and Webb would have enjoyed. The pleasant and appropriate cottages for Guild members, which Ashbee built, may still be seen.

It was a great thing to reject vagueness and be practical. From 1903 to 1913 he wrote annual reports on the work of the Campden School of Arts and Crafts, and printed them at the press. They make interesting reading, far away from hopes and general statements. The school worked alongside the guild, as the plan had been from the beginning in London. It is a commonsense history, rather sad through its final failure. Lead glazing had almost died out in that area where it should have been well known, so they started to teach it again. In

1904 we read about the laundry class for girls – 'It seems extraordinarily foolish that so rudimentary a craft as starching should have practically disappeared in a place of 1500 inhabitants, and that when the folk of Campden want their shirts and collars starched they have to send them by carrier to Evesham.' So they teach that too.

Thus Campden was not merely a retreat, a precious workshop away from noise for the making of frivolities in the style called art nouveau. Ashbee interested himself in the history of the place, and with Sidney Webb's help published a book called *Last Records of a Cotswold Community*, concerned mostly with the local and brutal celebrations called games which used to take place in that neighbourhood; rather as Tom Hughes had written *The Scouring of the White Horse* through an interest in similar head-breaking games at Uffington. His plans for education at Campden were admirably far-sighted.

'Our higher education should be planned so as to link technical and humanistic teaching in every possible way. Technical teaching by itself is narrow; humanistic teaching is often unpractical. Our purpose should be to get people to see the connection between the two.'

And behind the work of the Guild was a clear vision of the reasons why their activity seemed good and satisfactory. He brought these reasons into the classes for children at Campden:

'In an age of machinery and sub-division of labour, handicraft becomes a necessity in itself. Boys and girls are taught much more readily to think by using their hands and eyes than by learning lessons out of books. This is well illustrated by the complaints we often hear of farmers that the old "uneducated" labourer was a more valuable man than the "hand" of a later generation who has learned to read and write. There is much truth in this. The book learning of the elementary school has often been of little service. The object of our higher education centre should be to fill the want of handicraft, both in the elementary school and in the more mechanical conditions of modern life.'

They all helped in an experiment towards this good reform of life, and must have enjoyed it very much. Mrs New is thanked for 'her constant and kindly office as musical whip and organiser'. There are pictures of the boys drilling under a stout-chested soldier, on a garden

70

path in winter; still wearing their caps and working suits, doing press-ups with distinctly hollow backs. Perhaps Miss Pook's report on the shorthand and typing class 1907–8 allows a hint of exasperation to appear.

'Typists should always sit fairly high to do good work. The school was unable to supply any high chairs or stools, and we had to make shift with some wooden blocks taken from the carving class to place the chairs on. It would add greatly to the comfort of the pupils if the school could provide them with a long, high form to sit on when typing, and this would not be very expensive. The makeshift we had this year was extremely uncomfortable. The students continually had collapses on to the floor whilst they were typing, owing to the blocks shifting. Some of the pupils objected very strongly to this, and it certainly disturbed the class and hindered the teaching.'

These are parochial matters, important in the life of the Guild – just as the arts we call minor had equal rank with painting. But Campden was kept from pettiness by the need to survive commercially and be constantly in touch with the London shop; and by a flow of visiting lecturers. In 1905 Walter Crane talked on 'Design in Relation to the Crafts', and J. R. Barlow on 'The Bournville Village Trust'. Alex Miller gave a lecture called 'Notes on Craftsmanship from the writing of John Ruskin', and Gerald Bishop took the fascinating theme of 'Holidays and Holiday-makers from before Paganism to after Lubbock'. Edward Carpenter spoke about 'Small Holdings and Life on the Land'. All these were relevant. The subjects are predictably near to Guild ideas and Ashbee's taste. Four years later he and Miller are lecturing on 'The Pre-Raphaelite Movement', 'Arts and Crafts and Commercialism', 'The Relation to Life of Poetry Handicraft and Song', and 'The Work of G. F. Watts'.

The school had a mixed lot of pupils including, in 1905, thirty-two married women and two postmen, four lead glaziers and seventy-eight elementary school children who came by arrangement with the county council. He noted happily that 'all the subjects taught are such as are not provided in the Campden Elementary Schools, or for which the schools have no conveniences, namely: Swimming, gardening, cookery, carpentry, life and duties of the citizen'.

71

The Guild's failure at last was from loss of money, not lack of enthusiasm. 'In plain business terms,' Ashbee wrote in 1908, 'the Guild had dropped at the beginning of its twenty-first year and at the end of a period of acute commercial depression, a substantial sum of money, upwards of £6,000–£7,000, the money of its shareholders, many of whom are the workmen themselves, in the attempt to carry through certain principles of workmanship and life.' It was reorganized after a fashion in 1908, and hoped to continue, but it assumed the more easy forms of private enterprise of which something remains there unbroken now. Ashbee dedicated his book in 1908 'To those Members of the Guild of Handicraft, who, whether working in the Guild's Shops or not, have decided to stick to it and see it through'. He quoted from Cecil Rhodes, 'If you have an Idea, and it is a good Idea, and you will only stick to it, you will come out all right in the end'.

The Guild came out all right, for one looks at it with admiration now, but there was an end. One trouble was simply that when people are supposed to be working together in harmony it becomes very embarrassing to sack anyone. As Ashbee put it, 'In businesses where the market is secure, management with the cooperation of labour works very well, but when rapid change and adaptation to market conditions are needed it leads to difficulties.' He tried to solve the problem of redundancy by providing agricultural land nearby, so that highly skilled men would not have to go far away when times were bad and gave them too little to do. But that never had a chance to work, and the war came…

So many good plans inspired the Guild of Handicraft, such energy, one wishes it were possible to point to more influence and scope. Ashbee might have looked back, at the end, to his sad and beautiful parable which closed the book he published in 1894, called *Chapters in Workshop Reconstruction and Citizenship*.

'I was watching the other day,' he wrote, 'the lilies making their way up through my garden. It is a London garden, so at its best there is not much to be expected from it, but on looking closely I found that, by some accidental shifting of the soil, all the bulbs had got covered up with much more mould than they could bear, and, unburying the

72

surface, I saw leaf after leaf, pale and colourless, thrown off underground, and a most manful struggle going on for fulfilment. I have removed the soil, but I fear too late, the strength of the plants has gone out beneath, and this year there will be no lilies.'

The Essex House Press was thoroughly unpredictable, and produced an odd miscellany of work. Two styles by which its books can be recognized mixed strangely. We can roughly think of them as Ashbee's art nouveau and Kelmscott Caslon.

There were physical links with the Kelmscott press, in men and machines. Ashbee bought the two Albion presses Morris had used, and judged that the time had come, when Kelmscott was closed and disbanded by the Trustees, to start something new. Binning the compositor joined him from Kelmscott, becoming one of the long-serving active members of the Guild. Hooper and Catterson-Smith, who had adapted Burne-Jones's drawings into wood-engravings, came to Essex House. Douglas Cockerell, brother of the secretary of the Kelmscott Press, helped in the bindery at Essex House. At the end of one book, Ashbee's designs for silver work, a kind of joint colophon with Essex House running down one side and Kelmscott down the other, claims or declares the heritage.

So there are recognizably sound qualities in the paper, ink, close spacing and press work. Ashbee and Savage designed alphabets of brave and successful decorated initials, which are very commonly used through the range of Essex House books. Ashbee's especially have great charm and precision in design, generally using the dianthus emblem of the Guild, strapping and weaving the flowers and foliage among his letter forms. There was no special scholarship or prolonged study of incunabula, but the impression is rather that these woodcut letters freely adapt ideas taken from initials which Morris designed, yet they are quite original, and unlike the sort of imitation which became common in the decade when Kelmscott printing formed a taste in England and America.

Caslon type was a sensible choice for these Kelmscott-influenced books. It was the best of the generally available kinds of classical alphabet, common in the mid-eighteenth century and revived by the Whittinghams in books they printed for Pickering after 1844. In its old hand-cut forms it had a hint of irregularity and could be mistaken for the Fell type which Hornby was using at that time in his early Ashendene books. Pleasantly used and set close on a simple page, it was the successful foundation for many Essex House books, the slight heaviness responding to ink and pressure which the Kelmscott craftsmen knew how to apply.

And again, the woodcuts could be very attractive. Apart from Ashbee, there were Laurence Housman, William Strang and E. H. New. Drawings by New of stone houses in Campden, or sunny streets with shadows and a pony trap, are pleasantly evocative in the books and prospectuses of the later period.

As often we can find the character of the press very well in a few of its ephemeral pieces. Kelmscott paper was generally used. A very pleasant Caslon prospectus was issued to announce the magnum opus of the press in 1903, the *Prayer Book* printed on the accession of Edward VII. It was to be 'bound, unless otherwise ordered, in oak boards fitted with hammered iron and leather clasps and red leather back' – was indeed to be, and is, a thoroughly arts and crafts production. The middle pages of the pamphlet have two of New's most peaceful woodcuts of Campden in quiet days. At the back we read that an advance copy of the book is on view now at the Guild's gallery, along with other specimens of crafts; that 'Mr Ashbee superintends the designing of most of the pieces, but work by other artists can also be seen.'

Pride in the work, in Campden and the Guild experiment, is in these notices and invitations. The woodcuts show it and another pamphlet claims in blurb language how 'the Guild feels convinced that not only the quality of the work done will be improved by the more efficient workshops, but also that the beautiful surroundings cannot fail to influence the work of each individual craftsman.'

In 1899 a prospectus describes the second book from the press, the *Hymn of Bardaisan* – a little book less distinguished in the event than this four-page announcement. And that included an impressive mention of plans which were never carried out, such as Froissart's *Chronicles*, *Piers Ploughman* and the *Poems of Burns*. Every publisher learns the sense of counting his manuscripts before declaring them.

74

Two years later a single page in two colours announces one of the best books the press issued, an edition of Wren's *Parentalia*. Ashbee was passionately anti-scrape, and a large red initial attracts us to read that this book is chosen 'In view of the imminent destruction in London of some of the few remaining churches of Sir Christopher Wren, owing to the greed of new railway exploiters, the apathy of her citizens and the indifference of her churchmen for the beautiful things they still possess…' An urgent red note at the end adds that Parliament was about to consider 'four tubular railway schemes' and that the life of St Mildred, Bread Street 'is coveted'. St Mildred, Bread Street, had another forty years before Hitler coveted and wrecked it.

Books came in all shapes and sizes from the press, but the second style was quite different and Ashbee's type designs dictated it. The King's Prayer Book type was designed for that work, and the Endeavour type, a smaller version of it, first appeared in Ashbee's little book of essays called *An Endeavour Towards the Teaching of John Ruskin and William Morris*. Perhaps he believed these would have the importance in his books which the Troy and Chaucer types gave to Kelmscott books, but nobody has had many good words to say for them.

The critics have perhaps been rather unjust. Ashbee formed his types with very little reference to tradition and history – he shows no fashionable sign of having studied Jenson or imitated Ratdolt. It was an art nouveau letter, mixing very well with the style of other Campden work and true to his sense of form. Nobody followed his example, but Essex House books printed in his types are more typical of that period than other work from the private presses. Ashbee was not being medieval or doing homage. Printed very black on the page, with close and even setting in the Kelmscott way, it tends to dazzle, and fails to that extent; but the experiment was brave and attracts us now for its turn-of-the-century taste.

In one of the stranger works of the Press, an oblong folio, *The Masque of the Edwards of England*, Ashbee, with surprising levity, has a character called L'Art-Nouveau who describes himself with up-to-date cynicism:

75

I'm in the fashion – non-controversial,
And the fashion is nothing if not commercial,
Pre-Raphaelite once, with a tiny twist
Of the philosophical hedonist, –
Inspired by Whistler, – next a touch
Of the 'Arts and Crafts', but not too much.
Then Impressionism, the daintiest fluke;
Then the German squirm, & the Glasgow spook,
A spice of the latest French erotic,
Anything new and Studiotic,
As long as it tells in black and white,
And however wrong comes out all right,
'Id est', as long as it pays, you know,
That's what's meant by L'Art Nouveau!

Among the small pieces, a prospectus in 1902 for *The Flower and the Leaf*, printed in black and red, shows well the variety and range of use in the Endeavour type. One page in the eight calls 'the attention of the lovers of Essex House Press books to the Essex House Bindery, now opened under Mr Ashbee's direction, and in charge of Miss Powell in conjunction with the Press at Campden, Gloucestershire'. The bindings sound delightful 'in various leathers, and also in ebony, rose, and holly wood, and in silver with enamels'.

Perhaps the best use of Ashbee's types was in display work, and this is shown quite simply by comparing two forms of invitation to exhibitions of Guild work in London. One has a pleasant woodcut by New, and Caslon capitals for the invitation; in the other, a festive woodcut by Strang surrounds Ashbee's lettering and invites us with our friends to the private view of the Guild's second annual exhibition. Strang's design and Endeavour capitals are excellent together, suggesting the good sense and unity of a style. Caslon letters mixed equally with the design by New, whose work was traditional and outside the common Guild mood. It is time to look at the character of the books, and follow this muddle of manner in them.

There is a kind of philosophy in the choice of books the press printed. Some are concerned about destruction of old buildings, others with the Guild and its way of life. Hood's macabre poem of *Miss Kilmansegg and her golden leg* was a satisfactory parable for socialist members, and John Woolman's *Journals* brought a taste of selfless piety and anti-slavery from eighteenth-century Philadelphia. Shelley's *Prometheus* had the grand theme of man's freedom, and Erasmus *In Praise of Folly* appealed in the same way as *Utopia* which Kelmscott and Ashendene had printed already. *The Pilgrim's Progress* seems an obvious choice, and several books dealt with craft themes – Cellini's treatise on metal work, Ashbee's designs for silver. There were religious works, and an ambitious plan to print a two-volume bible in 1904 but unhappily that was under-subscribed and abandoned. Generally they avoided the common temptations towards Rossetti's sonnets, *Hand and Soul*, *Sonnets from the Portuguese*. Fitzgerald's translation only appeared on commission from a dining club of Omar Khayyam enthusiasts.

Apart from all this, the press is often remembered for its 'great poems' series. These were little books printed on vellum, coloured by hand with more charm than skill. Fourteen poems appeared in this way – *Ancient Mariner*, *Comus*, *Epithalamion*, *The Immortality Ode*, *Maud*, *The Deserted Village*, Gray's *Elegy* and others. They are pleasant evidence of local enthusiasm, but should not be treasured too seriously as examples of printing. Walter Crane made the frontispiece for Wordsworth's poem, Florence Kingsford coloured for Coleridge. About one hundred and fifty copies were issued of each, though the first in the series, *Adonais*, is much rarer. The most skilful and original of them all, a charming small work of art, is the medieval poem once ascribed to Chaucer, *The Flower and the Leaf*. Morris had enjoyed this and printed it, but there was no harm in doing it again. Edith Harwood made and coloured the decorations which run happily through the pages, in quite original simplicity of form and arrangement – large initials for each new stanza, with people and flowers in greens and pinks, purple and brown. Caslon was used for all this series.

Three splendid quartos may be taken as examples of the three types the press used.

The edition of Erasmus, *In Praise of Folly*, was edited by Janet Ashbee and printed in 1901. It was an appropriate choice, and set very simply in Caslon with side notes in italic but no headline. The result is a flawless page, and presswork was excellent. Designs drawn by William Strang, and cut on wood by Bernard Sleigh, have strength with just a hint of Guild style. A very powerful serpent twists about handsome Eve in a large triangle, its tail and her toe concluding the book. Ashbee designed a kind of harlequin cover which is printed on parchment. Father Time and a medieval peasant shake hands across the inner frame of a title page. Two hundred and fifty copies were printed. This may rank among the best made books of that time, and it is cynically amusing to read still.

'And fyrst, who is he but will confuse Childhode, the fyrst age of man, to be most gracious and acceptable unto all folks? for els, what is it in younge babes that we dooe kysse so, we doe colle so, we dooe cherisshe so, that a verie enemie is moved to spare and succour this age, unless it be the allurement of Folie? whiche, natures circumspection, even purposedly, hath adjoigned to children, to the ende that with some reputacion of pleasure, thei might supple the travaile of theyr bringers up, and provoke the benevolence of suche as tende unto theim'.

A good example of Ashbee's 'Endeavour' type, the smaller of his two letter designs – in the same relation as Chaucer to Troy type – is *The Psalter or Psalms of David* from the Bible of Archbishop Cranmer. This was produced in the year after Erasmus, edited again by Janet Ashbee 'in honour of David the great singer', bound in vellum which is not very happily stained blue. The reason for enthusiasm here is the splitting up and division of the pages of psalms which makes thoroughly enjoyable use of this type face. Just as a solid large page of Caslon was classical and right in the Erasmus, so the two-column arrangement here and the red leaves printed to mark verses give proper pause in the reading and balance to the page. Ashbee's type solid on a page dazzles with its even blackness. He cared more for shape in letter than variation in weight. Each psalm starts with woodcut initials which he designed for the book, and they, with his mannered letter forms, give this a happy unity. His own skill in books is best seen here or in the King Edward Prayer Book where again woodcuts and the character of the task make pauses and fragments and not foursquare pages.

For similar reasons this or the large version of it, called Prayer Book type, could be well used in setting poetry. Prayer Book type was chosen for the quarto edition of *Prometheus Unbound*, printed at Campden in 1904. This large dark letter looks imposing here and is rightly used, split by long and short lines of verse on the big page and by red which is used for notes and characters. There seem to be typographical undertones in Shelley's stage direction, 'A Train of dark Forms and Shadows passes by confusedly', but they are forgotten in the fineness of the song:

> Here, oh, here:
> We bear the bier
> Of the Father of many a cancelled year!
> Spectres we
> Of the dead Hours be,
> We bear Time to his tomb in eternity.

It is not necessary or possible to describe many of the sound and delightful books printed by the Essex House Press. The Essex House edition of Shakespeare's poems, in Caslon with Ashbee's leafy alphabet of woodcuts, is perhaps the finest version achieved by any of the private presses including Kelmscott. The fat little pocket books – only the loosest overcoat could have held them – *Pilgrim's Progress*, William Penn's sayings, and A *Journal of the Life and Travels of John Woolman*, are charming to read and bravely set in the usual size of Caslon with a smaller version of Ashbee's initial letters. Woolman is a particularly sympathetic character, making great and dangerous journeys when the missionary spirit moved him. It moved him towards England at last, but the sight of unnecessary decoration on the ship's prow made him think his passage money would in a manner be support for this luxury and the men who caused it; so he travelled steerage. His friends must have taken him as an amiable crank. 'In these opportunities my mind, through the mercies of the Lord, was kept low in an inward waiting for his help; and Friends having expressed their desire that I might have a more convenient place than the steerage, did not urge it, but appeared disposed to leave me to the Lord'.

The work of the bindery should be mentioned. Douglas Cockerell helped in the early days, his influence obvious in many Guild of Handicraft bindings – apart from those which are his own work, signed by him. Miss Felicity Ashbee possesses a beautiful copy of the *Essex House Song Book* printed on vellum and bound by Cockerell. The bindery at Campden was run by Miss Powell, whose bindings are blind-stamped at the end GH with the dianthus emblem between, and a monogram AP. I have seen two American books printed by the Elston press, bound by the Guild of Handicraft: blind-stamped with a hint of Gothic taste, serviceable amateur work, nothing to write home about.

More interesting is a binding in brick-coloured morocco, divided into sections which are charmingly decorated with the Guild's dianthus emblem and, oddly, sprays of holly leaves. This unsigned binding is very obviously Guild work, perhaps under Cockerell's care, and it protects the *Essex House Song Book*. This was the heart of it, printed part by part for their winter evenings – bravely using two colours for the music at first, but keeping red later for the chorus words. Ashbee was in this again, writing airs for Scott's words or words for Beggar's Opera airs. And there we can leave the Guild of Handicraft, shouting out William Morris's words through the otherwise quiet Campden evening sixty years ago, to the tune of John Brown's Body,

> What is this sound and rumour? What is this that all men hear?
> Like the wind in hollow valleys when the storm is drawing near,
> Like the rolling on of ocean in the eventide of fear?
> 'Tis the people marching on!

made to her husbande, feigned that hee was a yonge man, of comely stature, with a flex~ en bearde, & had great delight in huntinge in the hilles and dales by. And least by her longe talke she should be founde to trippe or faile in her wordes, she filled their lappes with golde, silver, & Jewels, & commanded Zephyrus to carry them away.

When they were brought up to the mountaine, they toke their waies home~ warde to their owne houses, & murmured with envy that they bare against Psyches, sayinge, Beholde cruell & contrary fortune, behold how we, borne all of one Parent, have divers destinies: but especially we that are the elder two be married to strange hus~

From *The Marriage of Cupid and Psyche*, Vale Press, 1897. Wood engraving by Ricketts.

From the title opening of *Poetical Sketches* by William Blake. Vale Press. 1899, Wood engraving by Ricketts.

VALE, ERAGNY AND A LINK WITH
THE AESTHETIC MOVEMENT

The course of the Vale Press was from 1896 to 1904. Charles Ricketts had designed books before his Vale Press began, and in much the same style as the Press followed. The books he designed for Osgood, McIlvaine in 1890 and 1891 had been 'unlike the ordinary books in the matter of title page, proportion of margin, and in the designs upon their boards'. The title page of *Tess of the D'Urbervilles*, with its long lower margin, is influenced by Whistler, but the honeysuckle shapes with wavy lines on the binding are in the style he developed.*

Those earlier books did not meet all the conditions of book design as he laid them down at the closing of the Press in 1904; they were not printed in his own type founts, and he did not see them through the Press. For Ricketts lived well within the arts-and-crafts view of the printing revival. In the 1904 Bibliography of the Vale press, printed by him privately but forming the last of the Vale books, he put it very clearly:

'The novelty of a book, made during the recent revival, lies in the fact that it shows design in each portion of it, from type to paper, and from "build" to decoration. Therein lies the difference between a book so understood and any other modern book printed before 1891: therein lies their affinity with the grand volumes of the Italian and German presses.'

Vale Press books tend to be quiet and modest – less obviously fine than Morris's books, less perfectly finished than a Doves book; it needs some sympathy to accept the claim he makes, about their affinity with 'the grand volumes of the Italian and German presses'. But Ricketts is one among them all who stands comparison with Morris, differing from him in the concept of a book but having much in common.

Like Morris, he was much more than a printer or maker of books. As an artist his range was wide and restless – wood engravings, stage design, oil painting, etching. Books were not likely to provide the

---

* I owe this example, and much else, to John Lewis. The title page and binding are clearly shown in his *The Twentieth-Century Book*, Studio Vista, 1967.

final philosophical answer. Forty-eight works appeared from the Vale Press, including as one work a complete Shakespeare in thirty-three volumes. It was an immense achievement. A discouraging fire at the printers destroyed many of his engraved designs, borders and initial letters, and the impetus dropped away. His own reason for stopping sounds peculiarly foolish – that 'the number of books which were suitable to the conditions of the firm had dwindled with time'. After so much energy the pleasure had evaporated, he had worked himself out, there was nothing to add to his last statement.

In several ways Ricketts belongs with Morris, and first because both were designers. As an artist he has received highest marks time and again – from Basil Grey in a history of prints (1939) and, most recently, from John Russell Taylor in his book, *The Art Nouveau Book in Britain*. But Ricketts has not always been accepted in his own claims, as maker of the whole book. Wood engravings and designs for borders or intitials give only part of the story and one which others also could manage. He is not only for the art critics.

He and Morris were the two printer-designers – with perhaps Lucien Pissarro, later and on a small scale. And though Ricketts was much younger (born 1868) they began making books at about the same time. He and Charles Shannon – as an artist merely, there is no evidence that Shannon offered ideas about the printed book – and Sturge Moore formed the trio for the Vale Press; with literary and editorial advice from John Gray, author of *Silverpoints*. So this takes them out towards Beardsley and the more typically aesthetic attitudes of the eighteen-nineties, where they half-belonged. Beardsley was not concerned with arts-and-crafts, and it is hard to imagine Ricketts as a socialist. Morris would not have spent, as Ricketts did, five hundred pounds in one year on flowers for the house. Yet their work is closely linked, and Ricketts says that Morris on his death-bed wept at the sight of Vale Press books. Their bond was this flair for making a thing wholly and mastering it, start to finish; and a scholarly affection for early printing. Again, except for Lucien Pissarro, he was the only important one among them all who could draw borders and decorations with something of Morris's skill, and might therefore have produced books which competed with his own. But

82

Ricketts, unlike the imitators in America, was an original artist and carefully developed his own style, differing from Morris also in several points of theory about type and printing.

Ricketts took a position which belonged appropriately to the younger man – if progress from one age to another has a parallel in the two generations. He rejected the earlier assumptions about calligraphy and its influence upon type design. Morris and Walter Crane had worked from the clear similarity between fifteenth-century calligraphy and early type; indeed, the first printed pages are almost indistinguishable from scribes' work of the period. And this had a strong appeal, linking this questionable invention of printing with the older ways of life which they both admired. It became important for Morris that modern type designs, returning to fifteenth-century perfection, preserve this link with pen letters.

Ricketts was so original as to point out extreme differences between punch-cutting and pen-pushing, and to put the view that there could be no need to follow a style which had been dictated by other tools and conditions. It is an important divergence, with a focus upon the well-known problem of the true arts-and-crafts man when he considers machinery or new materials – even though 'new' in this instance means late fifteenth-century, post-Gutenberg.

In his essay printed at the Vale press, *A Defence of the Revival of Printing*, Ricketts wrote:

'That trained scribes of the fifteenth-century were called in to design type, and that the efforts to recast the Carolingian writings of the ninth and tenth centuries benefited by their practice with the pen, is conceivable enough, but conjecture ends here, for penmanship was not of the highest quality at the end of the fifteenth-century. A student of form must study elsewhere (as the old type designers did) to note at what period shape reaches its perfection.

'At a charmed time in the development of man, in the Renaissance namely, the old vein was reopened, and reworked to suit the exigencies of the new material, i.e., type, and it is the duty of the modern student to note how this or that element was lost in the excitement of discovery, or else merely over-looked; to compare, reason and recast, that his type may fulfil the requirements and ben-

83

efit by the conditions of his proper medium, and so become type – type only.'

His interest in metal as the medium for type and borders shows absolute logic of argument, and appears in the fine delicacy of his borders – compared with the calligraphic flourish of Kelmscott borders. Applied to type design he felt less free, because people had to read his books and recognize the letters. He designed the letters which reflected his scholarly choice among ancient letter forms – believing that scribes had taken a lazy way with certain of them, and seeing no need to follow that laziness into type. So he went back to the period of development which seemed to achieve passing perfection, against the taste of all the other specialists, and made for the first and last time in type a half-uncial alphabet. He caught the phase between capital letters and what printers call lower-case – between majuscule and miniscule – in which several letters appear still to be capital, and most have developed the shape the scribes found convenient. This type face he designed appropriately for the thirteenth-century poem *The Kingis Quair*, one of the most interesting of the Vale books because love and taste went into it. He used it only twice more, though this was his favourite among the three Vale Press founts. All three, before the Press closed, went underwater where private press types seemed properly to rest.

The originality of the Vale or Kelmscott books can be discussed here, because Ricketts was several times articulate in claiming it. Morris had thought the edition of his *Roots of the Mountains*, printed modestly at the Chiswick Press in type copied from an old Basle fount, one of the outstanding printed books since the fifteenth century. To see it now, there is nothing obviously marvellous. Equally, a Vale book was far from the taste or manner of splendid Victorian books which are time and again described as the 'precursors of Morris'. One begins to question the qualities in these earlier books which are supposed to have pre-cursed him.

Kelmscott books are known for splendour, but neither Morris nor Ricketts could challenge the mid-century in that matter. Mr Ruari McLean has fascinatingly charted the century which Morris despised, pointing to its glories and opening our minds to what

84

Kelmscott rejected, until it seems worth putting the Kelmscott Chaucer side by side with a copy of the *Grammar of Ornament* and seeing where our own judgment lies. There was no lack of skill, craft, care or pride in the great mid-Victorian books. So what were they all protesting about, and what did the revival of printing revive? A wiser comparison might be to place the *Kingis Quair* beside the *Grammar of Ornament*.

Most simply, one might see it as an anti-technical rebellion. We can now admire everything from another age, for we generally despise our own, but our taste for it must still distinguish, choose and judge. Victorian publishers and artists must have been delighted by the sudden chances the technicians had provided, especially in colour-printing. No more need for gangs of students to add the water-colour, or for children to paint through stencils within printed outline. Four, six, twelve printings could be used upon one illustration. Chromo-lithography meant a millenium, books became larger and ever more ambitious. Whether we notice and collect them now, or dismiss them for poor taste, is irrelevant. The skill is not questioned.

But the focus turned upon illustration, which is only part of most books. Henry Shaw, Owen Jones, Digby Wyatt and other antiquaries produced picture books in the pride of their enthusiasm for medieval art, ornament and calligraphy. The textual job of a book half-disappeared, and some of the finest examples from Shaw printed by Whittingham might be indifferent in that respect, and the illuminating superb.

In all this just two characteristics are near to Ricketts and Morris: the great care needed for each copy where all the hand-work could not often be repeated – especially in the illuminated initials which Shaw enjoyed, and the common enthusiasm for medieval art. This medieval discovery, which Morris shared with them, took varying forms. One was a love of bright colours, where printing methods kept pace with Pre-Raphaelite tastes in painting.

But the changed philosophy turned upon a view of the printed book – not merely illustration. Marriage of type and decoration, quality of ink and paper – everything contributed. That is why the brilliant chromolithography of Owen Jones has nothing whatever to do with

85

the Kelmscott Chaucer – or with the most innocent book produced at the Vale, where quietness meant unity not lack of ambition.

The small and exquisitely colour-printed Victorian gift books had nothing to do with it either. Anyone who has hoped to enjoy them, to experience some of this precursor pleasure, knows what a chaos of incompetence they are; pages falling out, stiff card mixed miserably with flimsy newsprint, or even in the splendid works of gilding and hand-colouring, paint blotting the pages opposite or showing damp patterns through the opening before. All this means poor book making, in spite of a flair for certain techniques and their enjoyment. It is very far from the ideas and ideals of Ricketts. There was room for revolution.

But one can more easily compare Vale with Kelmscott. Both used borders – but Ricketts had infinite pains with his, and Morris enjoyed designing his decorations for relaxation much as other people plant bulbs in their gardens. So there are fewer ornaments in Vale books – though the title pages of each tend to be equally filled up with overall design. The Doves and Ashendene title pages represented a reaction against them both. And Morris's leafy flowery designs had a self-assurance which is some way from the precise and delicate line of the Vale Press. Ricketts's honeysuckle and his pansies are astonishingly clever in offering the feel and appearance of those flowers – rather as Morris's willow-bough wallpaper suggests the very tangle of hanging leaves which one needs to part with both arms to make a way through. Vale flowers are botanical, and Kelmscott structural. Morris gave the sense of a flower, without troubling with its identity – a sort of figurative abstract art.

The types came near to meeting in Golden and Vale founts, but the Ricketts half-uncial experiments have no kinship to Morris's half-Gothic. The difference in mood shows especially in these rather precious books, faintly effeminate to Morris's aggressive masculine. In the illustrations we could see closer connections; for Ricketts shared with Burne-Jones a sensitive line and sinuous view of drapery or anatomy – and both believed equally that the picture should form part of the text opening. Both pointed to (or from) the influence of Aubrey Beardsley and the style of art nouveau.

86

A decorative title page, Vale Press for Keats' *Endymion*.

Vale books never had the ambition – the masculine grandeur – of the Kelmscott folios, though that is not a difference of quality, but they failed by comparison in their choice of paper. The Vale Press paper – except for a couple of the large books – tends to be limp and soft now, foxed and inadequate. The strength and brilliance are missing, and this finally makes them humdrum beside the greater work of Morris. Bindings bear comparison also and here Ricketts wins because from of old he had interested himself in bindings and designed them for other people. The gold-on-vellum pattern which he made for Lord De Tabley's poems was an early and pleasant example – related to the work of Rossetti, Whistler and Beardsley. The geometric and spare pattern blind-blocked upon smooth green cloth, in which he clothed the Vale Shakespeare, is characteristic of a later style he used also upon his own books issued long after the Vale Press had closed. Between these two he used a style, quite varied within itself, which had some influence upon elegance in book covers over the next decades – the patterned paper boards with printed labels. It is likely that he took this style from Lucien Pissarro. Kelmscott books were always either in white vellum or grey paper-board and holland back. Morris intended the paper-board copies to be bound by the owner, in the old way of printers and private collectors; but clearly Ricketts meant his gay patterns to be enjoyed, not destroyed. One was thinking of present pleasure, the other of eternity.

Some of the small early Vale books have grey or blue paper board only; but the patterned papers are delightful and have all the skill of Morris's designs for wallpaper. *The Blessed Damozel*, 1898, a perfect little book on Kelmscott paper, has a pattern of angels and doves sloping across olive-green paper. The two volumes of Chatterton's poems, 1898, have swallows and roses in dark green and also a red geometric pattern for the spines. These were an advance from the attractive simplicity of the *Poems of Suckling*, two years before, where a dianthus which seems to sprout rose leaves and oak leaves slants in dark green across buff paper. The volumes of Michael Field's plays have splendid covers – bold oak leaves reversed through deep green upon a grey textured paper for *The Race of Leaves;* olive peacocks floating across a grey space, with sprigs of willow in their beaks, for

Julia Domna; an abstract suggestion of dot and flame in light green and orange for *The World at Auction.* The symbolism is not always clear, the effect is unerring. The arrangement of titles on spines can be odd and unorthodox too, unlike the propriety of Kelmscott. Michael Field's *Julia Domna,* which could most easily have run up its white label on the slim grey spine, is arranged across as

JULIA
DOMN
A

M.F.

But all in all these cover papers are extremely attractive, and it is unfortunate that we see so little of them – and that their condition does not improve with time.

Sturge Moore has described the energy and gaiety of Ricketts in in those years of the Vale Press. His reputation has gathered odd overtones to fit the place of his drawings with Beardsley's art, but the force and outward-turning fun, the capacity for work, seem nearer to Morris. Certainly the memory of his response in receiving an inscribed copy of *The Sphinx,* a volume of poems he had designed for Oscar Wilde, is in the Morris style:

'Ricketts never admitted any of Wilde's work into the first class, though he prized and learned much from his immense capacity for making the actual moment effective. Yet I can see his face crimson as he tore out the fly-leaf Wilde had inscribed from the copy of *The Sphinx* sent to him. "Vulgar beast!" he cried, for the signature ended in a straight-lined "Z" scrawled right across the leaf, an outrage to the exquisite niceties of the artist's book building, in blatant contrast also with the modesty of his insect-like autograph.'

And Sturge Moore's earlier description seems to bring a thought of Swinburne.

'I first met Charles Ricketts in 1887, his twenty-first year; he was even then, as he still is, for me incomparable. For Shannon, whom I had known a couple of years, had created a Ricketts in my mind, without report of any physical trait, but merely by frequent assertion of his ability to evolve compositions, to pick out good work and to remember all he had seen. A bodiless giant had loomed on my apprehension, dark-haired, because power associates with depth of tone... but this is already far too definite... At last I saw him, a short, ramshackle youth in a cloud of extremely fine tow-coloured hair which stood round his head like a dandelion puff. At 11 a.m. he had just turned out of bed and had no collar, no socks, and but just enough on to enable him to cross the two hundred yards from their rooms to the school. When he entered he was imitating an orchestra with gestures as well as sounds, a characteristic mode of progression from room to room all his life. Somebody began describing a picture of young girls with hay-rakes; he pretended to be shocked, "Young girls with rakes!" and danced about hiding his face in his hands and laughed even more than we did.'

As a scholar, outside the field of design, Ricketts had far less to offer than Morris. Both knew about early printing and writing, but Morris brought more of his own taste and standards to the choice of books which his press issued, and stamped a kind of appropriateness upon them. This cannot be true of his whole output – there is nothing particularly true to Shelley in the manner of a Kelmscott book – but certainly the grand Caxton reprints, Chaucer, the little medieval poems, and of course his own work were from the heart. Vale Press books seem to be a general sampling of likely taste among cultivated readers including Ricketts and his friends. We can be grateful that there are Vale Press editions of Campion's poems, of Suckling, Drayton and Constable. This looks like somebody's particular taste, but it spreads across to Wordsworth, Keats, Tennyson – and of course, the apprenticeship for so many of them, *Hand and Soul* and *Sonnets from the Portuguese*. No such guiding spirit cared for this choice, as designed its printing. That is what makes the airy sentence about

90

shortage of appropriate literature, at the closure of the press, look particularly silly. Sturge Moore had a sharper word for it: 'The £500 Ricketts inherited from his grandfather was invested in the Vale Press, which he had the sagacity to close down just before the fall in the prices of Morris and Vale books which followed the Boer War.' And although John Gray, Sturge Moore and Masefield at one time and another helped in the editing, the unscholarly nudity of Vale Press texts is in the common mood of private press work. No help with awkward passages (just the rarest footnote to explain a word), not one helpful introduction to the work or its author, nothing about the editing or previous editions, never a useful index. Almost the same could be said of the whole range of literature in the revival of printing. It points an astonishing focus upon the physical book as pleasure enough alone – or an assumption that we all know the backgrounds so notes and help are not needed. Whatever the reason, no help came. Nobody has yet turned to the private presses for confirmation in matters of scholarship. In our own period of excessive footnoting, where the teacher seems more highly valued than his author, some may turn back with a free heart to wander in pages which have not been tampered with; where the editor has worked, collected, enjoyed himself peacefully, resisted the temptation to interfere.

One of the most attractive Vale Press bindings came first of all – the small *Hero and Leander*, Marlowe's poem with Chapman's continuation, white vellum with the kind of geometric gold design of which Ricketts was a master. The vellum copies of Vale books, similarly, had limp vellum bindings with gold rules on the spines. The *Parables*, with excellent woodcuts by Ricketts in the quiet manner of Lucien Pissarro, appeared also in white vellum. But the white buckram bindings of a series of the Vale poets – three volumes of Shelley, two of Tennyson, one of Browning, and several more – had very little merit and generally seem soiled now.

On the whole, the list of Vale books suggests no special taste except in four separate volumes of plays by Michael Field. The aunt and niece, hiding in that name, were intimate friends of Ricketts and Shannon. They also appear in volumes from the Daniel Press, and from Eragny. But apart from particularly successful covers and title pages, the strained emotion and solemn tragedy of their drama add no dimension to our pleasure in Vale Press books. A passage from *The World at Auction* gives a fair idea of their manner:

> Mother, you stay or go, but I return
> Home from a palace where my will is mocked.
> My word claims no belief, my natural place
> Is filled by yonder god of print and lawn
> My sire is pleased to cherish as a son.
> Augustus, I, like you, disown our bond:
> You have no daughter, and my love is hate.

Dr Alan Fern has written the last word about the Eragny Press in his elegant little Christmas book from the Cambridge University Press for 1959. Lucien Pissarro and his wife Esther ran it together, in very different circumstances from that other couple, the Daniels, who had worked together to make their books. The Pissarros were poor, though Esther Bensusan came from a prosperous family. Lucien's father Camille, full of a painter's integrity all his days, never earning enough money until the end, quarrelling with his peasant wife but managed by her, sent help to Lucien in London, but he was only one of a large family.

Lucien had a long life, from 1863 to 1944. When he came to London for a year, in 1883, the family moved to Eragny between Paris and Dieppe. His London move seems not to have been any sort of rebellion, and relations with his father were always intimate and affectionate. But he came to learn more about wood engraving, and settled permanently in London after 1890. His particular friends were Ricketts and Shannon, and he worked with them on their journal *The Dial*. One high principle of the editors was that they would accept and encourage original print-making – reproductions were not wanted. All this chimed with the taste shown later in Vale and Eragny Press books.

'In a conversation', he wrote to Camille, '(when I go to their place we talk until long past midnight) Ricketts told me that the English

92

are not interested in engraving! that it was only in France that one saw those ardent amateur collectors. I disillusioned him, naturally, and told him that in France we imagined that only the English still interested themselves in engraving. Astonishment on both sides! What ideas we have of ourselves!! Ricketts will soon have his typographic press and we are all going to work on prints.'

Lucien's life work was as a painter and engraver, rather than printer; but it is clear from W. S. Meadmore's book* that the Eragny Press took most of his activity and hopes from its start in 1894 to the last book in 1914. It was always meant – unlike the most orthodox concept of private printing – to provide an income; but as it never did, he may be forgiven for that. Nobody could more thoroughly have identified himself with the working ideals of a private press. He mentions this in his letter to Manson in 1913: 'Hand-made paper printing is a very difficult thing to do; it is there where the machine falls short of the old fashioned presses, because the paper having to be used wet cannot support the rough handling of machinery.'

It was like no other press, working its way with all the integrity Camille showed in his single-minded theories of painting. After nine years of printing he was writing to his father of a hope 'to tell you that we could live without your allowance, but the time has not yet come. It is terrible to have to tell you this, but we must wait, wait, wait, until I can recover what I was able to do before my illness'; and 'you have no idea of the work needed to print a book'.

And the printed books are appreciated now, though he might have preferred better attention at the time they appeared. Those with an eye for them – among modern experts Alan Fern, John Dreyfus and John Lewis – see them with high admiration and affection. So did Camille Pissarro, who wrote to Lucien in 1897 after receiving a copy of his third book, the first volume of Laforgue, *Moralités Légendaires:* 'Your book arrived. Very beautiful, very polished, the first page with the ornament of Salomé, the typography, etc., has the stamp of a master. The cover is charming. It is a beautiful book'.

Nobody could miss the special charm of Eragny books these days, but

* *Lucien Pissarro*, London, Constable, 1962.

they may be a little over-praised. They remain a fairly minor matter in the whole movement, but unlike anything else. The illustrations form one single link with French impressionism, with the Normandy people and countryside and innocent recollections of another age than this. Yet Lucien has been oddly admired for his use of colour in these wood engravings and his experiments with gold printing. The Japanese had of course been doing it all, with infinitely more skill and sophistication, for more than a hundred years before he was born. Lucien caught the current and breeze from Japan; but Edmund Evans had known about colour printing from wood in England, and George Baxter before him, and Richard Savage some time before either of them. All this is well known and charted, but Lucien still receives tribute as 'a pioneer in using colour in wood engraving'.

The originality of his engravings, that which takes them away from all other book illustration, was his cross-fertilization from Japan to Normandy. To take the smooth with the rough in this way, formed Lucien's art of the book. The sturdiness of his French peasants, the trunks of trees which seem more Narnia than Normandy, and a flat formality of poise and composition which is wholly Japanese, give these pictures a place apart from anyone working near him and with similar enthusiasms. And the colours are always happy and flawless, influenced, Alan Fern suggests, by his father's long friendship with Seurat.

It is appropriate that he began with a children's story, *The Queen of the Fishes*. The text of this little book was photographed from Lucien's handwriting, and so gives the kind of unity with his illustrations which all of them were seeking – but it is a slightly muddly page to read. The engraved illustrations and borders, pretty and childish as they should be, are far more complex and carefully organized than at first sight; their shadows and forms always delicate and deserving a careful long look. In that way it is a beautiful book for children, though nobody is or ever was likely to let them get hold of it. His problems with the gold were like Cobden-Sanderson's in his binding days, but it succeeded very well. The simple vellum binding of copies which were not given to his friends has two irises peacefully sheltered by their leaves, in gold, and no title.

94

By the kindness of Miss Orovida Pissarro it is possible to reprint Lucien's short outline of the history of the Eragny Press, which gives its period and emphasis very clearly:

'The Eragny Press had its origin in the following circumstances.

'Over thirty years ago I had a desire to produce illustrated books and I planned two coloured albums for children. These were submitted to several publishers in Paris who objected to them mainly on the ground that they would be too costly to produce. So it occurred to me that the cost would be considerably reduced if I could engrave the line and colour blocks myself.

'My father gave me an introduction to Aug. Lepère who showed me the tools he used and the way to handle them. After a little practice I was able to engrave fairly well although in a simplified fashion.

'My first attempts were shown to the *Revue Illustrée*, the Director of which, M. F. G. Dumas, gave me a commission to illustrate a short story by Octave Mirbeau entitled "Mait' Liziard".

'Accordingly I executed (four) wood blocks which were published. At that time extra fine work was in vogue and the rather coarse manner of my engravings brought a storm of protest down on the Editor and my collaboration came to an abrupt end.

'Hearing that a movement was on foot in England towards a revival of wood-engraving and printing, I decided to come to London. This was in 1890, at the time when William Morris's "Arts and Crafts" movement was in full swing.

'I was introduced to Ricketts and Shannon who were also deeply interested in wood-engraving and printing.

'It was at their studio in The Vale, Chelsea, that, by their precept and example I got to know many of the rules the observance of which is essential to the production of the "book beautiful".

'At that time they were issuing an occasional magazine called The Dial and I gladly accepted an invitation to contribute to its pages.

'This taught me, among other things, that it is not absolutely necessary to depend on a publisher in order to produce a book or a magazine.

'So, in 1891, I made a portfolio of wood-engravings in line and colour, and soon after, a small booklet in line, colour and gold, the text of

95

which was reproduced by means of process blocks. Having finished the preliminary work, I determined to try to print it myself with the help of my wife who had learned wood-engraving in the meantime. 'We knew nothing of the art of printing and had to learn it as we went along – which meant that we were faced with endless difficulties. We bought a small hand-press, crown 4to, and started to print this booklet, *The Queen of the Fishes*, two pages at a time; the gold used in the book was real gold powder. Owing to the exceedingly imperfect tools we then had, the registration gave us a great deal of trouble. After many sheets of paper had been spoilt, the edition was achieved. 'It had been advertised that the binding would be in green leather but a strike in Germany stopped the supplies and we were able to secure only enough leather to bind the subscribers' copies; the rest of the edition was bound in vellum.

'This book, which was produced before the firm of Hacon and Ricketts was formed, was issued by Ricketts and Shannon from The Vale, Chelsea.

'Meanwhile, Mr Ricketts had founded the Vale Press and designed his "Vale" type. He generously put some of this type at my disposal on the understanding that it was to be used only for books issued by them. This arrangement worked smoothly until the Vale Press came to an end. Then I decided to have my own type. The "Brook" fount, as it was called, made no pretension to originality – my aim being restricted to a fount which would harmonize with my wood-engraving and which would, at the same time, be clear and easy to read. I also designed a very simple fount of music characters adapted to a simple form of music printing.

'The stave was printed in red and the notes in black. Needless to say, the registration of wet handmade paper presented great difficulties.

'We had to invent many improvements to our presses in order to secure perfect registration. These improvements allowed us, later on, to use gold leaf with colour.

'For lack of capital, I was not able to print the books I wanted to produce until the French began, at last, to take an interest in the revival of printing. Mr Roger Marx, who knew of my efforts, introduced me to Mr Rodrigues, the President of the Society of the "Cent Biblio-philes" in Paris. The latter asked me to produce a book for them, giving me carte blanche with regard to text, illustrations, size, paper, etc. This gave me the opportunity I wanted and with a quiet mind as to cost, I set to work on the production of the *Histoire de Soliman Ben Daoud et de la Reine de Matin* by Gérard de Nerval. For this book we used gold leaf in the printing of the initial letters. This gave us much trouble and we had to invent a technique to overcome the great difficulty of preventing the gold leaf from sticking to the wet hand-made paper and, after many attempts, we were successful.

'My father, Camille Pissarro, was always greatly interested in my books. He planned with me a book to deal with country work. For this purpose he designed twelve compositions to be engraved on wood in chiaroscuro. Unfortunately he died before all the blocks were engraved, but he had seen two of them and this gave me a clue to the rest.

'Another society in Paris, "Le Livre Contemporain", began to take an interest in the work. They asked Mr Moselli to write some stories round my father's compositions and so provide a text for the book. I was then asked to draw some head-pieces, initial letters and "cul-de-Lampes" to harmonize with my father's illustrations and the text. With this object, I adapted some of his drawings and studies and soon the book was complete.

'One of the books, which gave me particular pleasure to produce, was *Poèmes tirés du Livre de Jade* by Judith Gautier. For this little book I again used gold leaf; this time for the illustrations as well as the initial letters but, on this occasion, I tried Japanese vellum which, as it could be used dry, enabled me to avoid the tiresome tendency of the gold to stick to the wet paper.

'With the exception of the two books produced for the French bibliophiles, I printed a small edition on vellum of all the books printed with the "Brook" type.

'It is a source of special satisfaction to me that I discovered a way of avoiding the ugly effect of printing superimposed on vellum; the latter is a non-absorbent material, and the oil when drying produces a somewhat cheap, disagreeable and shiny effect.

97

'The last book printed at the Eragny Press was *Whym Chow* privately printed for Michael Field.

'When the war came, our activities ceased; the difficulty of getting paper, the cost of production, the loss of most of our continental clientele on account of the rate of exchange, seemed to present insuperable difficulties.

'For the time being, though with much regret, I have had to abandon a project I had in mind, to produce a final book to be illustrated from drawings by my father which are in my possession. Perhaps, some day I may be able to do it.

'In ending these notes, I must acknowledge the valuable assistance given by my wife, both in engraving and in printing.

'Her energy and skill have been invaluable in the Press Room.'

The first sixteen Eragny books were printed under the same conditions as Vale books, and with the Vale Press type (except for *Queen for the Fishes*). Bearing in mind the self-identification with a type design which formed an odd characteristic of these printers, this gesture from Ricketts suggests friendship and generosity. The Vale bibliography appeared in 1904. The first Eragny book to use the new Brook type which Lucien designed, the bibliography for that half-way stage, was printed in 1903. Thus the disappearance of one forced new life from the other. It is arguable that the Brook type, on the white paper of the small pages in Eragny books, was the most beautiful fount invented in this whole period.

Sturge Moore wrote a pleasant defence of the press and its ideals, at the start of this bibliography. Lucien made such books as a man would want to keep as his friends, not merely read and pass on. It was an anti-paperback sentiment.

'If they are precious, honour them, be liberal for them. We must have fewer then; but those few shall be beautiful upon the table, on the shelf, in the hand; while we muse on the meaning the eye shall rest happily on the page where fair proportions have been sought and established between margin and text, between type and page.'

But that would defend any of the private press books from obvious attack. Ricketts and Pissarro shared assumptions about the weight and place of wood engravings in relation to the printed page, though

98

as artists they remained far apart. The scale of their books is similar, but the Eragny books shied away even more from the ambitious or monumental – except in complex colour printing. The patterned paper covers are very similar, though Ricketts liked to use printed labels and Pissarro blocked finely in gold on the grey.

For the choice of work to print, the happiest Eragny books were in French. These, taken affectionately and without outside influence, lie away from the stream of taste and reflect the mood. In 1901, for example, *Les Petits Vieux* by Emile Verhaeren appeared – small wide pages, folded in the Japanese manner and printed on one side only; large orange initials and one in three colours, orange for the first lines of poems; one innocent pastoral French woodcut in four colours, the old man with his rake, the woman sitting at the tree trunk, a corn-field, red-roofed church far away – almost a nursery quality, but fresh as the fifteenth-century woodcuts Morris loved. This book is covered with a ranunculus pattern.

Two years later, the most obviously appropriate Eragny book was issued – the last to be printed in the Vale type – *Aucassin and Nicolette*. Hornby had printed a small edition of Lang's translation, as one of his early exercises at Ashendene, but this French book from Lucien Pissarro is a happier production – pleasantly printed music for the songs, a fine red initial and borders for the first text page, and a coloured woodcut – Nicolette sheltering alone, looking across at the fields and donkeys – perfect marriage of style and subject in every aspect. The cover has a design of irises, which seem to grow with crysanthemum leaves.

Two years later, in 1905, the Eragny Press issued a similarly appro-priate little book, having most of the qualities one identifies with their work – the music, red initials, a coloured woodcut, something of French and English. This was *Some Old French and English Ballads*, edited by Robert Steele. The picture, in a circle framed by a design of apples, shows 'Les Princesses au Pommier Doux'. Perhaps in this homely style the neat French ballads come a little more naturally than 'O mistress mine, where are you roaming?' – with archaic spelling – but all are charming and this, like the others, is a perfect book in its scope. The cover paper is an orderly tangle of winter jasmine, the climbing shoots wheeling about flowers and buds, a beautiful impression of its growth.

And a last example of this sort, more elaborate but still quite modest, is the slender volume from 1911, *Album de Poèmes Tirés du Livre de Jade*. These poems by Judith Gautier declare the other influence upon Lucien, the Chinese and Japanese. The upper and lower covers are limp jade-coloured leather wrapped rather than bound, the spine nipped in light brown leather and tied with brown silk cord. There are gold-blocked designs on the upper cover, and the recognizable Brook letters. Each page is ruled in red on the Japanese vellum, and gold is used as fourth colour in the pictures which are also formed in circles of gold. This gold printing is used here with elegant success. Gold initials give balance to the illustrations opposite; flower decorations, printed orange and green, end each poem. This is perhaps the climax of Eragny printing, because its elaboration came so clearly from the printer's taste and there is no hint that resources are strained. It is of its time, and ends a period attractively. Two more books were issued, the last of them – by Michael Field again – in 1914.

Within this range, or outside it, the Press chose writing of varying character, some of which seems little connected with Eragny style. The volume of Browning's poems, 1904, very charming to look at, rests some distance from the spirit of that poet. The coloured wood-cut, 'Women and Roses', has the style of a French nursery book. Rather away from all the others is the Eragny edition of *Areopagitica*, which can be compared interestingly with the Doves Press version. Apart from Johnston's fine opening to the Doves edition, there is more character in Pissarro's printing. It is in the Brook type ,1904 (a productive year) on a large quarto page in two columns. The severity of black initials, and spare use of red for shoulder-notes, takes away the customary prettiness from this Eragny book and gives a classical seriousness quite appropriate to the theme and the author. The beautiful initials to each paragraph divide the text agreeably, and al-together the success of this makes one wish that other experiments of such an ambitious kind had been attempted. The opening page, with its heavy, bold black flowery border and great red initial T, seems also to suggest the character of some tract, with its heading

FOR THE LIBERTY OF UNLICENC'D PRINTING. With such boldness inside, one is pleased to accept the patterned dianthus paper cover. And between these two, the happy medium of Eragny printing, are such elegant little books as Bacon's essay *Of Gardens* and *The Descent of Ishtar* by Diana White. Both are in the customary style of the press, printed in three colours which give scope for double-page borders of trailing green, mingling beautifully with the red initials and patterns of green and red flowers. Esther, Lucien's wife, engraved these borders. The books are an extension into text and ornament, of the mood of the coloured woodcuts.

Sturge Moore wrote, of Eragny books, 'The small edition is as essential to this art as the high price.' It was an odd point of view. By our horizons the prices seem sensible, and one supposes that in the days of low taxation they could not have been beyond range. Two hundred of the Bacon essay were issued on paper, at sixteen shillings. Of *Aucassin and Nicolette*, there were two hundred and thirty on paper at thirty shillings. *Areopagitica* with its large page cost thirty-one and six, and the one really complex production – *Poèmes Tirés du Livre de Jade*, with its gold printing – cost four pounds, but only one hundred and twenty on Japanese vellum were issued, and ten on vellum for eight guineas.

So the prices were not absurd, and with so much careful work over small editions they now look cheap; but this open question remains, about the small edition. Sturge Moore thought it 'essential to this art'. This was what irritated Francis Meynell, and inspired a different direction for the Nonesuch Press. Sparling explained in his book on the Kelmscott Press, and as its secretary he should have known. It was simply the limitation imposed by strict hand-work, 'when each and every sheet is pulled with as much care as an etching, being then tried over for the minutest fault, and replaced if it be in the least defective.' That is what governed the small edition, the discipline and in our days the high price. There was no overtone of snobbish exclusion in the matter-of-fact sentence from Sturge Moore's essay. These two presses, Vale and Eragny, stand together, private and self-contained, with an integrity which stretches even further than the great three, Kelmscott, Doves and Ashendene; for each was largely the work of one man from start to finish, including the engraving of decorations and illustrations. This fulfilled the conditions of the work. Doves Press ornament, where it came, was the work of an outside calligrapher. Hornby employed outsiders for his type and decoration, and Burne-Jones's drawing suffered interpretation before it appeared on the Kelmscott page. But Ricketts could speak for himself in his *Defence of the Revival of Printing*:

> 'I think the sweetness of effect procured by engraving is a desirable end in itself in the matter of ornament. In the handling of pictures, the rendering of flesh, hands, feet, and faces an original engraver has that chance of refining upon his design, that with an interpreter however skilful cannot always be relied upon, and that cannot exist at all in process work, however perfected.'

Quare non facimus? Tum ego, toties exci-
tatus, plane vehementer excandui, et Red-
didi illi voces suas: Aut dormi, aut ego jam
patri dicam.

CAPUT LXXXVIII.

Erectus his sermonibus, consulere pruden-
tiores cœpi ætates tabularum, et quædam
argumenta mihi obscura, simulque causam de-
sidiæ præsentis excutere, quum pulcherrimæ
artes periissent, inter quas pictura ne minimum quidem sui vestigium reliquisset. Tum
ille: Pecuniæ, inquit, cupiditas hæc tropica in-
stituit. Verum, ut ad plastas convertar,
Lysippum, statuæ unius lineamentis inhæren-
tem, inopia exstinxit: et Myron, qui pæne
hominum animas ferarumque ære compre-
hendit, non invenit heredem. At nos, vino
scortisque demersi, ne paratas quidem artes
audemus cognoscere; sed, accusatores anti-
quitatis, vitia tantum docemus et discimus.
Ubi est dialectica? ubi astronomia? ubi sa-
pientiæ consultissima via? Quis, inquam, venit
in templum, et votum fecit, si ad eloquentiam
pervenisset? quis, si philosophiæ fontem at-
tigisset? Ac ne bonam quidem valetudinem
petunt: sed statim, antequam limen Capitolii
tangant, alius donum promittit, si propinquum
divitem extulerit: alius, si thesaurum effo-
derit: alius, si ad trecenties HS. salvus perve-
nerit. Ipse senatus, recti bonique præceptor,
xxxix

Vale Press, a page of King's type first used in the *Kingis Quair*.

Opening of Sturge Moore's essay which gives its name to the book, Eragny Press, 1903. The first to be printed in the Brook type designed by Lucien Pissarro.

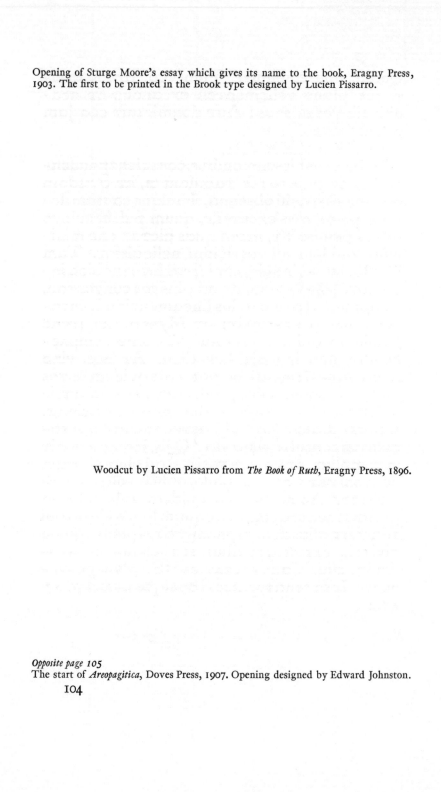

Woodcut by Lucien Pissarro from *The Book of Ruth*, Eragny Press, 1896.

Opposite page 105
The start of *Areopagitica*, Doves Press, 1907. Opening designed by Edward Johnston.

MR. PISSARRO first learned to draw from
his father, in the fields far from any art
school. One day M. Lepère, the well-known
engraver, showed him how his tools were held,
& finding him interested, gave him two gravers
and a scorper. Thus furnished with the means
he made a start and taught himself; with the result that in 1886 F. G. Dumas, editor of the «Revue Illustrée», commissioned him to illustrate
a story, «Maît' Liziard», by Octave Mirbeau.
Four woodcuts appeared, but the subscribers to
the Review expressed so much disapproval of
these illustrations, conceived and executed in
the uncompromising spirit of Charles Keene's
work, which Mr. Pissarro greatly admired, that
his collaboration was cut short there and then.
He learnt later that this epistolary demonstration against his work, which inundated Mr.
Dumas' office, was the work of some students
in the atelier of a well-known painter. Dis-
appointed, and having heard that in England
there was a group of young artists who were
ardently engaged in the revival of wood-engraving, he crossed the Channel with the intention of joining them, having in his pocket
an introduction from Félix Fénéon to John

4   Gray

HAND AND SOUL

BEFORE any knowledge of painting was brought to Florence, there were already painters in Lucca, & Pisa, and Arezzo, who feared God and loved the art. The keen, grave workmen from Greece, whose trade it was to sell their own works in Italy and teach Italians to imitate them, had already found rivals of the soil with skill that could forestall their lessons and cheapen their

Kelmscott Press, *Hand and Soul*, 1895, compared with (*opposite*) the same book by the Vale Press, 1899.

BEFORE any knowledge of painting was brought to Flor~ence, there were already painters in Lucca, & Pisa, and Arezzo, who feared God and loved the art.

THEY WHO TO STATES
AND GOVERNOURS OF
THE COMMONWEALTH DIRECT THEIR
SPEECH, HIGH COURT OF PARLAMENT,
or wanting such accesse in a private condition, write
that which they foresee may advance the publick
good; I suppose them as at the beginning of no meane
endeavour, not a little alter'd & mov'd inwardly in
their mindes: Some with doubt of what will be the
successe, others with feare of what will be the cen-
sure; some with hope, others with confidence of what
they have to speake. And me perhaps each of these
dispositions, as the subject was whereon I enter'd,
may have at other times variously affected; & likely
might in these formost expressions now also disclose
which of them sway'd most, but that the very attempt of this addresse thus made, and the thought of
whom it hath recourse to, hath got the power within
me to a passion, farre more welcome then incidentall
to a Preface. Which though I stay not to confesse ere
any aske, I shall be blamelesse, if it be no other, then
the joy & gratulation which it brings to all who wish
and promote their Countries liberty; whereof this
whole Discourse propos'd will be a certaine testimony, if not a Trophey. For this is not the liberty
which wee can hope, that no grievance ever should
arise in the Commonwealth, that let no man in this
8

THE DOVES PRESS AND HIGH IDEALISM

It is a kind of paradox that the Doves Press, simplest and purest of them all in style, was the creation of more passion and complexity of thought than the rest of them put together. Doves Press books have to be seen from more than one level, and the fascination grows upon acquaintance. Their common reputation, simplicity and a type face, comes first. 'The Doves Press deserves mentioning for their insistence on plain printing,' Mr Steinberg writes. The deduction is often made that these were the books which influenced our own. Morris and decoration and Gothic, it is said, showed great panache in a street marked clearly 'No Thoroughfare'. Walker and Cobden-Sanderson started upon the broad way to our own taste.

But various odd things have been said about the Doves Press. Most of its books were printed in the same format, all with the same type face and in only one size. This was of course a sign of great strength and assurance, a tour de force. It caused Sir Francis Meynell to say there was something of the literary Tiller Girls in these books. Readers have been grateful for a standard which came near to perfection; collectors have been known to get a little bored. But Meynell in his frivolous moment spoke inappropriately, for the Doves Press was a religious activity; its discipline one of prayer rather than of chorus girls.

The type they used is well known, and never looks attractive in reproduction. Its lightness seems heavy, its poise quite lost in those patches of photo-lithography so familiar in the history books from Updike onwards. The fact and experience is that this alphabet, beautifully adapted from Jenson's *Pliny*, is quite as fine as its reputation; but it must be seen on the strong white paper, somewhat lighter in weight than Kelmscott paper; on the broad page with a hint of roughness at the edge, and perhaps with the bright red shoulder note. This sounds precious, but something is lost when these red adornments are reproduced black. Emery Walker completed his designs most sensitively, and this was his chef d'oeuvre. His notions of close and even spacing and minimum leading prevailed. Cobden-Sanderson must have learned all this from him, as he learned binding from De

Coverly; only with the binding he made new styles of his own, and in printing took no such liberty. Walker and the compositor Mason, one assumes, kept him in iron control or converted him completely. There is simply no evidence that Cobden-Sanderson knew much about type, or contributed more than a craftsman's skill and his wife's cash to the physical printing of these books. This classic purity of page appeared as a form, distilled from much experience, into which whatever romantic and Germanic passions afflicting him, or coming from outside, could with art be ordered and disciplined. It was like Pope's verse forms. The simplicity of a poem is deceptive.

Doves and Kelmscott books are commonly compared; generally with a conclusion that Morris used excessive decoration for his unreadable types and, though marks go to him for trying, the true reform and benefit lay in the work from Cobden-Sanderson and Emery Walker. The Doves Bible is taken to be the highest achievement. As with all aesthetic matters, either view could be taken and defended. Alfred Pollard with some originality in 1921 described the Doves type as 'the finest ceremonial type ever cut', but regretted that the British have no talent for ceremony and he confessed 'to being unable to read more than twenty or thirty pages in the Doves Press type without feeling perceptibly chilled'.

In these questions it seems pointless to take sides. Morris might have been chilled by Doves books, but only Morris could have produced Kelmscott books. The interesting high common factor in both was Emery Walker. As the styles of the two presses were so sharply different, and Walker seems to have presided over the typography of each, one can isolate his taste and contribution. It is unlikely that his own taste shifted completely. The qualities in common are fine materials, a black impression, close spacing and the placing of type on the page. Except for the type face, an undecorated Kelmscott page is very similar to a Doves page – red shoulder notes, no headline, large type closely packed in a block. The visual merits of Doves Press books are from Emery Walker – and in discussing private presses, the visual qualities are usually valued first. Mason the compositor learned from him, and Cobden-Sanderson from them both. Walker was too modest to leave much record of his part, but everyone in his neighbourhood acknowledged it. Morris, and after him May Morris, Horn by, Kessler – he was behind them all, generously ready to advise. From the 1888 lecture which inspired Morris, to the Cranach Press *Virgil* and some work with Bruce Rogers, it will not be disputed that the taste and knowledge of Emery Walker guided and presided.

The other artist in the Doves Press was Edward Johnston. Sparely and carefully, he supplied something of what the Press lacked through absence of a decorator. He did this for the Doves Press, and Graily Hewitt for the Ashendene Press. The other important presses of the day – Kelmscott, Essex House, Vale, even the Daniel Press – had their own decorations from the abilities of their owners. It is odd that Cobden-Sanderson so inventive with his patterns for bindings, never applied himself to this though he had once studied calligraphy under Johnston at the Central School. He came to printing at the age of sixty, but so did Morris.

Johnston's red initial letters, often lying outside the text area to the left, were quite unconventional and they can still carry the force of invention. Mr Ronald Briggs wrote recently of Johnston's opening to the first book of the Doves Press *Paradise Lost*, 'The elements of this masterpiece are utterly simple and purely typographic, but the first glimpse of it as the page is turned is breathtaking.' Cobden-Sanderson saw clearly and responsibly the value of helping a reader through the book's text by attention to the beauty and decoration of its intervals; part of 'the whole duty of beautiful typography' was 'to take advantage of every pause or stage in that communication to interpose some characteristic and restful beauty in its own art'. This is what Edward Johnston was doing for the Doves Press.

His opening to *Genesis* in the Doves Bible is well-known through reproduction, splendid in its boldness and redness still. The books in which the initials are drawn rather than printed give special pleasure; and of them one thinks first of *Paradise Lost* where each book of the poem, apart from the complex opening Mr Briggs mentioned, has drawn initials. Another very beautiful opening was for the first scene of *Hamlet*, where the calligraphy of his green W is so elegant as to take away most of the alarm from Bernardo's 'Who goes there'? And many of the Doves Press edition of Browning's poems in two volumes, *Men*

¶ I BELIEVE IN INFINITE SPACE
AND IN ETERNAL TIME.

¶ I believe in the innumerable & infinitely
distant stars.

¶ I believe in the sun, & in the wanderers,
the planets.

¶ I believe in the earth, and in the silver
moon : & I believe in day & night, & in the
seasons, summer and winter, & spring and
autumn; and

¶ I believe and I see that as the earth turns
upon itself we pass into the light and wake
to life & die downward into darkness and
the sleep of rest, and that we are one in life
and sleep with the earth's self: and

¶ I believe & see that as the earth, turning
upon itself, whirls round the sun, the earth
wakes to life in spring, to the full pomp of
summer, and dies rhythmically downward

A page from one of three little books printed at the Doves Press,
Cobden-Sanderson's *Credo*.

and Women, were 'flourished by Edward Johnston'. That brought a variety of decorative pen-strokes in red or green, and took this work outside the range of common criticism about monotony in Doves Press books. It is astonishing that a line of calligraphy can give character to a book and change its quality. Johnston achieved this in his opening, quite simply printed in black, to the Doves *Areopagitica*. Milton was well served.

Morris never bound his own books, and probably the only bindings he would truly have approved for them were Cobden-Sanderson's. The Doves Bindery existed for the whole life of the Doves Press, and carried out splendid work for private collectors, but its routine work must have been in the ordinary binding of Doves books. These were generally in darkish vellum without ties, occasionally in grey paperboards with vellum backs. 'Doves Bindery' is stamped on the endpapers, and these bindings are very pleasant – superior to the vellum bindings Leightons did for Kelmscott books. They open well, handle easily, and the silk thread with prominent knots coming up through printed sections of the books are a feature of Doves bindings. Care and precision went into the forwarding of these simple bindings as into the same stages of more exacting work. The three little pocket-books of the first chapter of *Genesis*, Cobden-Sanderson's *Credo*, and the *Lord's Prayer*, were bound in plain brick-coloured morocco.

But it is not enough to look at the type face with admiration, or Johnston's red openings, or the bindings. If books were merely pictures, the artist would vary their form. If the Doves Press is reckoned a success, that must be because we can see that its structure was right for carrying the burden of thought and vision for which it was chosen. These were not designed for decoration, elegance or collectors. The design was an engineering job, the books a bridge across to mystic realms of cloud and God. And this is where Cobden-Sanderson takes over from Emery Walker.

His vision of the ideal book is difficult to express, and he quickly became woolly in attempting it; but Cobden-Sanderson had an astonishing gift of mystic communion, practising the techniques of yoga in his own life and with no effort realizing the wonder and mystery of a moment in the day – or hours at a stretch – when he chose to pause, to think and listen. Obviously his wife, in pushing him towards a handicraft, felt uneasy in the presence of so much seeming idleness. She must have been a wise and cheerful woman, active to his contemplative; and when he turned to printing at the age of sixty, the book became for him a symbol of those moments within the day, which contained eternity. Books could reduce God to a page of visible type, as sunlight on a still morning showed the river in His form; and that was the reason for making a book with immense care, and making it beautiful. He saw also a special aptness in the way several artists shared in producing books – calligrapher, typographer, painter, author; as in the world so many share in the work of a society.

'The wholeness, symmetry, harmony, beauty without stress or strain, of the Book Beautiful, would then be one in principle with the wholeness, symmetry, harmony, and beauty without stress or strain, of that WHOLE OF LIFE WHICH IS CONSTITUTED OF OURSELVES AND THE WORLD, THAT COMPLEX AND MARVELLOUS WHOLE WHICH, AMID THE STRIFE OF COMPETITIVE FORCES, SUPREMELY HOLDS ITS OWN, AND IN THE LANGUAGE OF LIFE WRITES, UPON THE ILLUMINED PAGES OF THE DAYS, THE VOLUMES OF THE CENTURIES, AND THROUGH THE INFINITUDES OF TIME AND SPACE MOVES RHYTHMICALLY ONWARD TO THE FULL DE-VELOPMENT OF ITS ASTONISHING STORY, THE TRUE ARCHETYPE OF ALL LIFE AND OF ALL BOOKS BEAUTIFUL OR SUBLIME.'

He is alone among the arts-and-crafts printers – perhaps among any in the five centuries of printing – in seeing so seriously the link of idealism between a finely made book and religious thought. Morris's affections were expressed in his press, and Hornby's taste most elegantly in his; but none of them approached Cobden-Sanderson in missionary seriousness of purpose. It is of course appropriate that he alone among the private presses (leaving Nonesuch aside) produced the Bible. Ashbee had planned it, and gave up for lack of support. But all the literary choice of the Doves Press was planned in the same earnest spirit – no story-telling for its own sake, such as Morris loved. And in this whole view, which includes the pleasure of Walker's type face, its printing achievement should be judged.

The two partners quarrelled half-way through the life of the press, and after 1909 Emery Walker had no hand in its work. This sad and absurd episode has been described enough. Papers in the possession of Mr John Dreyfus make it clear that the row began quite early in the life of the Press. Among them, a long but un-posted letter dated 1902 carries a weight of pent-up irritation with Walker for the small time and energy he managed to give to the work – complaining he had to do almost all of it himself. If this were all true, it would remove Walker a little from his place in the foreground.

But nobody has managed to find any difference between the quality and character of books before and after the famous split; which suggests that Walker's affectionate supervision had done its job, his pupils could take over. In a private press this looks startling, because they always depended upon the energies and spirit of one man; so we can reckon that after the skill had been learnt, the creative force continued to flow from Cobden-Sanderson who had always provided it. The life and work of Cobden-Sanderson are more relevant to the Doves Press than his quarrel with Walker.

The chief source is his Journals, published in two volumes in 1926 by his son Richard. It is an unfair publication and might almost have been called Saintly Thoughts from the Journals. As much is cut out, including every single reference to Emery Walker, nobody can go to it for balanced history; but it remains an astonishing and intimate document. Another source is his own exchanges of letters with Lady Amberley, back in the eighteen-sixties when as a puzzled young man his thoughts were always reaching into an O altitudo. This attractive self-portrait he issued from the Doves Press in 1914 in an edition of one hundred and fifty copies, under the title *Amantium Irae*. It is the most private and endearing of all books from the Press.

The quarrel with Walker is understandable when one sees in the Journals how curiously he identified himself with the Doves Press books and the type designed (by Walker) for them. In July of 1917, after the matrices of the Doves type were safely under the Thames so that nobody else could cast type from them, he reflects in a way which is curiously composed, as he was, of the holy and unholy.

'I stood upon the bridge, and I walked to and fro and bethought me of the time when I had crossed and re-crossed it in winter time, in the darkness, and as the buses brought protection – threw the type from the bridge to the river. Then I lifted my thoughts to the wonder of the scene before me, full of an awful beauty, God's universe and man's – joint creators. How wonderful! And my Type, the Doves Type was part of it.'

And one more example can help to show his feeling about books, not one of his own this time, but a copy of Humboldt's *Cosmos* published by his son Richard, which he brought home for his wife 'in remembrance of our betrothal in February 1882'. This is written thirty-eight years later, at the age of eighty-one.

'After the first thrill, and after I had given it to Annie, my heart sank, I know not why – it seemed after all so small a thing; and till this morning I was plunged in gloom, but with the morning my spirits rose again. I disbound the book, and let its spirit expand, and lying on my back in bed I looked upward to the heavens, and, myself disbound, I prayed that my little human life I might ever more and more bring into accord with the great life of the universe. Then free, released from all ambitions earthwards, my book became its contents, and I, content!'

One feels he would like to have disbound Walker and thrown him into the Thames from Hammersmith Bridge, except for a haunting thought of posthumous pleasure in the mud with all those matrices. He so closely identified himself, in later life, with the books, that we also must identify them with him.

It is encouraging for anyone in middle age, to read about great men who largely wasted the first half of their lives; Shaw forty before he wrote a play, Cobden-Sanderson forty-one before he learnt about book-binding. His father, working in the inland revenue, had adequate means and his son went up to Cambridge in 1858. Thomas Sanderson (the other half of the name came after his marriage to Annie Cobden) was only eight years younger than William Morris. At his birth, Victoria had been on the throne three years. He left Cambridge without taking a degree, abandoned theology and a career in the church, read for the bar and mooned about the Temple with a tendency to ill health, hating law and the committees he should have been attending. This somewhat futile bachelor life is described in the early pages of the Journal. It is also the fretful and morally puzzling period of *Amantium Irae*, the Amberley correspondence. And all his life, whether idle or in the middle of work, outside sounds and influences entered when he cared to pause and listen for them. This enviable and religious gift, losing the distractions of self, is present from the early aimless years in London.

'I am now sitting at my table,' we read from August 1881, 'the lamp sheds a cheerful light, and as I cut the pages of my new book I felt so happy, so longing that I could thus sit with the great in my mind thinking about them, that I naturally turned to thee, O my journal, to tell thee of it. Yes, it is at such moments, when all is quiet about one, when the lamp sheds her genial light around and upon my books, when the world and all that thereon is swings into vision, that I am truly happy. Then my prayers go up to Thee, O my God, and I bow in adoration, a rapt worshipper, before Thee.'

Obviously these ecstasies were followed by descent and depression, and the published diary tends to record more of one than the other – as if he were climbing towards heaven in fact – but there is no doubt about the frequent experience of a sort of religious communion. Here he is six years later by the sea at Westgate:

'And, by and by, when I had brought my chair and taken my seat alone on the lonely cliff looking seaward and sunward, my mind grew upward and outward, and the world's pure self came to intertwine and be one with it. And oh, the stillness then, and the beauty!'

At his fortieth birthday he was without hope or achievement 'horribly tired of my life'; but once or twice a clear flash of the future helped him, and the whole vision arrived before the first creative step towards it. Out of this gloom of 3 Paper Buildings, the fortieth birthday approaching, he wrote:

'Oh, not to create only, but to create things in sympathy with knowledge, to poise things beautiful and good as the universe is poised in all space and time! What other solution of the universe can there be, creation in the imagination and outwardly in unison with it? To know then first, and then to create, knowledge striking the key-note. What a longing the tossed soul has after tranquillity!'

The cosmic philosophy of the Doves Press is there.

This was his condition when one of Cobden's daughters most valiantly agreed to marry him, and she judged very well what his character was capable of. Nothing dramatic happened for a while; he seems to have continued his bachelor ways, his private confidences in the journal and the longing for moments of stillness when the sun came through the windows in Paper Buildings and shone upon his books. He was far from strong, and lived on her money. Annie pushed him towards a useful life.

'At last it dawned upon me that perhaps to justify our existence, to live a real life of helpful work, we should go and live in the east at Poplar, give up the Temple, give up the Bar, live upon our present means, and work for the people's good. I might, too – thinking it out in detail – as a ratepayer become a Guardian, and work in that way. I told Annie the scheme. She folded me in her arms, and said that that perhaps would be the best, but wait – do nothing rashly, say nothing about it, and after we came from abroad we perhaps would. But she feared she might grow sick of it – she hated the poor, they were only a degree more miserable and not a whit less wicked than the rest of the world. (But this was not either true, nor from the heart – it was precaution!) And she put out her arms again and again, and said she loved me more than anything, was quite happy here, only she was ambitious for me, and when I seemed not to care, but to fall into idleness, and inclined only to dream life away, she shot at me all the arrows which she thought would have most effect, but she really did not mean what she said.'

It was William Morris's wife one evening who suggested book-binding. Such a mournful face and strange clothes – the surprise is that she calmly offered such an excellent idea. He called on De Coverly the next day, to ask for an apprenticeship; so the intention to work with his hands was truly there, not merely a conversation for the Morris circle. And one guesses the decision was harder for Cobden-

114

Sanderson, a natural dreamer and a detached thinker, content in his study or a quiet garden. Morris had always been a compulsive worker, not long content in the conditions which brought peace to Cobden-Sanderson.

The change brought episodes of quarrel and doubt. He must have God as well as book-binding, not become merely a labourer with his hands. 'I must not forget, in taking to the handicraft of bookbinding, that there are higher things in the world, higher ambitions even for me than to produce well-bound, beautifully-bound books.' But he could enjoy 'the thinking of high thought the while'. The decision he had taken can be admired now as it was then; for though the demand for good work is the same, and the social stigma does not exist, how few people follow that path in our own time – except perhaps in pottery.

So he becomes an important figure in the arts and crafts movement, for which book-binding might be a symbol; for all the hard work of forwarding is pure craftsmanship and structural soundness, and the finishing is no less an art than other kinds of design. He liked to watch plant and insect forms, to get new ideas for binding tools. The working day was extremely busy, and he lost friends to whom this life looked peculiar. The new work became far more important than their small talk. He criticized Morris for a lack of socialism in his practical life. About the binding Morris was quite provocative, and failed to see the point. It is a very surprising entry.

'Morris called on Thursday, and we lunched together at Rule's. He began to talk about my prices. Premised that "people would go to the cheapest market", and almost as if he approved; thought my work too costly; bookbinding should be "rough"; did not want to multiply the minor arts (!); went so far as to suggest that some machinery should be invented to bind books.

'"The cheapest market!" Should I then go to the sweaters in the East End, and there buy my shirts and clothing?'

In all this middle period, between the early futility and later printing, Cobden-Sanderson was establishing himself as a book-binder; for the first seven years with his own hands and some help from Annie, and after 1893 as director of the Dovers Bindery. There is no obvious change of manner between two stages of his work, though early bindings done at home or in his workshop – one hundred and forty-three were completed in this way – are greatly prized. After March 1893, his son says, 'no book was personally bound by T. J. Cobden-Sanderson'. It was a surprisingly complete break. One would have guessed that he tried his hand now and then, for old time's sake. The total abstention looks like a row. But the patterns, by which most people know a binding, were still his own and there are common references in the Journals to his care for them. There is no decline in the standard of materials, but he found other occupations and had served his time in handicraft. It seems to have been, in Ashbee's terms, an ideal small workshop. There was no more reason for Cobden-Sanderson to do each stage of the work himself, than for Morris to compose type and become pressman for the books he printed. His standard was perfection, and from the start he worried about the good sense of spending so much time on the chores – he who had always appreciated quiet and passivity above all things. We find him fussing in language which recalls Holofernes, though the meaning of it is fine:

'It may be true that I am now engaged in work beneath my capacity; if it be, I am still very usefully employed in modestly so engaging myself. It must fall to the lot of many to be so employed, and to have no alternative. May it not be some solace to them to know that there are some others in the world who are voluntarily with them? Moreover, it cools the fever of desire. And shall the lowly capacities never be learned by fellowship in identical work with higher minds?' His bindings are of course beautiful, and it gave him pleasure to watch the collectors raise their value. He always worked consciously for posterity. He made a simple style of decoration, not derivative or imitative, and this was in some ways a greater originality than any work from the private printing presses. The simplicity of tools for elaborate decoration is impressive, and gave some unity within complexity; but beyond this he aimed for apt symbolism and relation to the book, and he never needed the luxurious effect of inlaid leathers or exotic material. Unlike his master De Coverly or such trade binders as Bedford and Zaehnsdorf, the manner was always his own

116

and he would not accept dictation from his clients about design. Doves bindings are easily recognized, though MacLeish could bind in a similar way when he set up on his own; but the style and work were forged with hard labour and failure – time and again the gold would not stick, or the spine turned out too short, or he made a hole through the surface in tooling the pattern.

'When turning the leather down at the headband I found it too short, and in a burst of rage I took the knife and cut the slips and tore the covers and boards off and tossed them to one side; then, in a very ecstasy of rage, seized one side again, tore the leather off the board, and cut it, and cut it, and slashed it with a knife. Then I was quite calm again; made so, I think by the wonder and awe and fear that came over me as in a kind of madness I cut and slashed at the leather.'

And after the Doves Bindery had been established for seven years, the Press began. As a binder he had worked in the arts and crafts ideal of classless labour, as an original artist. Now he joined with Emery Walker, and together for different reasons they attempted an absolute standard for printing different kinds of book. One can imagine very well the appeal for Cobden-Sanderson, after so much variety and invention in his bindings, of one single form which each work could accept. And beyond that, the higher unity of intention – Ruskin, Carlyle, Emerson, Milton, Wordsworth.

It must have been the least frivolous of all the presses. Morris had merry pleasure from most of the Kelmscott books – the medieval world he loved, the old poems and stories. There is aesthetic gaiety in some of the Vale Press books, French charm in Eragny, and Hornby's press could be domestic, entertaining, homely as well as serious. Nothing less than a fixed moral vision governed the taste of the Doves Press; with Cobden-Sanderson at the heart of it, using the precious type face only for the greatest thoughts and finding place among them for his own stray reflections, profound conclusions, and letters to *The Times*. The spirit of it is reflected in his Journal entry in January 1902, when subscribers were invited for the five-volume Bible:

'And so, with this new year, let me devote myself wholly to this great work. Let me desire for it the most beautiful frame possible for

117

the Bible as a whole – that composite whole, wrought with tears and laughter in the olden times, wrought again in the paroxysm of a nation's reversion by the blood and tears of its first translators; and now set forth, not ornamentally for a collector's toy, but severely, plainly, monumentally, for a nation's masterpiece, for a nation's guidance, consolation and hope.'

He made it so finely that it becomes, of course, ornamentally a collector's toy. I doubt whether a church in the land uses it for the nation's guidance. The white vellum covers would quickly be grubby on a lectern; by printing only four hundred it becomes an irreplaceable rarity, unusable in quite the way he meant. It has a humbler place instead – as his widow inscribed a copy of it, 'the magnum opus of the Doves Press'. As the finest expression of his intentions, it is a place of adequate honour.

We can judge the other books in the same way as this Bible, though they are all on a smaller scale. This was his only folio. It is a strange achievement. Bibles have obviously been looked after well by printers, from Gutenberg on; often with decoration, sometimes with care and sound printing when most books were not well printed – as at Oxford and Cambridge in the seventeenth century; or imaginatively divided into chapters with titles, as Bensley printed it a hundred years before the Doves Press. But nothing is so stark and pure, such unbending art as the Doves Bible. Walker's pure taste in type, and his partner's iron morality combined in this example of unadorned reverence. The red headings and Johnston's initials relieve the spirit when they come, but do not amount to decoration. It remains, as all the other Doves books, formal and formidable. There is not one illustration, no experiment with woodcut or border, from the start of the press to its close. This absolute refusal to enjoy or experiment suggests a peculiar tension.

It would be easy to mock these aims and hopes of the Press, and dismiss Cobden-Sanderson's crackpot ambitions. If he tends to write as if he controlled the Universe, we might see that his place is near the saints – at least in a consistent uppermost desire which he describes unrestingly through sixty years, whatever vice mixed with it. 'So I should slowly build up the idea of monumental thought, and

118

slowly would emerge the Vision of Cities dedicated in their public buildings to Thought, to the majesty of the Universe, to man's part in its imaginative creation.

And as I would nobly print so I would have thinkers nobly think, and set out in spacious terms, yet restrained and true, the wonders which are our Universe.

Then we should have noble music, noble architecture, noble adoration, and a noble goal set for man's education, the city of the world to be. Such is the Mission of the Doves Press.'

In moral terms, to perform minor tasks – such as printing – as a part of God's will, is a saintly limit in personal ambition. His eccentricity could be honoured, not mocked. And years afterwards he was very perceptive when one of the manic periods had passed. He saw then that the future, 'to which in a moment of enthusiasm the Press looked forward, is not, it is found, for the Doves Press itself. Not the realization, but the Vision, was, it would seem, the goal of the Press'.

That seems a humble and accurate observation.

One side street, not truly linked with the Doves Press, should be mentioned at the same time – the printed lectures of the Hammersmith Socialist Society, issued in the early years of the century from 7 Hammersmith Terrace, where Cobden-Sanderson was living. These were the results of his own dream, though the Chiswick Press printed them for him. Physically they are very like Doves Press books, and one assumes Emery Walker's hand guided them. The paper is excellent, the type an old face of similar weight and character to the Doves fount, and they were bound in brown paper board with vellum backs. These lectures are good in themselves, including Cobden-Sanderson on 'The Ideal Book' and Mackail on Morris – reprints of slender early Doves Press printing. They were sold for half a crown. They remain a fine example of applied ideals, in hope and type.

Looking through the whole history of the press, from its foundation through the visions and descents, the quarrels and absurdities, the Last Will and Testament in which the Doves type was bequeathed to 'the Bed of the River Thames' so that it might 'pass from change to change for ever upon the Tides of Time, untouched of other use and all else' – one can admire a type face and good taste in its use, with the mysticism of a fascinating mind which appears in all its work. The mixture of abilities made flawless books. As they fall among collectors rather than philosophers, Emery Walker's work in them is the more conspicuous – but that was not a part of anyone's plan. It is tempting to end with one more quotation from Cobden-Sanderson, of no relevance to the Press but typical of him and so oddly evoking London in the summer of 1914, which ended the quieter world he could appreciate. It shows his capacity for watching, withdrawing and keeping his inner eye upon the bridge between now and eternity. He is writing his Journal at 7 a.m. on July the First, at The Press.

'In coming home last night between 10 and 11 o'clock after dining with Stella, I at once felt myself in an atmosphere of excitement – motors were rushing past, and newspaper boys and men were rushing about on foot, and crying hoarse, and to me unintelligible, cries. As I proceeded towards Addison Bridge – I was on my bicycle – the crowd and excitement became so great that I had to get off and walk close to the kerb. Presently the crowd was impenetrable. I asked the reason why. The great fight at Olympia – which was indeed all lighted up, Bombadier Wells had just knocked Bell out in the second round, and that was it! I pulled to the side, and leaning my bicycle against the wall on the bridge, waited the passing of the crowd. Such a crowd! Old and young, rich and poor, evening dress and filth, and men, almost all, or boys, but some women on foot, in the latest limpest evening dress, some in motors; all hurrying by as if all were bearers, to some remote other world, of long expected news. Long expected, now at last, and theirs, to tell. The victory of Wells! And where, I wonder, was Wells, and where Bell?

What a victory, and what a crowd. Slowly it thinned, and I was able to go on my way, on my contrary way westward. Arrived at the river – at the Broadway there was again a crowd, and a long row of motors drawn up before the Clarendon; the river's self I found sublimely remote, and the half moon and the always patient stars, remote, sublime; the river's surface unrippled, receiving upon its dark surface the lights of the bridge, of the moon and of the stars: all one, quiet other-world. Oh, world of men, what is your destiny?'

120

Private presses at all periods, like marriages, might be for richer, for poorer, for better, for worse. The merit which made them better was more usually art in printing than taste in writing, and the urge towards doing the job had probably no link with a need to publish. There were censorable works which had to appear privately or not at all, but quality alone has never condemned bad work to silence. Printers have been ready to make books of bad writing, if the author could pay his bills, but the first impulse for doing it oneself was more typographical pleasure than literary mission.

Two bold exceptions were the Cuala Press in Ireland, and Leonard and Virginia Woolf's Hogarth Press in Richmond in the twenties. The Hogarth Press, starting as a therapy for Virginia Woolf and never passionate for good printing, falls outside this book. That it turned out the most interesting poems and stories of the century and had cover sketches from Vanessa Bell still does not bring it in. It bore less relation to the revival of printing than the Omega Workshops to Morris and Co.

The Cuala Press is another story, its place in dispute, and it lies half way between. Except for occasional work from Jack Yeats, of very unequal merit, these books were unadorned and should be judged by standards of pure typography. Much work from the Irish literary revival was first printed at the Cuala Press in its long life from 1905 to 1946. The coloured broadsheets have some decorative charm of a primitive sort which varies in manner from Sunday school to chap-book. Yeats's sisters founded the press, and ran it on very cheap female labour at Dun Emer outside Cork and in Dublin. It was more than a printing press – a craft guild, though from the record of wages paid it was hardly run on co-operative lines. Emery Walker from his distance in London advised about the typography, but such remoteness in this subject is far from control. The slender books, in Caslon type, generally using red for a second colour, seem a poor pale failure in the shadow of the Doves Press – perhaps nearer to the Hammersmith Socialist Society pamphlets, lacking their skill. Mr. Liam Miller, whose Dolmen Press in Dublin is the only enjoyable literary enterprise of a comparable kind these days, with very much more taste and ingenuity in printing than ever the Yeats sisters knew, is preparing a learned and sympathetic account of the Cuala Press. His views and his bibliography are more to be trusted than my biased paragraph.

For richer and for poorer will be considered in this chapter. Gregynog in Wales was about the richest of all. The grand mock-Tudor house and its park of splendid trees in a wild part of Montgomeryshire, is used now by the University of Wales. Members of faculties split among the colleges at Bangor, Aberystwyth, Cardiff and Swansea gather there for talks, seminars, reading parties and a pleasant life. It seems an appropriate use for the place, not far different from its twenty years between the wars.

In those years Gregynog was run by two unmarried sisters, Gwendolen and Margaret Davies, as a house where artists could produce and live at peace. They had hoped at first for a craft workshop, where weaving and carving might take its place with printing and music – something between Campden and Merton, but without the commercial pressures. Walford Davies seems to have been king of the music, and Gregynog services, madrigals and concerts must have been the happiest expression of the main hope. Orders of service were printed at the press; formes of type for pages of them are there in the racks now ready for proofing. Much of Gregynog is alive still, the ghosts of it present there; no sense yet of municipal gardening, painted notices, asphalt car parks. The grand house keeps its private feeling. Gwendolen Davies lived here till 1961. The comparison which comes to mind, established and continuing, is Glyndebourne.

Printing and binding were carried out together from the start of the press in 1924 to its close in 1940; and the bindery continued through the war, with George Fisher completing his careful tasks and the sisters next door to him covering Penguins for the troops. All this work went on in the old brick stables. Fisher's small room looked over a peaceful wilderness of rhododendrons. In a cupboard are still an armful of unused skins, the colours familiar from Gregynog books. Some of the finest bindings of the period were made there. In the printing room an Albion hand press – made for the sisters by Stephenson and Blake but looking far older, stouter and Victorian – remains, evidence of simple tools used for the first two Gregynog books. Reams of their hand-made paper are stacked against one wall. There must be a temptation to begin it all again, make something as fine in its way as The *Cyrupaedia* which appeared there under Loyd Haberly in 1936, or the crusader chronicle of Louis X which was James Wardrop's masterpiece one year later.

They would be different now, of course. Nobody would try to reproduce the way of life which characterized Gregynog. Helen Waddell and Joan Evans, Walford Davies, Shaw and Eliot were common visitors there. In the production of the books and bindings, and taste in their choice, affection and wealth and discretion are shown. The result is of its time – woodcuts, economy of means, Georgian poetry and Welsh literature. The Principal of the new College, Dr Glyn Hughes, generously gave me a pamphlet of which some copies remained, Helen Waddell's poem *New York City;* printed there in December 1935, containing a word-picture which seems like old history, with something of that period in the house. A large black woodcut by Stefan Mrozewski marks the occasion. The poem is printed in twelve point Poliphilus type, associated with the best books of the Press, with Blado italic. The lines call back another age, when skyscrapers were week-away miracles deserving report:

Look down.
But the floor of New York is surely the roofs of Notre Dame,
Crotchet and Gargoyle and spire,
The Gothic city of Bashan,
With small hard shiny beetles that creep about in the gutters,
Cadillacs, Lincolns and Packards, their varnished wings tight furled,
And small legs leap in and out of them. How did these mites in a cheese
Build these great gods to cow them?
But the mites in this cheese are not cowed.
They run up and down inside their gods in small rectangular boxes.

Their gods are snail shells that house them.
Their gods are hollow.

The Aquitania's due to leave at midnight.

Apart from generous surroundings which gave the Gregynog Press a happy position of scope and privilege, the special distinction was its bindery. The standard of work there may be compared with the Doves bindery, though style and purpose differed. Doves books appeared in bridal white, with special commissions designed and executed for particular clients. At Gregynog no outside work was invited, though Fisher bound a variety of books for the house. His chief care went into the binding of a few copies – fifteen or twenty-five – of each book printed at the Press. These special Gregynog bindings are very much treasured. The designs for them were sometimes by Fisher himself, more often by whoever had carried responsibility for the book – Maynard, Bray, Hughes-Stanton. Bindings were often signed with both names, designer and binder. The range of work is from elaborate inlay and tooling, to such simple single-colour covers as the special bindings for Lamb's Essays or Blunt's poem *The Stealing of the Mare*. But every binder knows the importance of forwarding over finishing, and the standard and strength of these Fisher bindings is beyond question. They are safe and noble works. At the house there is still a full collection of them. Another was lately dispersed at the sale of Major Abbey's library.
But a pleasure of the Press, apart from these treasures, is that every book was issued with an attractive binding made at Gregynog. The ordinary bindings are often as successful as the few Fisher made at greater cost, quite as imaginative and several times simply better. A magnum opus of the Press, the *Cyrupaedia,* is too complex in its special dress. The ordinary issue was notably well bound, in black lambskin with green and red inlay of a medalion and corner pieces, gaining from the simplicity. The poems of Fulke Greville, one of the last books from the Press have an original mixture of quarter leather with asymmetrical gold borders, blue paper with diagonal black stripes and black leather corners. The best example of a fine 'ordinary

binding' is Paul Nash's splendid design in black and orange morocco, with orange lettering, for the volume of Bernard Shaw's autobiographical essays. This striking experiment, more like a poster than a book, has a place in the development of modern binding styles.

All this raises Gregynog books to an aristocratic shelf of their own. Nobody else took the same trouble. Essex House had its bindery, but rather as a separate craft-workshop ready to carry out special commissions. The Caradoc Press and others had bound their own books, but never with this variety and freshness. To that extent the entire work of Gregynog, printing and binding, produced a better thing than anyone else had attempted.

In private press history, you take the rough with the smooth and each has its merit. Rough printing can be like farm furniture, perfect printing is Hepplewhite. The Daniel Press was far from technical perfection. Morris tried to combine it with a declared and evident hand-work. The Doves Press moved towards technical smoothness, but others made the stamp of one man's character appear quite waywardly – perhaps on a title page, or Hornby in the wording of his colophons and Ricketts in their arrangement. The conventional orthodox book, lacking any sort of signature, was rare. Between the wars, a rough technique of printing formed sometimes a deliberate accompaniment to primitive illustration – as with Lovat Fraser's woodcuts, like old chapbooks stemming from Field and Tuer's conscious archaisms at the Leadenhall Press, and the Cuala Press broadsheets with Jack Yeats's sketches.

In these matters again Gregynog showed independence. The famous 'dwell' of a hand press, pressure of black ink upon damped paper, meant nothing there. Except in one single instance, no experiments were made in type design. Nothing had to be secretly ferried to the Severn and dumped for the curiosity of future divers.

The interesting emphasis at Gregynog was upon hand setting, and most of the books were machine printed. It sounds nonsense, but attends to the sensible heart of the story; for the good appearance of a page depends upon close setting and careful spacing – avoiding the white 'rivers' between words, which flow as a chance from machine setting. By hand, the spacing can be changed and varied in relation to the page – not merely for a line, which is what the machine achieves. Machines cannot watch above and below their work.

And as the press existed in a period of excitement when newly-cut type faces came year by year from the Monotype Corporation – modelled upon the very books and works which Morris and Walker had admired – the printers decided to take advantage of these fresh tools and techniques. At that stage of history, to turn away from them and make one's own would have been unadventurous, the opposite of the impulse in 1890 which led to new design. That a man of Gill's genius still designed type for the Golden Cockerel Press is another story, for his life lay in lettering.

We can judge now, being further away, between punches cut by hand and by machine. There is a difference. The Monotype faces are adapted from old models, in a way which suits the Monotype casting process. In small ways the designer is not quite free to follow his taste. There are manifest differences between, for instance, Baskerville's own type and the Monotype version. The change appears to be pure loss in the direction of timidity and uniformity. Something of human error or character, the humanity of hand and eye, have gone. But these are minimal matters, and forty years ago a balance of interest lay the other way. New tools were there, and Gregynog used them.

But at first they were limited by the starting equipment and had to use Kennerley type on a hand press. The first two books, poems of Herbert and Vaughan – appropriately Welsh poets – were made in this way. That Albion hand press is still at Gregynog. Able and artistic small books they were, setting the style of the press with woodcuts and red initials. Gregynog is more thorough from the start, more like Morris in this; not marked by a time of experiment and house errors, as Ashendene books had been.

Then they bought a Monotype caster, but not the other half of that apparatus the type-setter. So the caster was simply used as a mechanism for making new alphabets of type from molten metal – a type foundry. Then the hand setting and printing began. In this way Gregynog could use a fair range of the newly machine-cut Monotype faces, as many as the matrices they chose to buy.

126

The exception to this rule or theory is the interesting edition of Bridges's poem *Eros and Psyche* issue at Gregynog in 1935. Three hundred copies were printed on stout Kelmscott paper, gaily using three colours – green for Graily Hewitt's initials and openings to each book of the poem, red for sub-titles and occasional emphasis. The ordinary binding was white pigskin with a gold medallion – a particularly foolish choice, for it gets uncleanably filthy. But the point of interest is Graily Hewitt's type, used here for the only time, designed for private press work and cut in the old way by Edward Prince. The design of the type came under fire, we are told, from Hornby and never appeared again; which was a touch too timid of it, for it looks very well now, a bit undisciplined but brave and different, calligraphic, splendid for Gregynog. They ought to have adopted it, and not been scared off by Hornby. Another attraction of this book is the woodcuts from drawings by Burne-Jones which had been made far back for that edition of the *Earthly Paradise* which never appeared. Cut with authority by Hooper, they still seem distant from the great Kelmscott days and some way from Burne-Jones. It may only be, like Gere's woodcuts in Ashendene books, that one misses the surrounding decoration Morris provided. This is a notable book, with all its faults, bringing together almost sentimentally the old players – Kelmscott paper, a type cut for the press, Graily Hewitt, Burne-Jones, Bridges. But the Burne-Jones girls seem far too short in the thigh, he could never have drawn them like that.

These principles – hand-setting, machine printing and the casting of available Monotype faces – with a generally straightforward style of printing, and enjoyment of coloured initials made the manner of Gregynog, though the same hand was never in charge for very long. The sisters bought Gregynog in 1919, and the first book appeared four years later – 'finished on the ninth day of November, MCMXXIII'. There were three regimes at Gregynog, with other distinguished entries and exits from time to time. The first in charge was Robert Ashwin Maynard, and he soon recruited Horace Walter Bray. Both had been painters at the fringe of the Campden Group, and wanted work after the war. Maynard learnt printing at the Central School under the great J. C. Mason of the Doves Press, who suggested his son John Mason as Maynard's assistant at Gregynog. John Mason recalled the first years there:

> 'The printing studio was converted from a stable at the back of the house. A folio Albion hand press, a composing frame, a few founts of Kennerley type, an ink table, an imposing stone, a bookbinding bench, a nipping press and a standing press comprised the equipment of the studio.'

Mason was the first binder, until George Fisher's arrival in 1925. For the next five years, Maynard and Bray were in charge of the printing. They left and founded their own Raven Press at Harrow.

From 1931 for three years Gregynog was under a quartet – Blair Hughes-Stanton and his wife Gertrude Hermes, William McCance and his wife Agnes Miller Parker. Both wives were artists, but Gertrude Hermes, possibly the most important artist of the quartet, unfortunately never illustrated any of the Gregynog books. There seems to have been some discord between the four of them, and exciting books appeared. For a short time, 1934–6, Loyd Haberly took over; but with other academic and literary interests, he had only come to help at a difficult moment. The magnum opus in his time was the *Cyrupaedia*. In the last four years of the Press James Wardrop was in charge, working there part time only. He had a connection with the Victoria and Albert Museum, and managed to combine both activities. Papers at Gregynog and Aberystwyth show his delightful handwriting. The best evidence of his taste as a printer is the Joinville *History of St Louis*, translated from the French by Joan Evans.

In the days of the Doves Press, type and paper may have been enough – Cobden-Sanderson thought them so, and initials appearing here and there were not the focus of design. Twenty-five years later at Gregynog, the balance had changed. With no special revelation in the founts of the press, some freedom in decoration lifted the character of the books above ordinary decency. The text page with its margins and press work might be enough, but could not become especially memorable. Initials, wood engravings and bindings give their style to these books. The style varies with changing hands which formed it, but gaiety and lightness seem to remain in the books and the place, expressing the life of Gregynog between two wars. And this recog-

128

nisable quality carries from one regime to the next. Hand-colouring of initial letters was typical. The letters Maynard designed for *The Stealing of the Mare* are very like others designed by Loyd Haberly for the *Cyrupaedia*. It is not like going from one press to another.

Bray and Maynard, artists by training, decorated the early Gregynog books most charmingly with their woodcuts and engravings. The style varied, but within their differences these illustrations are interchangeable from one hand to the other – no obvious manner identifies Bray or Maynard. For Herbert's poems Maynard made an engraving of Montgomery Castle not far from Gregynog, where the poet was born. It is interesting to compare its appearance in the book with the reproduction in Thomas Jones's bibliography of the press. From the wood block it looks so much blacker, stronger, rougher.

The Bray-Maynard period produced many of these decorated books, outline woodcuts as for Peacock's *Misfortunes of Elfin*, or a rougher primitive style for the *Life of Saint David*. Those Saint David woodcuts appear on each page of the book, gaily hand-coloured, making that perhaps the bravest experiment in decoration from the private presses. The volume of essays by Edward Thomas too, has homely engravings by Maynard and Bray.

Bray used a far more sophisticated and precise style to illustrate the *Autobiography of Lord Herbert of Cherbury* – just slightly satirical, mocking the little boy who works at his desk to the great admiration of his tutors, as he 'made an oration of a sheet of paper, and fifty or sixty verses in the space of one day'. But perhaps the most finished craft is shown in Bray's engravings for the two volumes of Lamb's Essays, 1930, near the end of his time at Gregynog. These, 'adapted from contemporary prints in the collection of Edward J. Finch', printed on Japanese vellum, have a lightness and neatness which fit their subject and help to make this, printed only in black, among the most successful works of the Press.

And in the art of printing it points to the next period under McCance and Hughes-Stanton. The wood engravings by Mrs McCance (Agnes Miller Parker) for the edition of *Aesop's Fables* make it the most conspicuously decorative volume of that kind; but the period is remembered for the delicate technical mastery of Blair Hughes-Stanton as a wood engraver. He refused an invitation to take charge as controller of the press, choosing to spend all his time in this art. Mr John Lewis, after reading a draft of this chapter, writes:

'Blair Hughes-Stanton is perhaps the most *skilful* wood engraver who has ever lived. The son of a famous artist a consummate craftsman, his interest in the naked body was somewhat obsessive, his manner of drawing owed much to Leon Underwood at whose school he and Gertrude Hermes studied. These incredibly fine engravings were most difficult to print and it was only as a result of Hughes-Stanton obtaining some very fine German ink and combining that with Japanese vellum that he was able to get the kind of result he wanted.' Mr David Bland, who watched him working on them, writes that in illustrating the *Book of Revelation* at Gregynog 'Hughes-Stanton's astonishing skill produced wood engravings so fine they might have been engraved on steel'.

This is praise for technique, but the art of it may not be so obviously successful. These long-drawn figures of light and shade seem overbearing for the printed page, and to carry more mannerism than wisdom. It is easy to admire the books from his period of the press – Milton, Revelation, Job – but the style of those engravings may keep them at a distance. The little decorations by the same artist for *Erewhon* are different, in another scale, apt and charming.

These were the source of supply, though others contributed – Reynolds Stone for instance, with some heraldry for *St Louis* and little typical engravings for the *Praise of Country Life*, and John Farleigh with a portrait of Shaw for the volume of autobiography, *Shaw on Himself*. The Burne-Jones designs for *Eros and Psyche* have been mentioned.

Woodcuts, bindings, initials – the gaiety of these books is a quality of Gregynog. Anyone may enjoy the Welsh books printed there, even when nothing in them can be understood but the title. The initials which Bray designed for *Psalman Dafydd gan William Morgan*, published in 1929 in an edition of two hundred, make that a delightful book to examine. The irritable husband in *Love*, by Elizabeth of the German Garden, says his wife 'has no idea about books – always reading them'. That echoes with some sympathy among collectors,

130

who may feel at home among the eight books printed in Welsh at Gregynog.

We can look at examples in one or two others. The volume of Vaughan's poems printed there in 1924, compares with the Vale Press edition of Vaughan from 1897. The Ricketts version was, perhaps properly, more solemn. The colophon at the end was arranged like a cross. Initials and text, black heavy woodcut and a black renaissance border – no relief of second colour, bound all over in grey paper-board and serious label printed black. It is Ricketts who looks like a Welsh Sunday. The Gregynog volume, with no more colour on the paper-board, overprints a design of HV and S for Henry Vaughan Silurist and a rough cut of a swan rides at the point of focus. There are charming wood engravings of the Vaughan country, which Maynard and Bray could so well do by wandering in the neighbourhood, and bright red initials for each poem. Red italic is used for biblical quotation. This from the early years, Kennerley type and the Albion hand-press, is a happy production.

The Life of St David, described above, is in its way the most ambitious of all the books. Only one hundred and seventy-five were printed – quite enough repetition for the chore of painting all the woodcuts in this short and merry work. The text is in three colours.

Another good use of colour is in *The Stealing of the Mare*, a large quarto from 1930. The spine is a sandy lambskin which quickly soils, but that is the only fault in a gallant book. The 'foliated pattern boards, specially designed at the Press and printed in three colours' are echoed in the initials Maynard designed for the book, and suggest Gill's manner in the foliage. It is an opulent production, with gold in the printed version of the Gregynog medallion on the title page, and gold in the large initials. These are so nicely coloured that it is hard to tell where printing ends and brushwork starts. Maynard designed them with precision and white space, forms of flower and leaf with Persian tiles in their ancestry. These on the large page of Garamond type, printed on Japanese vellum, are almost enough to lead one through this peculiar work 'translated from the original Arabic by Lady Anne Blunt and done into verse by Wilfrid Scawen Blunt'. Blunt saw to it that he was decently printed – by the Chiswick Press years before (published by Kegan Paul), then Kelmscott and lastly by Gregynog.

All the talents gathered in Wardrop's day to make the edition of *St Louis* of which two hundred were printed in 1937. 'The initials and headings were designed by Alfred J. Fairbank and cut in wood by R. John Beedham. The hand-coloured armorial ornaments, identified by A. Van de Put, were drawn and engraved in wood by Reynolds Stone. The maps were drawn by Berthold Wolpe and lettered by Alfred J. Fairbank.' That ought to have been enough to satisfy anyone, and it is beautifully printed in 16pt Monotype Poliphilus. This grand and well-spaced book has red and blue initials, and the coats of arms appearing in the lower margins were hand-coloured. It is the tour de force of the press, a bold expression of ability and control. The opening on page seven, with Fairbank's splendid lettering in red IN THE NAME OF ALMIGHTY GOD, and the French king's coat of arms at the bottom, is an extension of the sort of effect which Johnston initiated years before in the Doves Bible and *Paradise Lost*. But nothing there was so fine as this page from Joinville. The same coat of arms appears boldly in the front of a stout binding in 'dark maroon Oasis'. In the special binding in 'light blue levant, polished. Tooled with all-over pattern of fleur-de-lis in gold', this is the most striking exhibit of them all.

But perhaps the best quality at Gregynog, within these decorations and excitements, was straightforward merit. It is not easy to find – as a routine it becomes dull, and with too much care it grows pompous. The ordinary excellence of Gregynog books remains a noticeable pleasure. This is where the Doves Press had an influence, though its maker needed the emphasis of private type elaborately thought out and carrying a weight of mystic meaning. In Wales they bridged it more naturally.

This cannot be analysed, the excitement of the ordinary. A book which shows it well is the account of the Quaker wanderings of Richard Davies, a Welshman much like the American John Woolman whose Journals had been printed at Essex House. It is called *An Account of the Convincement Excercises, Services and Travels of that Ancient Servant of the Lord Richard Davies*. One hundred and fifty copies were

132

printed in 1928. One of the simple books of the press – no second colour, except for the press mark on the title page; no specially designed initial letter, just Baskerville type on good paper, with the right margins. And it stands as a flawless achievement, appropriate for its subject, a pleasure to hold and read. The Jewish prayer at Passover begins, 'Wherefore is this night different from all other nights?' Why is this book different from all others? Rough edges of hand-made paper come out almost to the edges of the binding; the blue buckram is round unusually stout boards; Baskerville type, wrongly used on rough paper, is so carefully printed that the choice seems right; and the book about a Welshman was affectionately made in Wales, 'Compositor: Richard Owen Jones'.

This Welsh taste tended to dominate the choice of books at Gregynog. There was less wandering in the forest of books, pulling up a few for careful replanting, than among most private printers. Welsh writing in both languages took charge at first, and only in the Hughes-Stanton period we have a caper round the common field – *Comus*, *Four Poems* by Milton, *The Revelation of St John*. A small fault, and *Comus* anyway had been written for performance not far off at Ludlow. Omar Khayyam arrives in Welsh.

Honesty of taste and sense of place were there. Among the attractive books of poems were *Caelica* by Sidney's friend Fulke Greville – a quiet and beautiful example of printing in small Perpetua type, with red initials – and the last book from the press, *Lyrics and Unfinished Poems* by Lascelles Abercrombie. Gilbert Murray seems an appropriate figure in Gregynog society, and the two folio volumes of his Euripides translations were the major works of the press though never the most popular and some had to be given away.

There must have been something about Gregynog, as about Glyndebourne, which successfully took its guests away from progress and affairs and allowed retreat for thought. The mixture of singing and pictures and a splendid house helped, but it remains in the books. It comes with a little of the recognition Richard Davies felt, that Ancient Servant of the Lord, for his wife:

'So the Lord gave me a little Time, and he alone provided an Helpmeet for me; for I prayed unto him, that she might be of his own providing, for it was not yet manifest to me where she was, or who she was. But one Time as I was at Horselydown Meeting in Southwark, I heard a Woman-Friend open her mouth, by way of Testimony, against an evil ranting Spirit, that did oppose Friends much in those Days. It came to me from the Lord, that that Woman was to be my Wife, and to go with me to the Country, and to be an Help-meet for me.'

It is in the sonnet by Joan Evans which appears at the beginning of the Gregynog bibliography:

> Only here
> Where all our different ways for once can meet
> In orchestrated beauty, can we hear
> The measure of our great Conductor's beat.

And the poem is called *Gregynog*, not Walford Davies.

Gregynog expressed the gentlemanly resources of peace and money. The revival of printing has been achieved, and a conventional language of equipment established. Private printing continues, but the search for new extension with the old sense of excitement becomes difficult. Printers have travelled to the limits of grandeur and excellence. For richer, for poorer. A modern survey is outside the subject of this book, but Morris Cox and his Gogmagog Press succeed in pushing their way in.

He is a poet of originality and force. His home shared nothing with Gregynog – bright and white-painted above a shop in Walthamstow. His printing tools are home-made, and Mr David Chambers describes the Press in an article for *The Private Library:* 'He will often have written the text, and nearly always have designed and cut the illustrations, the type is set by hand and painted on home-made presses; the binding cases ase immaculately hand-made; the finished books are given acetate jackets and then lovingly wrapped in coloured tissue, sealed with red paper seals and neatly parcelled off to their purchasers.' Morris Cox has an equal talent in painting and design, and he sensibly gave up the dull battle with commercial publishing to produce what he wanted in the way he chose. This intention, apt in private printing, has provided about fifteen experiments of genius which lie beyond the range of most printers. The illustrations to poems or moods, printed from blocks in which all sorts of odd bits of texture are used, combine with careful use of heavy type in bright subtleties bearing no connection with other people's books. As he writes in one of them, 'They prove nothing except that it might still be possible for a dedicated hand printer to remain in essence at the incunabula level and start adventuring again from there, particularly in the field of illustration.' But that was also the spirit of the Kelmscott Press.

Morris Cox has moved forward from simple experiments in printing and coloured illustration (with two of his own poems, *Yule Gammon* and *The Slumbering Virgin*) to varying demonstrations of possibility in the kind of work he has discovered. Its simplest exposition was in *Crash*, made for the Society of Private Printers in 1963, in eighty copies. After the statement of intent, his method is shown in eight double pages of varied illustration threaded with captions of a semi-story; and the method used in each block is then explained – as 'Birds of card and crepe paper. Wire mesh impressed into card and removed'. Or 'Disk inked with brush background lightly sprayed with petrol before printing'. No trade secrets, and no imitators. That disk and the petrol spray produce a strange moon in a grey night.

There are more conventional little books than this from the Gogmagog Press, poems with borders, a beautiful *Medieval Dream Book* of dream and meaning; and recently the seasons in four books of absolute discipline, abstract illustrations expressing four of his short poems. In these panoramic double pages which spill from one opening to the next, there is a link with the relief printing, the gauffrage, of prints and books from China and Japan.

Now that the method has been stated in these books and asserted, perhaps Morris Cox may feel free to use it as a form of art and literature in a wider context, freed from any need to demonstrate what he is doing. The method exists, with genius to use it, and one looks forward now to the excitement of its use in perhaps more extrovert ways.

A successful private press depends upon art and excitement not upon money. Gregynog and Gogmagog have sailed for the same harbour.

Opening of *Joinville's History of St Louis,* a Crusader Chronicle issued by the Gregynog Press, 1937. Poliphilus type, with headings and initials by Alfred Fairbank, and 'armorial ornaments' engraved on wood by Reynolds Stone.

Overleaf
Eric Gill's design for the opening of *The Reves Tale,* from volume I of the *Canterbury Tales,* Golden Cockerel Press, 1928. The type is Caslon.

Overleaf
A page of initials and headings used at the Caradoc Press, from a book of such examples issued by the press in 1908. Only seven copies were printed.

Overleaf
From volume II of the Shakespeare Head *Spenser,* 1930. Green, red and raised gold are used for the ship in the vellum copy from which this was photographed.

IN THE NAME OF ALMIGHTY GOD

I, JOHN, LORD OF JOINVILLE, SENESCHAL OF CHAMPAGNE, HAVE CAUSED THE LIFE OF OUR SAINTLY KING LOUIS TO BE WRITTEN ACCORDING AS I SAW AND HEARD FOR THE SPACE OF THE SIX YEARS THAT I WAS IN HIS COMPANY ON PILGRIM-AGE BEYOND THE SEA AND AFTER WE CAME BACK.

And ere I tell you of his great deeds and his knightly prowess will I tell you what I saw and heard of his godly sayings and his good precepts, so that they may be found set one after the other to edify those that shall hear them.

This holy man loved God with all his heart and followed His example: as appeareth in that even as God died for the love He bare His people, so put he his body in jeopardy many times for the love he bare his people; and he might well have avoided it an he had wished, as ye shall hear hereafter.

The great love that he had for his people appeareth in his saying to my lord Louis, his eldest son, in a dire illness that he had at Fontainebleau: 'Fair son,' said he, 'I beseech thee to make thyself beloved of the people of thy realm; for in sooth I had liefer have a Scot come from Scotland and govern the people of this realm faithfully and well, than that thou shouldst govern it manifestly ill.'

The saintly King loved truth so well that not even to the Saracens would he lie concerning his covenant with them, as ye shall hear hereafter.

So sober was he of his mouth that on no day of my life did I know him give thought to the ordering of any dish, as many rich men do; but he patiently ate whatsoever his cooks dressed and set before him. In his words was he temperate; for never in my life did I hear him speak ill of another, nor did I ever hear him name the Devil, which name is spilled about the kingdom, which methinks pleaseth God ill. He watered his wine in measure, according as he saw the wine would stand it. He asked me in Cyprus why I did not put water in my wine; and I told him that the physicians were the cause, who said that I had a thick head and a cold stomach, and that therefore I could not get drunk. And he

b   7

For every clerk anon right heeld with other.
They seyde, 'the man is wood, my leve brother';
And every wight gan laughen of this stryf.
Thus swyved was the carpenteres wyf,
For al his keping and his Ialousye;
And Absolon hath kist hir nether ye;
And Nicholas is scalded in the toute.
This tale is doon, and God save al the route!

WHAN folk had laughen at this nyce cas
Of Absolon and hende Nicholas,
Diverse folk diversely they seyde;
But, for the more part, they loughe and pleyde,
Ne at this tale I saugh no man him greve,
But it were only Osewold the Reve,

132

Oliver Goldsmith

Quia amore langueo

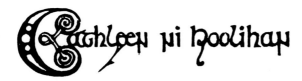

Cathleen ni hoolihan

The Proverbys of
Saynt Bernarde

COLIN·CLOUTS COME·HOME AGAINE····

By Ed. Spencer.

1595.

GOLDEN COCKEREL AND
SHAKESPEARE HEAD

The life of the Golden Cockerel had three periods, starting in 1920 at Waltham St Lawrence near Twyford. The pressman, Mr A. C. Cooper has pleasantly described that time:

'The Golden Cockerel Press was started in 1920 by the late Harold Midgeley Taylor in a large wooden hut partitioned into composing room, press room, office and packing room. It was lined inside and well heated, and situated at the rear of his house, Three Elms Cottage, Mill Bridge Road, Waltham St Lawrence. As there was no electric light laid on in Waltham in those days, the lighting for the evenings in the winter was hanging paraffin oil lamps, and the heating system was by two anthracite closed stoves, one in the press room and one in the composing room, with a Valor oil stove in the packing room when it was used.'

To that oil-lit hut Taylor's authors were supposed to come and share in the composing and printing of their own books. It was a good guild-of-handicraft thought without much strength of organization at the back. The authors came and their books appeared – no great splash, the ripples invisible now. The first three books from the press were twelve tales by A. E. Coppard with the title *Adam and Eve and Pinch Me*, *Terpsichore and Other Poems* by H. T. Wade-Gery, and a book of tales from J. D. Beresford called *Signs and Wonders*. The trouble about being contemporary, Taylor might have agreed, is that you so quickly get out of date. And as Mr Cooper explains, 'they were all enthusiastic at first; but as hard work became apparent they left him one by one, and he and his wife were left holding the baby so to speak'.

So he engaged a staff and the character of the place shifted towards soundly printed editions of well-known works – four volumes of Sir Thomas Browne, poems by Spenser, and that great standby of the private presses *The XI Bookes of the Golden Asse* translated from the Latin by William Adlington. *Daphnis and Chloe* followed soon after, and it looks as if Taylor was set on the road which led to *Sonnets from the Portuguese* and *The House of Life* – but at that time he had to withdraw through illness and in 1925 he died. The Press was taken

137

over by Robert Gibbings and his wife Moira. From then until the late summer of 1933 when Gibbings had to give up, and Mr Sandford changed its home from an active printing-press at Waltham St Lawrence to publishing offices in Staple Inn – seven productive years – this period forms the splendour of the Golden Cockerel as a private press in the terms of this story. Taylor's books were agreeable but not remarkable, and his ascent from the co-operative idea must have been a disappointment. Gibbings with the friendship of Eric Gill, raised the work to another level of ambition.

The achievements of the Golden Cockerel are varied and conspicuous, though most of them lie outside the terms of this introduction to private presses. In the three phases of the bird's life his character entirely changed.

Mr Christopher Sandford owned the Press after 1934 and all the books for which he was responsible are displayed in a room of his peaceful house, Eye Manor in Herefordshire. There is a thick Donegal carpet designed by Walter Crane, a splendid collection of old English costume, and the books with their grand title pages and varied woodcuts open for any visitor to examine. These works for which he was responsible may be remembered at a future time as we look back to the productions of the Baskerville Press; they were a development from the private press movement, the rational use of its example.

The language of a colophon has to be sifted. 'Oxford, at the University Press' means that the book was printed at the University's own press in Oxford. 'Printed by William Morris at the Kelmscott Press' means just what it says, except that Morris was at the head of a small group of workers, supervising and sharing with them. 'Printed at the Golden Cockerel Press' may mean that Mr Christopher Sandford designed the book and, say, the Chiswick Press or Shenval Press printed it.

'The survival of the Golden Cockerel' he said in a lecture, 'since I and my friend took it over in the midst of the great depression, has been due in large measure to the method of production we adopted. By working in with the Chiswick Press, a famous old firm of trade printers, we arranged that the Cockerel schould have the use of their plant and their skilled labour as and when we wanted it, without the necessity for capital expenditure on plant or of providing the wages

138

of skilled craftsmen, week in week out, whether or not fully employed.'
In other words it ceased to be a private press for this passage describes the connection between any printer and publisher. In another lecture, *Printing and Life*, Mr Sandford describes the joys of a publisher then as now, 'the intimate and personal contact I have all the time with the authors and the artists who are working on the texts and the illustrating of the books which I am producing'. He also describes the hazards and, it looks now, the mistakes of a publisher in choice and rejection.

Those books from the long final period of Mr Sandford's control, nearly thirty years, stand with Sir Francis Meynell's at the Nonesuch Press as examples of excellence for any printer or publisher now, their typography varied but always attractive, paper and binding giving pleasure each time, and a constant stream of experiment and achievement in book illustration. Mr Sandford's concern with the woodcut and other forms of art continued the tradition of the Press as it had developed under Robert Gibbings and Eric Gill. The work of the engravers of Golden Cockerel books gives the Press its greatest distinction and made a whole period of woodcut revival. Looking through the books now, or the three volumes of bibliography in which they are represented, one is impressed by the skill and beauty and their air of mild between-the-wars eroticism. These books were a happy house for the talent of the time, with work from David Jones, Dorothea Braby, Eric Gill, Gwenda Morgan, Eric Ravilious, John Buckland-Wright and Blair Hughes-Stanton.

Woodcut illustration has tended to be accepted with too little criticism, because of an orthodoxy which insists that it is the right medium for the printed page. It goes well with the text, we are constantly told, because both are a kind of relief block and can be printed together in one act. The balance can often be questioned – as in Walter Crane's illustrations for the Kelmscott Press *Story of the Glittering Plane*, or Mary Groom's in the Golden Cockerel *Paradise Lost*; but very often the balance is there for acceptance, because the medium seems fit.

The orthodoxy might be questioned, because there are different kinds of fitness. Another sort of excellence in illustration is that it perfectly explains the text. John Leech's drawings in the Surtees novels are a fair example. Time and again, reading Surtees, a new character is introduced and the drawing which follows brings the confirming fun of recognition – he is just how we imagined him. But those coloured etchings have nothing to do with that other fitness for which wood-cuts are praised – they do not balance the text. Again, the splendid coloured lithographs of Gould's birds facing common sense setting of a charming text form a grand double page to eye and mind, but have nothing to do with the orthodox balance which so much concerned the revivers of printing. Robert Gibbings had it in mind when he described Eric Gill's decorations for Chaucer's *Troilus:*

'The engravings are in the form of very delicate borders almost identical with the weight of the type, so that the page is of an entirely even texture picked out here and there with accents of rubrication and coloured intitials.'

This was indeed a sound thing to have managed, but not the only sort of success in illustrating a book.

Where so much was produced in such wide range it seems best here to look only at a few of the most splendid, and the same scheme can be followed in examining the Shakespeare Head Press at Stratford and Oxford which ran through the same time.

For an aperitif before this feast one could consider the folio twelve-page prospectus issued by the Press in Spring 1930, the high point of Robert Gibbings's time. For the front, Eric Ravilious cut a large black floral border and signed it with his initials. Drawn title lettering looks like the work of Eric Gill. Page two is blank, and a fine cock crowing in a field, Ravilious again, to full type measure, heads the text opposite. A general message signed by Robert and Moira Gibbings is in that curiously hearty prose (or verse?) of artists with an eye on commerce.

'Of editions de luxe there is no end and much fine printing is a weari-ness of the purse, nevertheless the Golden Cockerel hails the New Year with radiant comb and bristling spurs, fortified by the ever-increasing appreciation of connoisseurs.'

A new type has been designed for the press by Eric Gill. Ravilious on the front is a glossy black, on page three rather grey from imperfect inking or a nervousness over fine lines. The whole document is on heavy Kelmscott paper – what a pleasure to have received it in the morning's post! And apart from such ephemera as *My One Hundredth Tale* by A. E. Coppard, a grand gathering is heralded. The woodcuts and specimen pages alone make this a memorable prospectus. Perhaps the magnum opus of the press was its edition of the *Four Gospels*, decorated by Eric Gill. Here it is announced, with an excellent specimen page in Gill's new type and with one of his most impressive historiated initials – for that is how one must see them, not quite illustration but far transcending decoration. Over the page again, and we have a particularly interesting decoration, because this is its only appearance, by Robert Gibbings for the opening lines of *Paradise Lost*. Somehow that plan fell through, and the ambitious book was issued years later with woodcuts by Mary Groom. One wishes, seeing this, that Gibbings had carried it out.

And the next sample page is taken from *The Canterbury Tales*, a typical woodcut by Eric Gill at the head of some apt lines for a spring list:

> He wiste it was the eightetethe day
> Of April, that is messager to May;
> And sey wel that the shadwe of every tree
> Was as in lengthe the same quantitee.

One is pleased to see that in this fourth volume the printers had to follow the manner of the other three and use Caslon; for Gill's heavy Golden Cockerel letter is not his most sensitive invention, and that balance which Gibbings boasted might have been in danger by its use. And the perceptive *London Mercury* is quoted earlier – 'This first volume of the Canterbury Tales can fairly be put beside the same Press's noble *Troilus and Criseide*, and there can be no doubt that collectors of the future will scramble feverishly for them.'

On the back cover Ravilious has another cockerel in a fight with pages of a book, plucking and chucking them about.

So this list enshrines the finest Golden Cockerel books in its life of more than forty years. It becomes identified with Robert Gibbings and Eric Gill. We shall leave aside some good printing and much ephemeral writing, and look more carefully at these great Golden Cockerel editons of *Troilus and Criseide*, *The Canterbury Tales* and *The Four Gospels*.

For their achievement needs more careful analysis than the prospectus or the bibliography gave. The balance of text and illustration goes further than typography. In Gould's bird books, the text explains the pictures. In a Surtees novel, John Leech's engravings explain the text. Neither form of art had to do with book design, though they contribute to the delight of books. But Eric Gill's work in Chaucer and *The Four Gospels* goes back into the history of printed books and manuscripts, joining two arts with unique success. That is the balance he achieved, greater than the even weight of engraving and type.

In early illumination, one finds no frontier between decoration and illustration. The work of the artist surrounded the text, explained and ornamented it – sometimes within scrolls and borders, sometimes in historiated initials; and as calligraphy is itself a kind of illustration to explain meaning, text and picture formed one thing. With the invention of printing, painters found work in decorating the new books – more work than ever, no redundancy yet but their contribution moved a step nearer to Gould's birds.

Printed borders, straps and scrolls, leaf designs and arabesques, replaced them in time and give a pleasant taste to some early printing – in the work of Gunther Zainer at Ulm, and Ratdolt in Venice. They do nothing to the books except embellish them unnecessarily, rather in the way of Victorian ironwork upon buildings of the last century. Border and picture are now divided, and if they find their way together, one enclosing the other, the old unity is lost. When William Morris, looking back to his collection of fifteenth century printed books, drew rich borders for his own, they had nothing to do with illustration for which he always invited outside help – Burne-Jones, Walter Crane, Gaskin. Eric Gill in these Golden Cockerel books uniquely fused these two arts again, illustration with decoration. His borders in one work, and initials in the other, mark the point of balance, inseparable.

They rank very high in the range of Gill's work and Mr Robert Speaight has done less than justice to them in his recent and excellent

142

biography. The carvings for the Stations of the Cross in Westminster Cathedral might appear, physically and to one who is not a Roman Catholic, quite minor and of doubtful success by comparison.

Gill seems to have worked deliberately to these two forms, making examples of each. Having set the style of illustrated border in *Troilus*, and continuing it through the four volumes of *The Canterbury Tales*, he had intended something of the same sort for the Gospels but changed his mind; and, as the prospectus puts it, 'instead of floreated borders to every page as previously announced it has now been decided to decorate the book with a large number of engraved initials, printed in red, blue or black, many of which will contain pictorial devices illustrating the themes of the narrative'. And the decision changed again, for this book has nothing but black, and anything else for these bold woodcuts is unimaginable.

Troilus appeared in September 1927. Two hundred and twenty-five copies were printed, six of them on vellum. *The Canterbury Tales* followed in four volumes between February 1929 and March 1931. Of these five hundred were printed, including fifteen on vellum. A set of the Chaucer volumes on vellum sold at Sotheby in the spring of 1967 impressed those who saw them by their brilliance and clarity, by the success of this first Golden Cockerel attempt in such a difficult task, and by the fitness and blackness of Gill's engravings as they appear on vellum. With the fine lines common to his engravings, a smoother surface than hand-made paper allows seemed perfectly appropriate. The text is set throughout in 18 pt Caslon.

Most of the borders are leaf and stem, but among the leaves, hiding or beckoning, climbing or leaning out, are girls and men, kings and boys, priests and nuns who take part or seem to be commenting upon the stories. A young man is whistling across the page, two fingers at his mouth, to a girl; Chaucer himself waves to a little god of love facing across his own poem; a sad lover looks over to Christ crucified; Pan blows pipes and a naked girl, hearing him, prepares to climb her tree; a nineteen-twentyish girl climbs up, and a sad young bearded man looking like Robert Gibbings sits, supporting the whole tree's weight, opposite; Chaucer is writing with confidence under the leaves, taking it down by dictation from the naughty spirit looking down and over the lines. So the pattern continues, affectionate and cheeky, erotic, enjoyable and relevant, decorative and explanatory, a balance of taste and eye. Borders are repeated, sometimes in new combinations. To start a new tale we have more elaborate and descriptive work with a red or blue initial letter. At the start of the Reeve's tale, for instance, there is a half-accurate design of the big bed, the cradle below, the angry miller peeping from one side and his wife from the other, one of the young clerks from Cambridge embracing the miller's daughter and the other waiting with his hand up, playing it by ear. There they are, the characters in the tale, with their stage scenery. Turning for comparison to the same story as it appears in the Kelmscott Chaucer, not one stroke of the pen is there for illustration. Morris must indeed have enjoyed Chaucer in all his light as well as softer moods; but as for the problem of illustrating his obscenities, that was passed over as simply as the boat in the Man of Law's Tale passed across the rough seas, with its Christian princess, from Asia to England. And there it is in Burne-Jones's engraving of course, a lovely boat on the wild waves – but not the miller's daughter with the clerk from Cambridge.

One other quality in these borders should be noticed – their mannerism, the distortion of human figures sometimes so that they almost share the forms of leaf and stem – and sometimes grow from them. It is another, rather touching aspect of Gill's idea and all these manners work towards a single art – the poetry, people, leaves, decoration and explanation. Author, artist and printer have shared one concept and expressed it.

The Four Gospels is no less startling and original. Gibbings once said his only regret was that the book might have been a little taller. One problem in printing bibles must be to split up chapter and verse sensibly, breaking the convention of a new paragraph after most sentences; for as it is not poetry, 'verse' cannot be our right word to use. 'I must have chapter and verse' people say, from days when bible reference could settle an argument. My single complaint against this Golden Cockerel volume concerns the little black stars used to relieve the text page and divide one's reading. They stand out almost like small ink blots and distract.

144

I have carried out an experiment, examining passages from five bibles as a test of pleasure in reading – Baskerville 1760, one known as Bowyer's bible printed by Bensley in 1790, The Doves bible, *Genesis* printed at the Riccardi press and this edition of the *Four Gospels*. Baskerville, immense, orthodox and immaculate, stands monumentally as the finest lectern bible. Bensley's work, a kind of 'bible designed to be read as literature', with chapters and chapter titles as in a history ('Chap. XXII Isaac Offered Up') and divided conventionally into verses, is a delightful quarto to open on one's lap and use, with copper engravings from old masters. The Riccardi book has its pleasant type face which Herbert Horne designed, but leaves no strong impression otherwise and Russell Flint's illustrations add nothing. As an experience in reading for sense or pleasure, in this test I placed the Doves bible comfortably at the bottom – its fine printed type in blocks unrelieved by any concession to a less perfectly high-minded character than was Cobden-Sanderson himself. Reading *Genesis* in the Doves bible is like hearing a sermon spoken in absolute monotony. The Golden Cockerel book, by the same standard, has endless fascination and variation built into the printed text. Its three distinctions are the type face which Eric Gill had designed for the press, rather heavy in itself and suitably used here; unjustified lines which only now begin to be accepted in the printing of books, and the initials which in varying scales and elaboration adorn the pages. No woodcut decoration or illustration is here for itself, but always forming a part of the printed bible with one poetic exception, in the Gospel According to St John, when Pilate writes on the cross the title, 'Jesus of Nazareth the King of the Jews', and Gill gives most of his page to a leafy and spring-like crucifixion. This service to the words, unlike his Chaucer borders, appears as an act of humility.

There were problems in the mating, as Robert Gibbings has explained, between these two men who could not lightly join in a religious work – over the text at first, as Gill asked awkwardly 'Authorised by whom?'. But the result may be in Mr Sandford's words, 'the book among all books in which Roman type has been mated with any kind of illustration'.

The engravings, in Gill's art, meant absolute discipline. They give one more balance in this book, between primitive and modern. His discipline led to a mannerism of precision, an influence from ninth-century manuscript distilled into woodcut. His pictures beautifully explain their letters, as leaves spring from branches. This work is a wonderful extension of typography. And, as in his Chaucer, there is no long mood of reverence but it comes to the nineteen-thirties.

To take a few examples:

From St Mark, 'And when a convenient day was come, that Herod on his birthday made a supper to his lords, high captains, and chief estates of Galilee; And when the daughter of the said Herodias came in, and danced, and pleased Herod and them that sat with him, the King said unto the damsel, Ask of me whatsoever thou wilt, and I will give it thee'. Gill's AND has a gay short-haired girl dancing through the large A, the king and his guests standing at the supper table which runs through ND, gazing back at her. The clothes are anything – pantomime, primitive, Waltham St Lawrence.

At the end of St Mark, 'And he said unto them, Go ye into all the world and preach the gospel to every creature'. No illustration here but a stark and immense GO YE across the page width.

In St Luke, when Jesus asks Simon to let down his nets, 'Now when he had left speaking, he said unto Simon, Launch out into the deep…' the first N curls out to a marginal fish-hook, and a struggling fish curves down the length of those lines. In a similar example soon after – 'Now it came to pass on a certain day, that he went into a ship with his disciples' – a ship in high formal waves decorates the first letter. These are fairly simple in their range, but the style could rise to any symbolism and tragedy. Examples are Christ praying within the O of Our Father, in St Luke, and his portrait of St John the Baptist, in the Gospel According to St John – 'There was a man sent from God'. And for the scope this type face gave to his method, one could look at the two men who went up into the temple to pray, in St Luke. One is humble, carrying the pillar of his letter T as a burden, the other walking under its shelter and well satisfied with his piety. Both are in long folds of heavy black, impressive but by no means too dark on the page. These two works extend Morris's vision of ornament in borders and initials, carry it beyond his limits.

If there is life after death, Morris and Gill must have joined to make such books as it will one day be a pleasure to be allowed to see.

The Shakespeare Head Press was founded by A. H. Bullen in 1904, with the ambition of printing the complete works of Shakespeare in Stratford-on-Avon. This was managed and other interesting books appeared over the next sixteen years – among them several volumes of Yeats, Gabriel Harvey's *Marginalia* and the *Works of Mrs Aphra Behn* in six volumes. Bullen died in 1920, and the press was bought by Basil Blackwell and his partner Mott. They engaged Bernard Newdigate as designer, and for the next twenty years this became the most mature and sophisticated of the private presses, producing some works in the grand manner which are a great pleasure to read and examine now. The books were designed by Newdigate, for the press in Stratford. Nothing was farmed out. 'But it was printed at the Shakespeare Head Press' Sir Basil answered, when I questioned whether his could be called a private press. All the ideals of fine work and materials were in it. Sir Basil is a lifetime admirer of Morris, and this was a chance to practise one aspect of his teaching. Another aspect, pleasure in labour, is familiar to his staff in the Oxford bookshop. A third appears in the mighty scythe which hangs, for use not ornament, by his workshop door. And these books are a monument to the style and ability of Newdigate as a designer – very recognizable, from the use of simple means.

Newdigate had gained experience with the Arden Press at Letchworth, under the firm of W. H. Smith. And as St John Hornby held a degree of control there, some scope for interesting design was encouraged. One of his tasks in these years had been to design the complete edition of Morris's writings, published by Longmans and edited by May Morris. The same steady eye, the disciplined use of Caslon type, a close-set page and no headlines, are here as a link between Emery Walker's vigilance and the Shakespeare Head style.

In 1930 the press was moved to Oxford, and a free range of books appeared between the wars including whole editions of Smollett, Fielding, Defoe and the Brontes – fifty-five volumes between them. These formed the steady publishing activities. Punctuating them are three major works in the private press story – Froissart, Spenser and

Chaucer. A little short of this, two fine companion labours in editions of Boccaccio and Malory, and sewing these together, appearing appropriately at the start and finish of this rich time, a book on Ernest Gimson and twenty-four engravings by F. L. Griggs. This is not the whole story. It included a grand edition of Bede, and one of those Elizabethan translations from the classics without which no press is truly private – *The Loves of Clitophon and Leucippe*, 'by Achilles Tatius, translated from the Greek by William Burton; reprinted for the first time from a copy, now unique…' From time to time other friends dropped in, among them Omar Khayyam and *Sonnets from the Portuguese*. The style had a classic fineness of manner, born of orthodox behaviour and good taste. They sound dull qualities, but the secret of these books is quiet clothes well made. They are masculine and bold like Malory's heroes, with a gesture to red colour and decoration appropriately. Newdigate must stand as the best user of Caslon in the history of book design, of pure type as adequate in itself. What makes the page his, when that appears to be the whole of it, is hard to tell. Yet it was his own way, detectable any day, and the style appears through other type equally; as in the folio of Bacon's essays produced at the Shakespeare Head to his design for the Cresset Press. There the type face is Cloister, but no mistaking Newdigate's plain design.

Here is a difference between his work, the tradition in which he worked, and Sir Francis Meynell's designs for Nonesuch books. Morris, Cobden-Sanderson, Hornby, Newdigate – a certain strength of will stamps their books, as if the literary work were privately digested as well as printed, and it reappears in the form proper to this process; as grass is turned into milk by determined cows. Sir Francis Meynell perhaps listened more to the book and its period, less ready to impose his own view upon it. This is not a judgment of quality either way – one could seem arrogant, the other imitative – but it suggests the changing attitude to a task and the passions which drowned several type faces in the Thames and the Channel.

The earliest of these fine Shakespeare Head books, in its Blackwell period, was the *Loves of Clitophon and Leucippe*, 1923. About five hundred were printed on Kelmscott paper, five on vellum. It has all the character of Newdigate's best work – the close-set page well leaded, grandeur of large sizes on the title pages, brave use of a second colour, and absolute blackness on the white page. This is simple maturity at the start. Five books of Ovid's *Metamorphoses* in the following year appeared as a companion volume. The three great tasks by which the press is remembered – Froissart, Chaucer and Spenser – appeared steadily between 1927 and 1930. They were extraordinarily productive years.

Froissart, like Malory, has a special place in this chronicle. It was the favourite reading of William Morris, and inspired many of his best poems and stories – among them *The Haystack in the Floods*, and *The Tale of King Florus*. The Kelmscott Press had planned it, but nothing remains except the double page opening and some specimens to show what might have been. Now the Shakespeare Head Press issued its eight volumes in two years. Its pages are easy and unbroken, helped by shoulder notes as subject guides on the right hand side; and bringing a discreet bright chivalry in the painted crests of the Knights as each enters the story. Otherwise the daring of this design appears in its plainness, the refusal to go to town with a gothic flourish. Paper and print and the coats of arms take us through without a pause for boredom. It is a classic of Newdigate's skill, bound simply – 'made up', Morris would have said – in holland back and blue paper board. Chaucer equally lay in the English affections of the printers, and these eight volumes appeared in the next two years. It is a more flamboyant plan this time, with liberal use of calligraphy in headings and pauses, but of the three notable Chaucer editions – placing this with Kelmscott and Golden Cockerel – Newdigate's is strikingly the simplest. It is most readably designed in 18pt Caslon. The first impression is of care in planning, of thought for the reader. A friendly craftsmanship comes from all the pen and brush work in these books. The illustrations enter as pleasant surprises, rather than necessary parts of the plan. The edition seems complete without them, but we are delighted to find them. 'The figures representing the Pilgrims in these volumes of the Canterbury Tales', we are told, 'have been freely rendered from miniatures in the Ellesmere Manuscript of the Tales'. There they are at the start of their stories, ambling through the bottom of the page to Canterbury. But in several volumes, especially *Troilus,* some of the minor poems and the *Romaunt of the Rose,* something much more ambitious appears. For them Lynton Lamb took his designs from early editions or old French manuscripts, and the result is very rich – especially in the vellum copies, for which the local art school at Stratford provided students who could colour and lay gold with brilliant effect. The illumination seems as fine as the old French work it imitates, and nothing in the private press movement gives quite such jewelled splendour as this.

The eight volumes of Spenser, 1930, are equally good – different, as the character of the author is, but in merit nothing to choose between them. Calligraphy in both sets was by Joscelyn Gaskin. Hilda Quick made woodcuts for the Spenser. Perhaps the small devices below Spenser's sonnets, printed in black and in the vellum copies beautifully laid with gold, are the most discreet and opulent form of decoration, fitting and in flawless taste. They recur too in the wedding poems. At the end one feels this to be, in his own words

     a goodly ornament
    And for a short time an endless monument.

The two volumes of Bede, 1929, set in Cloister type, show the same hand but are more nearly related to the volume of Bacon's essays which Cresset published. The Boccaccio volumes, 1934–5, express a different mood with delicate economy, returning to a hint of the fifteenth-century Venetian book. A smaller size of Caslon, two columns, the use of blue for second colour, and the woodcuts most happily reproduced in facsimile from the Gregorii edition of 1492, produce a kind of elegance which goes out to meet the world of these renaissance stories. They are companions to the two volumes of Malory, successful also but rather less adventurous, and they link the more monumental books of this press with its one volume Shakespeare, also designed by Newdigate in two columns, in its more workaday way an equal record of his typography.

These are a few examples chosen from many others which include North's Plutarch and Chapman's Homer. If it is judged by numbers of volumes issued, this must be the most active of the careful private presses. As the major works stand out in any view of the labours of these five decades, the Shakespeare Head holds a place of high honour.

150

This chapter may end where it began, with a word about private presses. The point has been made, that according to arts-and-crafts ideas a book should artistically be the work of one man. To draw a frontier, the printing press should be owned by that man or in his control. Beyond that, it is not a private press, so the Nonesuch books are not described here – which is of course no judgement upon their design. This was the vital bridge from heaven to earth, which the pioneers had invited; otherwise their work would over the years have been wasted time. To list fine books from publishers' lists is not part of this introduction to a subject, but very high among them would come such works as *The Anatomy of Melancholy*, the *Astrophel and Stella* sonnets, Cowley's poems, Thomson's *Seasons*, George Herbert's poems and the five volumes of North's Plutarch, all from the Nonesuch Press, and its splendid *Nonesuch Century*, a bibliography which compares with the Ashendene Press volume of 1935. And it is just to quote from what A. J. A. Symons wrote there on this theme of private printing – though he misses the minor art, arts-and-crafts point of it. 'Although the Nonesuch Press does possess an old Albion printing machine, and a stock of type for hand-setting, and has in fact subsequently produced some publications on its own premises, its first twelve books were all produced by trade printing houses... This *direction*, from a central point of the resources of numerous printing establishments, was a resumption of the Lane-Mathews method, not the Kelmscott. The fact was not disguised; but it was criticised, and this is perhaps the most convenient point at which to deal with the objection, more frequently urged against Nonesuch in those early days than now, that because in general it does not print its own books, it is not truly a "Press". The charge, even if admitted, is entirely without weight as a criterion of the Nonesuch achievement. There is no virtue in a press, as such... It was because Kelmscott was *Morris's* Press, not because it was a *Press*, that it made fine things. Francis Meynell, who directs every detail of the production of Nonesuch books, and used printing firms as printing *tools*, is as much a press-master as Morris, even if not so precisely master of a Press.' It was the position of Mr Sandford at the Golden Cockerel.

G. S. Tomkinson, whose *Bibliography of the Private Presses* appeared in 1928 and remains the most valuable guide to the subject, made a collection of a hundred single volumes each representing different presses; but one cannot report on all of them, and after a few giants the more important are anyone's choice. It is tempting to mention some which seem specially to deserve it – of which one would say, like warmhearted Americans after brief acquaintance, 'It's been awfully nice knowing you'.

Twenty books were issued at the Caradoc Press in the ten years after 1899, and they have a secondary but recognizable character in the wake of Kelmscott. The care appears in the working notebooks the printer kept, a record of progress with pulls of wood engravings and designs for borders or initials. The little '*Kalendar: MDCCCC*', the first book from the press – small pamphlet really – was worked out in detail and invented from start to finish. It was not a notable invention, but H. G. Webb and his wife achieved some mature and sophisticated books so one is interested to watch their apprenticeship. They lived in Bedford Park, late arrivals at a progressive community from the eighteen-eighties. The blocks were cut, books printed and bound at home without help, and Tomkinson says 'the type used is founded on Jenson's' though the foundations seem to have shifted since Jenson's time. I have heard Caradoc Press books described as 'Morris gone wrong', but there is an integrity and success in them which may tempt the collector.

Webb's taste tended towards religion. Several of the little early books, conspicuously home-brewed (in a different way from early Ashendene books) are Christian – the *Collects*, *In Praise of Wisdom*, the *Communion Service*, the *Proverbs of Saynt Bernarde*. Though these are modest, five copies of the *Collects* printed on vellum were illuminated and sold at prices up to twenty-two pounds. Compared with the Kelmscott Chaucer at about the same poice, this seems expensive. The most interesting of the early books is Yeats's play *Cathleen ni Houlihan*, of which this forms the editio princeps. Yeats also lived for a time at Bedford Park, had known and admired Morris, and could easily have

152

been talked into this poorish private printing of his play – but he regretted it, and thought the effect not worth the money. (The title-page of this one reads 'Printed at the Caradoc Press for A. H. Bullen'.) Their best produced books were four reprints of classics – *The Vicar of Wakefield*, *The Compleat Angler*, Sir Philip Sidney's *Defence of Poesie* with his *Sonnets*, and Lord Brooke's *Life of Sir Philip Sidney*. Gold-smith's novel has a slightly absurd border to decorate each chapter opening and the book seems an odd choice for the treatment it re-ceives, but *The Compleat Angler* with its fish etchings is a happy pro-duction. Webb seemed equally at ease with woodcut and dry-point. The two companion volumes on Sidney have some literary importance as reprints. They are clearly printed with red ruled borders and, in this plain format, a sensible scattering of Webb's woodcut initials. Another interesting work from the Press, though few collectors are likely to find it as only seven copies were printed, is the volume of *Woodcut Borders and Initials* used between 1899 and 1908; and this, printed but not sold, serves as a kind of bibliography to close that phase of Webb's work.

Birmingham had been of particular importance to Morris since his Oxford days because most of his friends came from there. Burne-Jones, Dixon and Faulkner had all been pupils at King Edward School. One of his best-known lectures was delivered at the Birmingham School of Design. Two small presses in Birmingham date from the nineties and should be mentioned, the Vincent Press which produced only two books, and the Birmingham Guild of Handicraft which closed in 1902 after issuing five.

The Guild of Handicraft made two woodcut books, worth seeing because so curiously of that time and place. Bernard Sleigh whose work is also linked with the Guild of Handicraft at Campden 'dec-orated with designs' a slim book of poems by Amy Mark, *The Sea King's Daughter*. Poems and book have a loving care and naivete which is ruined by quotation ('We love the pretty buds that take your places/But they are not so beautiful as you') – yet this is one of the beautiful books of that time, in a fragile medium which could not often have been attempted.

Another woodcut book – words and decorations in both were cut in wood – from the Birmingham Guild is a quarto which has only six pages of text, *Good King Wenceslas* with illustration and ornament by Gaskin whose drawings were so successful in the Kelmscott Press edition of Spenser, *The Shephearde's Calender*. It would be interesting to know how that came about. Morris writes an introduction to this Birmingham book, which is amusingly tepid in praise of the author of the poem which 'is a good specimen of his manner and its limitations'; but of Gaskin's drawings he writes, 'I cannot help saying that they have given me very much pleasure, both as achievements in themselves and as giving hopes of a turn towards the ornamental side of illustration which is most desirable'. That introduction is dated 1894, and the book appeared in the next year. *Shephearde's Calender* was issued by the Trustees of the Kelmscott Press just after Morris's death in 1896. Perhaps these *Good King Wenceslas* decorations, in the same manner, suggested the invitation to illustrate Spenser's poem. Gaskin's style is as if Walter Crane had been disciplined, or as if Eric Ravilious had been asked to design in the style of Walter Crane. The Guild of Handicraft also printed, more conventionally, a handsome edition of Shakespeare's Sonnets.

From the Vincent Press in Lionel Street appeared two oddly contrasted books in 1898 and 1899, the entire oeuvre of the press, Johnson's *Rasselas* and *Five Ballads about Robin Hood*. Johnson dressed up to look like Morris is unexpected, but he does look very like and it remains a good reading edition. This close imitation of Kelmscott printing was more common in America than England. The initials, where they depart from simple cribbing, tend to be feeble and without roots. But it is a finely printed book on Kelmscott paper, in a face which resembles the Basle fount Morris used at the Chiswick Press for *Roots of the Mountains*.

The Robin Hood book is easier to digest in this format, a natural choice for the hearty medievalist –

> As Robin Hood in the forest stood,
> All under the green-wood tree,
> There he was aware of a brave young man,
> As fine as fine might be.

154

The book is a jumble of old spelling and new, caps and lower case, with dark woodcuts which derive from Beardsley's *Morte Darthur* rather than Morris – a bold semi-absurdity of post-Morris and art nouveau bound in vellum with green ties like the Kelmscott books and in every way pleasant these days to have and to hold.

The mock-Morris manner of the Vincent Press appears more commonly in early American echoes of the printing revival. Thomas Mosher of Portland, Maine, used it conspicuously in his edition of Arnold's play *Empedocles on Etna*. The fashion had travelled east to west by slow boat and established itself as a fresh movement unworried by comparisons. Portland and Hammersmith were far apart in those days. Mosher printed in other ways over the years and made his own style of neat reprint, often taking his notions from the English private presses – sometimes pirating against anyone's will, as in his edition of *Garland of Rachel*, sometimes making useful reprints of scarce works, as when he re-issued the Pre-Raphaelite journal from 1848, *The Germ*. Mosher reprints are quite pleasant little books now, but not a vital part of the printing renaissance.

Other examples of Kelmscott imitation in America at that time are easy to find, and interesting for the speed of the taste in establishing itself. In 1894 Copeland and Day issued their edition of the *House of Life* sonnets, with type and initials and decoration cribbed from the Kelmscott Press but no note of first source in the colophon where we read of 'three borders and one hundred and fourteen initial letters, designed by Bertram Grosvenor Goodhue'. In the Beardsley manner, very flamboyant with black border designs round over-delicate drawings, we have for instance a quarto edition of Keats's *Isabella* published by Lippincott of Philadelphia in 1898 – but these stray out from the private presses to ordinary, or extraordinary, publishing.

But much American book-making at the turn of the century came from that frontier between the two. We cannot ignore the Roycrofters, a strangely commercial arts-and-crafts affair which seems as if Ruskin had been taken over by public relations consultants. That might have done Ruskin no harm at all; but Elbert Hubbard who ran the Roycroft place in East Aurora, Erie County, and used to call himself Fra Elbertus, had more energy than discretion, more ambition than taste.

155

He undertook journeys to the houses of the great, alive or dead, and reported in a peculiarly valueless way at the end of them. He and his wife wrote unremarkable moral tales. All these were given sumptuous typographic exhibition in the hand-made style of the period. Their advertisements are fascinating and entirely familiar with their rib-ticklers in our own day – Hubbard would have worked as a television advertiser in the nineteen-sixties or started the Butlin Press. Here is the first paragraph from one, headed *For the Illuminati Only!*

'The Roycroft Reminder or Calendar is very Roycroftie. It contains for every day in the year an orphic by Fra Elbertus and a blank space for tickler, or Friendship's Garland. If you do not like the orphic, just write a better one yourself in the blank space provided. Ideas make the world go 'round. The Two Dollars we ask for this Calendar is simply to cover expenses for salt for putting on the tails of the Ideas. Three Hundred and Sixty-Five Ideas for Two Dollars – one-half of a cent each! Some of these Ideas will cash you in a thousand dollars or more, otherwise you are a has-wasser, which the same you aren't.'

That dates from 1907. A good thing Morris never lived to watch his influence.

But the point of mentioning these people at all is that they made some charming books. A whole series in small octavo, reprints of minor classics, seems successful and enjoyable now. Emerson's essay on *Self-Reliance*, in soft overlapping leather covers, is discretion itself with pale green decorations of chestnut leaves. The colophon explains a little ambitiously that it was 'completed on August the eleventh of the year ten, from the founding of the Roycroft shop'. Emerson on *Compensation*, same format, has innocent borders most gaily hand-coloured in green, blue, yellow and gold.

Forget good taste and these Roycroft books are delightful. One of the early Journey books, 'to the homes of Ruskin and Turner', was issued in 1896. It is a large quarto with painting and illumination all over the place. The title page has what looks like a freehand water-colour sketch of daisies. There had been nothing like it since Mrs Daniel. We must be grateful for all the work, though sorry for those slave-driven Roycrofters who had to produce four hundred and seventy-three copies of it – the number itself seems a typical folly. Fra Elbertus's tributes to Ruskin are as embarrassing as his advertising: 'His opposition to new inventions in machinery has not relaxed a single pulley's turn. You grant his premises and in his conclusions you will find that his belt never slips and his logic never jumps a cog.'

When they had a truly complex task, such as *Hamlet* or poems by Edgar Allen Poe, they dealt with it simply and completed it ably. Both these are sound, well-printed books on good paper and nicely bound.

Some imitation of the Kelmscott style was admirable and natural. One of the truly fine and comparatively little known American presses from the first years of this century was the Elston Press of New Rochelle, and the work there of Clarke Conwell as printer, and H. M. O'Kane as designer, showed this influence from Morris or Beardsley along with the skill and taste which make good books. These two, always working together, began with the wilder style of Beardsley and settled into a manner of their own, quite quickly recognisable from its qualities and heritage, with a letter derived from Golden type and rather more red than was usual for initials and side-notes, and a discreet Burne-Jones-Beardsley woodcut here or there. Excellent hand-made paper was always the rule, except for a few copies sometimes on thick Japanese vellum which were no improvement upon the ordinary edition.

One of the early Elston books was the *Philobiblon* of Richard de Bury, an amusing choice. They printed it in something remarkably like the Chaucer type, with romanesque concessions to the American reader. This 1832 translation of the fourteenth-century book speaks to and from the hearts of private pressmen – in Chapter XVII for instance, 'Of Handling Books in a Cleanly Manner and Keeping them in Order':

'He has a nail like a giant's, perfumed with stinking ordure, with which he points out the place of any pleasant subject. He distributes innumerable straws in various places, with the ends in sight, that he may recall by the mark what his memory cannot retain. These straws, which the stomach of the book never digests, and which nobody takes out, at first distend the book from its accustomed closure, and being carelessly left to oblivion, at last become putrid. He is not ashamed to eat fruit and cheese over an open book, and to transfer his empty cup from side to side upon it; and because he has not his almsbag at hand, he leaves the rest of the Fragments in his books. He never ceases to chatter with eternal garrulity to his companions, and while he adduces a multitude of reasons void of physical meaning, he waters the book, spread out upon his lap, with the sputtering of his saliva. What is worse, he next reclines with his elbows on the book, and by a short study invites a long nap; and by way of repairing the wrinkles he twists back the margins of the leaves, to the no small detriment of the volume. He goes out in the rain, and returns, and now flowers make their appearance upon our soil. Then the scholar we are describing, the neglector rather than the inspector of books, stuffs his volume with firstling violets, roses and quadrifoils. He will next apply his wet hand, oozing with sweat, to turning over the volumes, then beat the white parchment all over with his dusty gloves, or hunt over the page, line by line, with his forefinger covered with dirty leather. Then, as the flea bites, the holy book is thrown aside, which, however, is scarcely closed once in a month, and is so swelled with the dust that has fallen into it, that it will not yield to the efforts of the closer.'

The press began in 1900 with *Sonnets from the Portuguese*, followed a year later by its jolly companion the *House of Life*. In the days of both these productions H. M. O'Kane was under Beardsley's spell. Mrs Browning's passions appear in black letter like the Troy type, with thick Morte Darthurish borders of lilies or irises on the large quarto page. They suit her brave style –

> The soul's Rialto hath its merchandise;
> I barter curl for curl upon that mart,
> And from my poet's forehead to my heart
> Receive this lock which outweighs argosies, –
> As purply black, as erst to Pindar's eyes
> The dim purpureal tresses gloomed athwart
> The nine white Muse-brows.

This experimental and slightly ridiculous book should satisfy art-nouveau revivalists. The Rossetti sonnets are similar, from the same mood, but with borders and decorations lightly pen-drawn and a use of very large black initials at the start of each poem, printed from the wood. Copies of these two books bound at the Guild of Handicraft are evidence of exchange between the two movements at that time. Other books from the Elston Press in the first five years of the century appeared in the quieter style printer and designer discovered, and in slightly varying dress. *Daphnis and Chloe*, a very finely printed book from 1904, is bound in vellum with green ties like the Kelmscott books. The Vale Press had printed Thornley's Elizabethan translation. This one is 'that of the unique copy, dated 1587, of Angell Day's translation'. One hundred and sixty copies were printed, with admirable evenness and beauty of impression.

In the same manner but bound in grey paper-boards with holland backs and printed labels, were *The Cenci*, *Samson Agonistes* and, a more private choice, *The Patterne of Painefull Adventures, Gathered into English by Laurence Twine*. All these were excellent examples of hand printing and of the proper use of decoration and colour. Three more, similarly designed, but bound simply in dark blue cloth, are *The Rape of the Lock*, Greene's *Pandosto* and – reasonable tribute – Morris's five Arthurian poems from *The Defence of Guenevere*. But I would choose from them all, for the plentiful use of red in a well-disciplined book, *Poems Selected from the Hesperides* by Robert Herrick. This suggests comparison with the Kelmscott Herrick, and comes out from the test quite well. Red titles at the side in upper and lower case are happier than the black capitals above each short poem in Morris's version. A circular woodcut device at the end reminds one of Lucien Pissarro, and a rectangular one at the start recalls Burne-Jones, so all are present and correct. These fragments of poems gain independence from the use of red for label and initial.

> Lost to the world; lost to my selfe; alone
> Here now I rest under this Marble stone;
> In depth of silence, heard, and seene of none.

There were many attempts to carry Kelmscott into commoner life, in Britain and America. 'Fine printing' became an average ambition, and the notion of it spread from alpha to beta. The Nonesuch Press began in a similar spirit years later. One example was the De la More Press founded by Alexander Moring in 1895 in London. He produced some very pleasant large quartos, in a series edited by Israel Gollancz – Roper's *Life of More* among them, and the long volume of Ovid's *Metamorphoses* in the Elizabethan translation by Golding. Vellum copies of these were given grand illuminated initial letters. Nearer to the private press style and better known are the books from Philip Lee Warner at the Riccardi Press, and from Chatto and Windus's Florence Press. They were not strictly private presses, but very near in heritage and example. Types for both were designed by Herbert Horne, whose designs for the Century Guild *Hobby Horse* had made their mark twenty-five years earlier, and cut by Edward Prince. Both these type faces have a clear and rational beauty, more economic in use than the Doves type but based upon the same models. Most of the Riccardi books were printed by Jacobi at the Chiswick Press, much of the Florence Press work came from the Arden Press under the care of Newdigate.

Chatto and Windus declared themselves in May 1908:

'Believing that the time has now come when beautiful books in the choicest types can be published in larger editions, and at a less cost than has been usual with such monuments of typography as the issues of the Kelmscott and other similar but less notable Presses, the Florence Press has commissioned Mr Herbert P. Horne to design a new fount modelled upon the finest types used by the Italian Master-Printers of the Quattrocento and Cinquecento.'

But these publishers with new intentions tended to return to the style of origin. More copies were sometimes printed, not always – one thousand was the normal limitation, but Stevenson's essays appeared in a paper edition of only two hundred and fifty. In the expected way a few came on vellum. No startling editorial plans suggested the choice of books – Poems by Swinburne and Blake, a translation of St Francis, eighteen books from 1908–25. The same could be said of the Riccardi Press, and the productions of both are very similar in other

160

ways than a common type-designer. Riccardi brought out several major works, in the tradition of its forebears – *Canterbury Tales*, Malory, – and had a slant towards Greece and Rome; but it did its duty also with *Omar Khayyam*, *In Memoriam*, *Atalanta in Calydon*, and *Sonnets From the Portuguese*. Mrs Browning served as repertory for the management to bring back in lean times.

Both these two presses are remembered also for their coloured illustrations, especially the series of forty-eighty water-colours by Russell Flint reproduced in the three volumes of *Morte Darthur*. They are in the revived Edwardian taste of our time, though another eye may judge they ruin the books.

I would choose as examples from the Riccardi Press three which show different kinds of illustration: *The Book of Genesis*, 1914, with drawings by Cayley Robinson; *The Heroes* by Kingsley, with drawings by Russell Flint; and a strange one to find there, *Alice in Wonderland* for which electros were made from the original wood blocks of Tenniel's illustrations. That is an admirable book, and the drawings are especially well shown in the few copies printed on vellum.

One would give higher praise to the Florence Press for Newdigate's work, than to the Chiswick Press work for Lee Warner. The close and even setting which became a rule of life for Emery Walker is more faithfully carried out by these few books from the man who was sharpening his skill for great labours at the Shakespeare Head Press years after. *Virginibus Puerisque*, in the large quarto edition of 1910, is a particularly fine instance of his work and it has effectively strange modern-dress illustrations from Norman Wilkinson. These were interestingly printed by collotype upon good text paper, a far better arrangement than the mounted shiny paper of Russell Flint's work in the Riccardi books. At a future time good collotype work may be collected, the last of the excellent hand processes, as aquatint is treasured today. Another beautifully printed work from the Florence Press, though the lines are really too long for good reading, is *The Little Flowers of St Francis of Assisi*, 1909. The use of red for initials and the long chapter titles distinguishes its design, and there is good sepia collotype at the end to reproduce an early manuscript.

But these presses never attempted much more than an inferior following of mighty models. For all their comprehensive policies, they were chiefly interested in the grammar stream. Their books are delightful, but it was left for Sir Francis Meynell to show how the great example could be directed into different forms.

Germany followed the English example, but not in the same spirit as the Americans. There was no wide sweep towards the Morris manner, very little superficial copying. It became a German movement, built under the care of English tutors. Emery Walker's mark is there all the time.

The affinity is most obvious between Doves Press and Bremer Presse. This German enterprise is described in the Gutenberg Museum at Mainz as the Queen of the Private Presses. Dr Willi Wiegand founded it at Bremen in 1911, and designed the type faces. The level excellence of simple type use was its clearest characteristic – page after page of serious purpose like Cobden-Sanderson's, and relieved only by the mannered initial letters of Anna Simons – who began her working life as a pupil of Edward Johnston, and ended it with calligraphic birthday tributes to Hitler. One of the Bremer Presse publications is a folio of initials and designs by Anna Simons, but they suggest monotony. The familiar Bremer Presse type was a beautiful letter, leaning towards Gothic in the shadow of Hornby's Subiaco type. A smaller form of it had typical use in the immense work of setting St Augustine's *De Civitate*, six hundred and ninety folio pages of impeccable type which very few people are ever likely to read. Hölderlin and Hofmannsthal had their places in its history, and several of the religious books showed a pleasant use of red as second colour.

The issue of classics from other languages came as a compliment among printers from time to time. Bodoni had presented Grey's poems, *The Castle of Otranto* and Thomson's *Seasons*. *Faust* and *Iphigenia* appeared from the Doves Press. Notable English books from the Bremer Presse were Bacon's *Essays*, and, more oddly, a *Book of English Ballads*. This large quarto in the half-Gothic type gives a mood far away from its words, suggesting libraries and professors rather than fields and shepherds. But the immaculate pages of these books impress us now, bringing German care and exactness to a friendly English origin which had sometimes wandered into the merely ama-

162

teurish, the homespun and the hand-made. Folio editions of the *Iliad* and *Odyssey*, in Greek type from the same hand, are magnificent examples of controlled printing.

Other German examples were the Janus Presse at Leipzig under Walter Tiemann and Carl Ernst Poeschel, clearly linked again with Emery Walker and his founding influence upon the Insel Verlag, and the Ernst Ludwig Presse of the Grand Duke of Hesse in Darmstadt which produced several handsome tall volumes of Shakespeare plays. But the most interesting among them was the Cranach Press at Weimar under Count Kessler.

Only a few books were undertaken there, in a perfectionist spirit. It seems far from the energetic gaiety of Morris and those who worked with him. Mr John Dreyfus has written a close and fascinating study of Kessler, Emery Walker, Edward Johnston and Edward Prince as they worked towards the cutting of the Cranach Press italic. The attraction of such detailed research is that the character of the people comes through so much more clearly than in word-pictures. Kessler becomes a most tiresome pedant pushing these craftsmen, Prince especially, into moulds of exactness which really needed machines not men; and Prince complains most gently, but is rapped back to where Kessler thought he belonged. And the truth of it appears, that this precision instrument of German judgment was not suited to the form of a private press at any time. The proper alliance would have been Kessler and Cobden-Sanderson, solemn mechanism of highest purpose. But the meeting of mind and hand at the Cranach Press produced landmarks in the movement, especially *Hamlet* and the *Eclogues of Virgil*. Aristide Maillol made forty-three woodcuts for the *Virgil*, Eric Gill engraved a line for its title page, Walker designed the type and Johnston the famous italic. This brilliant quartet comes again for *Hamlet*, with the vital addition of Gordon Craig's woodcuts. Its colophon expresses time and scruple which are hammered into this book:

'Count Harry Kessler planned the typographical arrangement of this volume. Edward Gordon Craig designed and himself cut on wood the illustrations. Eric Gill cut the title. The type (18 Point, 12 Point and 10 Point black letter) was designed by Edward Johnston after that

163

used by Fust and Schoeffer in their Mainz Psalter of 1457, it was cut
by Edward Prince and completed after his death by G. T. Friend. The
paper was made of pure hemp fibre and linen by a process devised
in joint research by Count Harry Kessler and Aristide and Gaspard
Maillol. The book was printed on the handpresses at the Cranach
Press Weimar from February to October 1930. Count Harry Kessler,
J. H. Mason and Max Goertz supervised the setting of the type and
printing. The proofs were read by F. G. Hutt of the Cambridge Uni-
versity press and H. Wengler-Dresden. Compositors: Walter Tanz,
H. Schulz, Ernst Rudolph, P. Neubert. Pressmen: H. Cage-Cole, M.
Kopp, Gustav Lepenies, Gustav Loeckle, Assistants: Hugo Bergmann,
Franz Horwik, Walter Prunnel, Rudolf Richter.'
And if all this looks like film credits, it shows the joining of English
and German craftsmen under the old masters – Prince, Johnston,
Mason, Cage-Cole.
Anybody who examines the Cranach Press *Hamlet* must agree it is
worthy of its reputation. The paper, superficially like Bachelor's
Kelmscott, seems softer and more friendly, appropriate for the expressionist style of Craig's woodcuts. It is an expressionist book.
Kessler had admired Craig's theatre work in London before 1914. The
simplicity and structural clarity of his ideas for stage scenery fitted
the conception of this printed *Hamlet* and had been employed in the
famous 1911 production under Stanislavsky in Moscow. Sometimes
the woodcuts appear like suggestions for sets and costume. Sometimes they enter the page in a kind of stage setting of type, as the
sources for Shakespeare make their way round the edges of the type
area as a frame for the text. Red headlines and captions relieve the
severity of the vision. The wood grain, and shadows from varied
depths of engraving, bring valuable informality to a formidable
scheme. These designs, and Gill's in the Golden Cockerel Chaucer,
form the bravest artistic adventure among all private press books.
Original spelling is appropriate in the calligraphic fount Johnston designed. Apart from an inexplicably feeble title page, which must have
been the product of much thought, this book is a flawless monument.
Another work of comparable splendour was the volume of Dante,
printed by the Officina Serpentis in Berlin between 1921 and 1925.

164

Many woodcuts were made from drawings of Botticelli, and a beautiful semi-Gothic type, adorned in a few copies with fine hand-painted initials.

While so much expert and exact work came from Germany, the other aspect of arts-and-crafts expressed itself happily, casually, irresponsibly from many presses in England which were simply the do-it-yourself versions of earlier specialist experiment. Some rose high into more lasting notice. Some of Jack Lindsay's books from the Fanfrolico Press, some from the Swan Press, and from the St Dominic Press at Ditchling deserve careful attention which they cannot receive here. The Vine Press at Steyning has produced interesting work, typical of this free and enjoyable period, and its first book, *Lillygay*, issued in 1920, expresses the character of what followed. It is an anthology of anonymous poems. The woodcuts by Percy West are cheerful and chapbook in style, like Tuer's books from the late nineteenth century or Lovat Fraser's more recently, or Jack Yeats in the Cuala Broadsheets. Forty special copies were bound delightfully in pink paper boards and green buckram back, with printed labels and hand coloured. The type is nothing to write home about but the book is a success – ballads and rough woodcuts, the beautiful and carefree colouring.

> One morning very early, one morning in the spring,
> I heard a maid in Bedlam who mournfully did sing;
> Her chains she rattled on her hands while sweetly thus sung she;
> 'I love my love, because I know my love loves me'.

The Beaumont Press, which Cyril Beaumont ran from the cellar of his shop in Charing Cross Road, produced a crop of interesting books including new work by Edmund Blunden, A. J. Symons and Walter de la Mare. The type was Caslon, and the books have pleasant patterns for their paper boards with vellum backs. Perhaps the most remarkable among them was *After Reading; Letters of Oscar Wilde to Robert Ross*, and a similar volume called *After Berneval*. There is finer literary taste here than in most of the other private presses put together. One especially attractive little book, of its time and interesting in itself, is *Eclogues* by Herbert Read. This early collection has simple woodcuts by Ethelbert White brightly hand-coloured. The imagist poems seem sometimes scarcely to deserve the gaiety of their illustration – as for instance, one called *The Pond:*

> Shrill green weeds
> float on the black pond.
> A rising fish
> ripples the still water
> And disturbs my soul.

It was of course a grand thing to be disturbed by the fish, so soon after life in the trenches. The assumption seems to be that after the first flush and impulse one may as well stop. Here is another poem splendid for a start, called April:

> To the fresh wet fields
> and the white
> froth of flowers
> Came the wild errant
> swallows with a scream.

More remarkably, in 1924 came *Madrigals and Chronicles*, a choice from the many unpublished poems of John Clare, edited with an introduction by Edmund Blunden. This was a significant book in the growth of recognition for Clare. There are charming wood engravings by Randolph Schwabe. Anyone who read such a poem as ends this volume, must have looked forward to more of John Clare over the years. It is the one which ends with these two verses:

> I loved, but woman fell away;
>   I hid me from her faded flame,
> I snatched the sun's eternal ray
>   And wrote till Earth was but a name.

In every language upon earth,
　　On every shore, o'er every sea
I gave my name immortal birth
　　And kept my spirit with the free.

As a last example of these sympathetic and secondary presses from
the twenties, one might look at the Stanton Press run by Richard
and Elinor Lambert. They only printed a few books, of a rather
esoteric sort, mostly Richard Lambert's translations from late Latin.
Elinor Lambert's woodcuts decorate them pleasantly. Two books
take them quite outside this run of taste, and remain as important
editions of excellent poems – Sir John Davies's *Orchestra*, of which
175 were printed in 1923 and Binyon's long poem *The Sirens* 1924,
of which two hundred were printed on paper and five on vellum. The
light fantasy of the Elizabethan poem is in odd contrast to Binyon's
sad and puzzled philosophy. Sir John Davies must have been an
adaptable Renaissance man, and delightful as a talker in his young
days when he wrote this poem. Later, defending Tonnage and Pound-
age, perhaps the mood changed. This was a happy choice for the
Stanton Press. Dancing is the theme, music of the spheres, the whole
harmony of all living and active things, their union in the dance of
life:

Loe this is Dancings true nobilitie
Dancing the child of Musick and of Love,
Dancing it selfe both love and harmony,
Where all agree, and all in order move;
Dancing the Art that all Arts doe approve;
The faire Caracter of the worlds consent.
The heav'ns true figure, and th' earth's ornament.

And Binyon, the heavier handed, gets a tall quarto of dignified
Cloister type, Kelmscott paper and a fine double-page opening with
strapwork borders for the title and first stanza. Second to Bridges he
is the modern poet of the private presses with three appearances
over a long period – Daniel Press, Golden Cockerel and this philo-

167

sophical poem which might remind one of Bridges at the time of *Now in Wintry Delights*. The mood is far from Sir John Davies:

> I saw them clouding up over the verge,
> Ghosts that arose out of an unknown grave,
> Strange to the bouyant seats that young they rode upon
> And strange to the idle glitter of the wave,
> Magically re-builded, rigged and manned,
> They stole in their slow beauty toward the land,
> Mariners, O mariners!
> I heard a voice cry; Home, come home!

The spread of private presses between the wars, as printing became a happy home alternative to more orthodox ways of life, is too large a subject to be attempted here. There were notable presses everywhere, which deserve examination – The Grabhorn in California, Victor Hammer in Florence and later at the Anvill Press in Lexington, A. A. M. Stols at the Halcyon Press in Maastricht and, perhaps the finest of all for the quality of his press work, Mardersteig at the Officina Bodoni in Padua. Mardersteig's editions of poetry by Eliot and Pound in late years have been particularly admired by English book-lovers, who look to him as the most superb letterpress printer and also a considerable scholar.

In this introduction it will be better to avoid any vague round-up of great names in recent printing. The work goes on all the time – Grolier Club, Limited Editions Club, Folio Society and endless hand presses which are found to be more enjoyable at week-ends than gardening or car-washing. Some of the Rampant Lions books from Will Carter at Cambridge are in the great tradition. The scholarship and taste of David Chambers at his Cuckoo Hill Press give much pleasure.

Equally important is the excellence which appears from publishers occasionally, inspired down the years by the private press revival. One might mention especially the noble edition of *Marius the Epicurean* issued in three hundred copies by Macmillan in 1929, with dry-point etchings; the well-loved and recognized edition of *Urn Burial and the*

168

Garden of Cyrus by Sir Thomas Browne, published under Desmond Flower's care by Cassell in 1929 with wonderful stencil illustrations by Paul Nash, a book which brings the spirit of the thirties as it flowered in abstract art; and most recently, the grand folio from Oxford University Press, in preparation one way and another for forty years, recording the work of Dr Fell and the history of his types in the hands of the Press; forming a memorial at the time of his death, to the work of Stanley Morison who kept it as a background task for so long.

Some phases in the history of British printing stand out for anyone concerned with physical books and their production, rather than with early editions of particular writing – though the two can run together. After the earliest printing, which will always attract whatever the standard of work, we may look for great folios of the seventeenth century with their baroque engravings such as Dryden's Virgil translations published by Tonson in 1697, or the three volumes of Clarendon's *History of the Rebellion* at the turn of the century. In the eighteenth century, Baskerville's reforms appear in a kind of private press which leads to others – the Foulis Press at Glasgow, Bensley and Bulmer in London. These merge into the fine period of aquatint illustration identified especially with Ackermann and MacLean as publishers, and after it the several Victorian forms of lithography and woodblock printing and illumination which Mr Ruari MacLean has described; and through the nineteenth century comes a pleasant stream of sensible and experimental books issued by Pickering.

None of these makes a subject with clearer borders or more natural purpose for a book collector than the private presses. It was from the first a collector's subject, with excellence the intention. Morris never laid himself out for collectors, but they overtook him. Here is a paragraph from *The Times Review of Literature*, 16 April 1898. Morris had died two years before, but the work of the Press had not yet ended:

'Although Mr William Morris made no profit by his artistic printing, the same cannot be said of the subscribers to the beautiful books which issued from the Kelmscott Press during the seven years of its existence. During the past two years all the books have been gradually increasing in value, and in a short time some of them will probably attain prices which the daily Press will describe as "simply scandalous". On Tuesday, the 5th of April, Messrs Sotheby sold a number of Kelmscott books at prices which show a distinct advance on those of only a few months ago, while if we go back a year or more the increase is most marked. In 1896, for instance, Keats' Poems, 1894, went for about £4, a price which has now increased to £12. *Poems by the*

170

Way, 1891, brought then about £3.15s., now £6.10s. is not considered too much, while the difference in the cases of the *Book of the Ordre of Chyvalry*, 1893, is as £1.15s. and £3.8s.; *Sidonia the Sorceress*, 1893, £1.18s. and £3.10s.; *News from Nowhere*, 1892, £2 and £3, and More's *Utopia*, 1893, the same; Shelley's *Poetical Works*, 3 vols, 1895, £4.4s. and £8. The most expensive and difficult book to acquire from this press is the folio Chaucer of 1896. A good copy of that brought £28.10s. at the recent sale mentioned, and that too, is a great advance on recent prices. The works issued from the Kelmscott Press have already proved to be the best literary investment of modern times.'

Hornby seemed quite happily conscious of producing collectors' pieces. In the Bibliography he writes, of the little edition of Bacon's essays *Of Building* and *Gardens*, of which only sixteen copies were printed:

'I cannot say why so few copies were printed. I regret now that there were not more, as it is a pleasant little book and deserved a wider circulation. It provides at any rate good sport for collectors!'

At the end of a letter to a friend he writes, in January 1925,

'I also send you a copy of a little story of Tolstoy's which I did this Christmas, which may one day become a rarity, as such things are apt to be thrown away or lost!'

This very deliberate resurrection of the best from the start of printing, produced with utmost care in a modern idiom, forms a single subject with beginning and end, though it had introductions and the epilogue continues. In such themes collections are made. If this was the last flowering of the finely printed traditional book, after which new methods and other subjects arrive, collectors are not likely to ignore it. They can look back now and see it as the ideal modern subject, before the books become too rare to be found; before the institutions and 'public' libraries wolf them for glass cupboards in their directors' rooms.

A myth that the books may be fine to look at, but that nobody wants them for reading could be answered in detail but there is no need. At the moment we may find Morris's prose romances witless and absurd, but that will pass. We can enjoy his Caxton reprints (the major works of the Kelmscott Press), the little medieval poems, the volumes of Spenser, Keats, Shelley, Coleridge, Herrick, Blunt, Shakespeare, Tennyson, the prose of Cavendish's *Life of Wolsey* or More's *Utopia* – to mention a few. The philosophical works Cobden-Sanderson printed – Emerson, Carlyle – keep their interest, as well as his editions of Shakespeare plays and poems, of Browning, Tennyson, Wordsworth, Milton, Ruskin and the Bible. The Ashendene *Morte Darthur* is the most delightful form that work is ever likely to take, and Cervantes and Thucydides are not contemptible presences in anyone's library. Some of the smaller Ashendene works – Milton, the *Three Elegies*, the poems Bridges wrote in 1913, the Tolstoy story and the volume of Wilde's stories for children – cannot sensibly be called eccentric or unreadable choices. These printers, with their large visions and ambitions, did well to avoid ephemeral writing. The movement forms a grand collection of classic work, with a large entry of modern poets – shows, indeed, the background of these civilized lives. It needs no more defence than that.

Another attraction for collectors is that one may enter at any level of ambition or humility. As the aim all the time was good printing and paper and this appeared as much in the lists, prospectuses and trial sheets as in the finished books, an entire collection could be formed of these ephemera of the private presses. The character of the printing can be seen well in that way. Such examples should be kept as one would store a print collection, a few framed on the wall and changed for others from time to time. They can be bought without great expense at auctions or found sometimes in half-forgotten envelopes in booksellers' shelves. They are always worth looking at carefully. Some are interesting rarities, as the first Kelmscott prospectus in May 1892 which includes the first use of Troy type in its announcement of *The Recuyell of the Histories of Troye*. The type is described there simply as 'Black Letter'. It became the custom to announce these books in the appropriate type, so that a page from one of the leaflets gives the best view of each of Morris's type founts together. Four books in the list of December 1892 appear for the first time in a flourish of Chaucer type – *The Order of Chivalry*, *The Well at the World's End*, *The Story of the Glittering Plain* and Chaucer's Works – mentioned there as having 'about 60 designs by E. Burne-Jones'. The whole series of these prospectuses is a kind of history of the Kelmscott Press, its plans and alterations. In the long list of 2 July 1894, we have four books 'in preparation', which went no further than that, and a fifth, *The Chronycles of Syr John Froissart*, described hopefully as 'in the Press'. That may be the one which is most to be regretted, 'In black and red. With Armorial Borders and Ornaments designed by William Morris'. Shakespeare in three volumes folio, 'Probable price Twelve Pounds', is another.

There were many Essex House leaflets and stray pieces, invitations and exhibition notices, and interesting collections from the Vale and Eragny Presses. Doves Press ephemera are plentiful and serious as one would expect, and Hornby gives a record of the Ashendene lists in his bibliography. That he did so suggests the care he devoted to printing them. Golden Cockerel announcements have been mentioned earlier, and often showed the woodcuts for which the books are remembered.

One could advance from there to the minor pieces which came from these Presses, and for which a bibliography would be of great interest. Cobden-Sanderson lovingly reprinted his letters to *The Times*, for instance. The Ashendene Christmas pamphlets are already much prized. The Guild of Handicraft had its share of semi-books, as for example the bound statements of rules of the Guild. Daniel Press minor pieces were a fair part of its whole output and are listed in pages of Madan's bibliography. The orders of service at Gregynog, too, are of this kind. The point to recall is that at each level this is a fascinating and possible subject to anyone who finds a taste there. At the opposite end, as ever in such searching, the finest books in the best condition whatever their prices will probably turn out to be the safest and merriest things to buy.

The roots of collecting are choice and taste, rather than snatch and grab. A child in a pile of stones will choose, pick and reject. Endless wealth would be an endless nuisance, and proper balance is vital to accurate aim.

It may be hard to recognize a true wish. One week-end I planned to write an article, 'On Not Buying the Kelmscott Chaucer,' but the book was in my shelves three days later. There are such subtleties as discovering why other people appreciate a thing, rather than seeing vacantly whether you happen to admire it yourself. Buying can range from the need for reference to an equal need to prevent a rival from enjoying the same reference. As all motives are absurdly mixed and cooked in it together, morality may as well be left out of our thoughts. But the problem in taste remains. Completeness would be an absurd aim – all the books of the private presses, in paper and vellum. No point in attempting that. Balance, at a certain point along the pole, is necessary and the proportion of one press to another will suggest itself to anyone's choice. It would be foolish to attempt a collection of the books without possessing quite early one or two from the Kelmscott Press, which will remain the clear point of departure. It might seem sensible, as a foundation, to get one book in the Troy type, one in the Golden type, and one in Chaucer type. There is no high need to get the Chaucer itself, though it may be reckoned a safe and admirable monument. It puts the others out of scale, and eight or ten are needed to balance it! My choice of three would perhaps be Morris's poems, *Guenevere*, as a pleasant volume in Golden type, from the heart of the matter; *Psalmi Penitentiales* as a beautifully printed book in Chaucer type; and for a grand folio in Troy type, a marvellous book to read, the *Crusader Chronicles of Godefrey of Boloyne*. They would not be so very hard to find, in a year of looking, at the time of writing.

Something from the Doves Press, and a couple of Ashendene books, might complete this laying of foundations. A fine start in the Doves Press would be, for example, the two Milton volumes and Cobden-Sanderson's little *Credo*; after which it could be said, in political language, he had nothing to add to his last statement. The range of Ashendene books being more varied, one might feel ambitious to find a splendid folio such as *Morte Darthur* or *Don Quixote*, with a choice from such smaller examples as *Songs and Poems from the Old Testament*, *Fysshynge with an Angle*, or the Oscar Wilde stories. *Ecclesiasticus*, in orange vellum and with so much calligraphy, would do very well instead of the *Morte Darthur*. A rare early Ashendene book could happily be added – *Three Elegies*, *Aucassin and Nicolette*, or one of the

174

sixteen copies of Bacon's essays. Of all the presses, Ashendene gives most temptations towards extravagant buying and obsessional vice. All its books have become expensive.

Beyond this, nobody can plot directions for collectors. The ways tend to make themselves known, with a sort of integrity whose origins are mysterious. A few time-honoured rules are wise – as

1. Never buy a second-rate copy, or anything you don't absolutely want, because it seems cheap. The best is cheapest, whatever its price.

2. Don't ignore the secondary reputation, if it seems to you underestimated.

3. The only reason to buy a book is because you love it.

Through much of the nineteenth century the price of books stayed the same, or fell. In the last thirty years they have very sharply risen, and a fall may be due again. They are not sensible subjects for investment.

One's own taste of course, and no outside advice, must rule. I am not advising apart from those first three roots in Kelmscott, Doves and Ashendene. But it is amusing to observe the unreason of book values, giving high honour to some and strangely abandoning others. The Vale Press is certainly undervalued in 1969. Most of these books which Ricketts designed with such love, and of which only two or three hundred copies were issued, can be bought for less than £5. They are probably as good as anything in the arts-and-crafts movement, and they chime with current taste for the style of the nineties. Their comparative neglect is hard to understand. Pissarro's little Eragny books go soaring ahead, having for long been underpriced.

The Essex House Press, apart from its amateurish poems on vellum, also seems underrated at the moment. The Daniel Press, with smaller editions, lies outside the main stream and is less well known. It rests there, neglected except for two or three books for which collectors will fight.

To mention these seems justified, when most of the books have become rather highly priced, and one could go further in suggesting parts of the subject which seem greatly over-valued, but anyone is likely to discover those quickly for himself.

175

Rarity is a temptation, impossible to assess. Sometimes, it dropped to reasons of commerce – as when any machine printed edition appeared in a limited number of copies. That unfailing recipe for collectors had nothing but solvency to commend it. The earlier and better reason, a careful interest in each printing process, could always be defended in hand work. Years before these private presses, for example, in the splendid folio volumes of Roman Antiquities in England which Samuel Lysons issued, he had written:

'Only 200 copies of the whole Work have been printed off, and most of the Plates are cancelled; not with the view of making a scarce book, but from the great difficulty of getting even that number properly coloured under the Editor's inspection.' Where every page of a hand-printed book is searched for faults like proofs of an engraving, the same limitation appears.

In the pure mathematics of collecting, rarity means merit. Stamps which may have slight aesthetic interest but are certainly not desired for that reason, become attractive to stamp collectors exactly in relation to their rarity. Some departments of book collecting suffer in the same way, from obsessional concern with errata slips or a full ration of advertisements. Private presses, on the whole, attract for other reasons and rarity is some way from their excitement; but a collection without special treasures lacks heart. There are several sorts of likely treasure.

The privacy of the presses meant that people were printing quietly for themselves and their friends; that was the spirit of it. 'Printed for my Friends, whom God preserve, and not for sale by myself or any other Bookseller'. Often the few copies went out to friends, with the printer's inscription. Collectors will come upon these association copies, more and less interesting but never negligible. Copies in Cockerell's possession can be amusing, with leaflet or specimen pages 'loosely inserted', the unconsidered trifles he snapped up. Inscriptions can tell their story. I have seen a copy of *News From Nowhere* inscribed 'To Philip Webb from William Morris', which would be adequate in itself, but on another page had been added, in Emery Walker's hand, 'To S.C. from P.W. via E.W.'. That is a charming and typical touch. The book must have come to Walker after Webb's death, and he was giving it to Cockerell; but rather than present it from himself, he chose the modest fiction of presenting it as if it had been the gift of Webb, himself merely the agent.

It can be simpler than that. Morris is known to have liked the vellum covers which showed a scattering of marks, like freckles, where the wretched animal's hair had been. To find a Kelmscott book with his bookplate and in this darker cover, instead of the pure white, brings the link of an association copy. Equally and more obviously satisfactory is a copy of the Chaucer inscribed, 'To Algernon Charles Swinburne from William Morris and E. Burne Jones' with both their signatures and the date a couple of months before Morris died.

Hornby was a letter writer, and his notes about the books may be commonly found inserted. It is pleasant to see in a copy of Ruskin's essay *Unto This Last*, printed at the Doves Press, Cobden-Sanderson's inscription: 'To S. C. Cockerell in memory of John Ruskin 15 July 1907'.

The more private the press, the likelier the inscriptions. Many of the Daniel Press books are inscribed by the printer or his family. Mrs Daniel's initials and decorations almost make these into association copies wherever they occur.

Another kind of special copy of course is the one printed on vellum. Some pure-hearted printers feel this is a decadence, but collectors are always likely to enjoy it. Paper is the right material for books, the printer says. But Morris was not seeking a collectors' market when he bothered with vellum again and investigated its making. The long tradition existed, of special copies printed on vellum. They were meant to be the summit of achievement, the finest copies. It was a hit or miss method, expensive through error and the cost of material. When it succeeds, the absolute black on pure white is unrivalled – because, on such a surface, no pits or creases can reduce the strength of ink or absorb its richness. Put them side by side and the clarity of impression upon vellum can be startling. The risks and failures were in show-through, which sometimes appears as a serious fault – as it could also in early manuscript. No vellum book will be perfectly consistent in the material or impression. When all this is said, the collector who would put aside the chance to get a vellum copy is himself a great rarity. A few illuminated vellum copies, such as the Shakespeare Head Press made, stand alone in opulent gaiety. As it was usual, because of problems and cost, to limit vellum copies to about six or ten, they tend to be extremely expensive.

And the other kind of treasure is a special binding. A Kelmscott or Doves volume bound at the Doves Bindery will be among the aristocrats of these, and close to the idea of the book. Morris left aside the responsibilities and fascinations of binding, satisfied if Cobden-Sanderson's workshop took over that side of it. His own copies of Kelmscott books were not re-bound. His famous binding he designed for the Chaucer, executed at the Doves Bindery, is the one exception from these years. The sympathy between these two tastes in the movement, represented by Morris and Cobden-Sanderson, is pleasantly given in a Kelmscott book bound at the Doves Bindery. These might range from elaborate and symbolic designs, such as Cobden-Sanderson made for *Atalanta in Calydon*, to the simple and geometric tooling, quite original and surprising of him, for *The Flowre and the Leafe*. The fine leather and finishing, economy in the tools used, and affection for gold upon leather without the fuss of inlay or overlay, characterize this work. The forwarding is said to have been less splendid, but I have no fault to find.

Doves books specially bound at the Doves Bindery, too, are admirable. Others followed the style, but these have authority. I have seen a copy of *Amantium Irae* that most private book of Cobden-Sanderson's letters as a young man to Lady Amberley, with his worries about life in the world, bound at the Doves Bindery and inscribed to Edmund Holmes 'in aff. memory of the Summer, 1913. C-S'. One way and another, his spirit is there. These letters were 'now after an interval of half a century printed by him who wrote them'. And now it is over a century since the last of them, August 1867.

The other notable bindery allied to the printed books was at Gregynog. Fisher worked for the press there, and had no time for commissions from outside except when he bound or repaired for the library of the house. About twenty-five specially bound copies of each book from the press were issued, to designs by Fisher or one of the illustrators. Certainly a collector who can find a Doves and Kelmscott

178

book in Doves bindings, and a special Gregynog binding, will very pleasantly adorn his group of books from these presses. There is no need to seek one of the mighty Gregynog books. I might choose, as perfectly appropriate for Gregynog and fine in itself, Fisher's binding of *The Lovers' Song Book* by W. H. Davies. The dark green levant with a formal arrangement from the base, almost like a graph, of straight stems and leaves deeply tooled to varying heights, seems to me a grand example of modern binding – thirty-five years old now, branching away from great traditions but feeding from their root.

Many beautiful bindings of private press books appeared in the thirty years after 1890, because the printing movement went in hand with a revival of interest in the art of binding. Ricketts interested himself in it, and designed bindings for his books and others though he was not a binder. A group of Vale Press books appeared in Sothebys lately, bound by Sybil Pye to designs by Ricketts. He also designed bindings for Kelmscott books – and so did most of them, ranging over the work of the private presses appropriately. A careful collection would be well balanced by a few of these bindings from such artists as Sarah Prideaux, Katharine Adams, MacLeish, Cockerell, De Sauty and Gwladys Edwards. Work from the private binders upon the private presses is a subject by itself which deserves thorough record.

The link between the Ashendene Press and Douglas Cockerell was similar, though less directly traced, because he had command of the W. H. Smith bindery where Hornby, as a director of the firm, arranged for the books to be bound. Some of the vellum copies and special bindings of Ashendene books, signed W. H. Smith, are certainly Cockerell's work. Katharine Adams also made a number of glorious bindings for these books in Hornby's own collection, though nobody is likely to be able to find or buy one.

The Daniel Press is often interesting for bindings, simply because most of the books were issued in paper and people liked to have them bound. Mrs Daniel's bindings turn up here and there, in the style of Katharine Adams from whom she learned. A collector may pure-mindedly insist upon original paper covers as issued, or enjoy himself among the variety of pleasant bindings in which these books have been preserved. Excellent bindings by Morley of Oxford are common,

179

others by Maltby not rare. Two exceedingly elaborate pieces of work by the Club Bindery of Chicago, more slip-case and leather and silk doublure than printed book, were in the possession of Major Abbey. Cockerell's work at the Guild of Handicraft should be remembered, and the bindery he helped to establish there under Louise Powell. Essex House books bound at the Guild are of obvious interest, but not great examples of the art.

And all the time the fine trade binders who worked in these years, and nearly all of whom have now disappeared, were producing a whole range of work for private press books. Occasionally we find a special link, as in the Golden Cockerel books so beautifully bound by Sangorski and Sutcliffe who remain the single and splendid survivors from the great days, peacefully working away above five flights of exhausting stone stairs in Poland Street, as though the years had not passed and destroyed all quiet and courtesy. And one may come upon fine bindings of any of the books by Riviere, Zaehnsdorf, Morell, Fazackerley, De Coverly, Birdsall and such great names as these. Again, the choice between original state and a good binding is for anyone to make. Booksellers have it all their own way by quoting either condition as a high point in its favour.

Yet one should be clear about the meaning of original state. Daniel's overlapping paper covers squash and fray in a bookshelf. Nothing but bibliographical reverence preserves grey paper board and linen back, and we know that Morris meant them to be bound from his instructions to the binder on a slip in the *Golden Legend*. At the end of a letter to Gilbert Redgrave he says 'Of course the book is issued "done up" and not bound: and under the circumstances it would have been a mistake I think to have trimmed the edges'. If the right skill is available I see nothing against having such a book bound now or at any time. It seems that the *Golden Legend* was not even well 'done up'. Anthony Gardner bound a copy of it recently, and wrote at the end in his apologia: 'It is to be noted that in the original bindings the 4to gatherings comprising the end sections had their two outer leaves glued to the boards, with the half titles on the reverse of the inner leaf, as now bound in'. This glue caused some damage, which had to be repaired in the course of the work.

And whenever such bindings are invited, careful instructions should be given. For a precious book, it may be well to insist upon absolutely no trimming. Cropped edges in bright gold are far less estimable than original margins, which for Kelmscott books anyway tended to be barely enough on the pages where borders or illustrations appear. Much fine work since the start of books has been damaged by a passion among binders to crop delicate edges instead of protecting them. It is like beheading a child instead of educating him.

As a last word on bindings it is worth adding that the joints of leather bindings should be given British Museum ointment from time to time, to stop them from cracking; that any new leather-bound addition to a collection should be so treated before it is opened, and that each book mentioned in any of these chapters should be carefully opened and supported, never pulled open to the sound of glue splitting. For book and binding, damp cold or damp warmth should be avoided. Women welcome nice books in winter because a room has to be kept reasonably warm for them. Unless you choose shelves with metal grilles which look like a form of quarantine from infection, glass doors are best. I could never see the least intelligence about leaving a book unopened. It should of course be read, and the pages cut with a paper-knife.

For one last simple possibility in collecting, bibliographies may be mentioned. Presses which issued their own tended to make them among the most useful and attractive of all their work. Probably the finest was the Ashendene Press Bibliography, 1935, with its many examples set again from original equipment. *A Note on The Founding of the Kelmscott Press*, issued by Cockerell in 1898 as the final gesture from the Trustees, is in every way a beautiful and necessary book. The Doves Press Bibliography, 1916, has all the character one would expect from Cobden-Sanderson with such a chance to use. The Vale Press, Essex House, and Eragny half way through its life all produced typical and excellent book lists with essays about the works of the press, in their volumes of bibliography. The *Nonesuch Century* is an important book. Slightly outside these borders we find Madan's book about the Daniel Press, Tomkinson's *Bibliography of the Private Presses*, Richard Steele on the *Revival of Printing*, and the two useful works of reference by Ransom published in America. These few form an attractive and helpful group. Recently a well produced bibliography of the Bremer Presse has appeared in Germany.

Nobody in any of this should hope to find bargains. These books will not be luckily picked up from the sixpenny tray, or discovered at the back of a shop where the bookseller didn't know what he had got – a dubious form of morality at the best of times. But they exist and change hands, and are to be found in the catalogues of good booksellers, in which England abounds. The wanderer may find particular pleasure in the astonishing richness of London's bookshops and especially, if names may be mentioned, in the company of Mr Newton of Quaritch, Mr Russell of Francis Edwards, Mr Fletcher of H. M. Fletcher, Mr Lent of Maggs, or the Joseph brothers; and with Mr Fenemore of Blackwells antiquarian department in Oxford. They have produced consistently fine collections and catalogues of private press books in the last years. On a fair London day after lunch, or at week-ends near Oxford, there has often seemed no happier form of civility than to talk with these scholar booksellers and be educated a little by their treasures.

SELECT BIBLIOGRAPHY OF PRIVATE PRESSES
WITH SOME RECENT AUCTION ROOM PRICES
compiled by David Lincoln

ABBREVIATIONS

C. = Christie, Manson & Woods; H. = Hodgson & Co.;
M. = Morrison McChlery & Co. (Glasgow); P. = Phillips, Son
& Neale; S. = Sotheby & Co.; n.f.s. = not for sale; l.p.c. = large
paper copy; h.m.p. = hand made paper
Unless described otherwise, auction prices refer to copies of the
largest issue of the edition.

DANIEL PRESS

Frome Minor Pieces

St. Jude.1845.

Psalm XXIII. 1850.

Frome Miniature Gazette. 1850.

Hymns. By a Poor Woman of B......y. 1851.

Hymns for Divine Service, used at Kingston Deverill Church. 1851.

Christmas: A Vigil. By C[harles] J[ames] C[ruttwell]. 1851.

The Busy Bee. 3 nos., and 2 supplements. 1852.

W. C. Cruttwell. *Sir Richard's Daughter...* 1852.

Sonnets. By C[harles] J[ames] C[ruttwell]. 1856.

St. John the Divine. *Epistles...* 1857.

Confirmation. 1861. 200.

Daniel Press Oxford

C. H. O. Daniel. *Notes from a Catalogue...* 1874. 25.

— *Notes*, etc.... [a continuation]. 1875. 25?

New Sermon of the Newest Fashion. 1876. 50.

Erasmus. *Colloquia Duo.* 1880. 40.

The Garland of Rachel. 1881. 36 (18 in bevelled vellums bds.)

Preface to the Garland. 1881. 20?

Hymna Ecclesiæ cura H. Daniel. 1882. 100.

Theocritus. *Sixe Idillia.* 1883. 100. 12s.

R. Bridges. *Prometheus...* 1883. 100. 10s.   H. 1963 £5 10s.

R. W. Dixon. *Odes and Eclogues*. 1884. 100. 5s.

H. Patmore. *Poems*. 1884. 125 5s.

R. Bridges. *Poems*. 1884. 150 8s.

J. Webster. *Love's Graduate*... 1885. 150 8s.

W. Blake. *Songs*. 1885. 40?

R. W. Dixon. *Lyrical Poems*. 1887. 105 6s.   S. 1965 £6.

R. W. Dixon. *Story of Eudocia*... 1888. 50   S. 1965 Cont. vellum gt. £14.

Margaret L. Woods. *Lyrics*. 1888. 125 n.f.s.

R. Bridges. *The Growth of Love*. 1889. 22 n.f.s.

W. Blake. *The Lamb*. 1889. 12

R. Bridges. *The Feast of Bacchus*. 1889. 105 12s.

F. W. Bourdillon. *Ailes d'Alouette*. 1890. 100 5s   C. 1963 £4.

R. Bridges. *The Growth of Love*. 1890. 100 in black letter 12s 6d.

Psalm CXVII. 1890. 6?

Herrick, His Flowers. 1891. 100 2s 6d.   C. 1963 hf. mor. unc., orig. wraps. prsvd. £10; C. 1967 £10.

Christmas, from... Robert Herrick. 1891. 60

Our Memories: Shadows of Old Oxford. 20 nos. 1888-1893, 100/110 n.f.s.

Our Memories... 2nd series. 2 nos. 1895

R. Bridges. *Founders Day*... 1893. 30 n.f.s.

W. Blake. *Songs of Innocence*. 1893. 100

R. Bridges. *Shorter Poems*, Bk. I. 1893. 150

R. Bridges. *Shorter Poems*, Bk. II. 1893. 150

— *Shorter Poems*, Bk. V. 1893. 150

Sir T. H. Warren. *A New Year's Greeting*. 1893. 100 n.f.s.

R. Bridges. *Shorter Poems*, Bk. III. 1894. 150

— *Shorter Poems*. Bk. IV. 1894. 150

— *Shorter Poems and Index of First Lines*. 1894. 150 issued with the preceding five pts. at £1 5s.

W. Pater. *An Imaginary Portrait*. 1894. 250 6s.   C. 1963, with prospectus lf. £10.

J. Milton. *Ode on the Morning of Christ's Nativity*. 1894. 100 5s; 100 2s 6d.   H. 1966 £2.

L. Binyon. *Poems*. 1895. 200 10s.   S. 1962 with A.L.S. £10; S. 1965 £11; S. 1966 £8.

J. Keats. *Odes, Sonnets and Lyrics*. 1895. 250 12s 6d.   H. 1965 £7 15s.

T. H. W[arren]. *All Amidst the Gardens Fair*. 1895 50?

Margaret L. Woods. *Songs*. 1896. 200 5s.

Fancy's Following, by 'Anados' [Mary Elizabeth Coleridge]. 1896. 125 7s. 6d.   S. 1966 £28.

A. à Wood. *Life of Richard Lovelace*. 1896. 50 for the Lovelace Club.

H. Warren. *By Severn Sea*... 1897. 130 7s. 6d.   S. 1965 £7.

Keble's *Easter Day*. 1897. 12 n.f.s.

Rosina Filippi. *Three Japanese Plays*... 1897. 125 10s.

Christmas Carols. 1897. 120 incl. 50 at 5s.

R. Bridges. *Hymns*. 1899. 150 12s 6d.

M. Field. [Edith E. Cooper & Katherina H. Bradley] *Noontide Branches*. 1899. 150 7s 6d.   S. 1965 £7.

Outlines, by W. S[tebbing]. 150 incl. 45 at 7s 6d.

A Christmas Welcome... c 1900. 95 2s 6d?

A Royal Guest. 1900. 110 5s.

R. Jones. *Muses Gardin for Delights...* 1901. 130, wrpprs 10s; limp vellum £1.

A[lice Mary] Buckton. *Through Human Eyes: Poems.* 1901. 130 wrpprs. 7s 6d; limp vellum 17s 6d.   S. 1965 £6.

Hon. Mrs. Wedgwood. *Wind along the Waste.* 1902. 130, wrpprs. 10s; limp vellum £1.

F. W. Bourdillon. *Ailes d'Alouette.* 2nd series. 1902. 130, wrpprs. 10s; limp vellum £1; morocco £1 10s.   S. 1965, title and imprint supplied by hand £7.

R. Bridges. *Now in Wintry Delights.* 1903. 300 10s.   S. 1965 mor. gt., silk fly ll. £42; S. 1966 £2.

Peace Ode... by R. B[ridges]. 1903. 100 5s; 10 on vellum.   S. 1965 mor. gt., mor. doublrs., orig. wrpprs. prsrvd. £45.

In Laudationem Benefactorum... 1906. 140; 4 on vellum.

The Queen Majesty's Entertainment at Woodstock... completed by the Clarendon Press. 1910

Sir Nicholas Bacon. *The Recreations of his Age.* 1919. Completed by the Clarendon Press and publ. by L. Chaundy at 10s 6d (130).

Falconer Madan. *The Daniel Press. Memorials of C. H. O. Daniel...* 1921. 500 £1 1s; 60 (50 for sale) h.m.p. £ 2 2s.   S. 1965 L.P. (60) £16; S. 1966 £3.

W. Morris. *The Story of the Glittering Plain.* 1891. 200 £2 2s; 6 on vellum (of which all but 2 were sold at £12 12s.) £15 15s.   S. 1963 £36; S. 1964 £55.

W. Morris. *Poems by the Way.* 1891. 300 £2 2s; 13 on vellum about £12 12s.   S. 1963 £17; S. 1964 £18; S. 1965 £12.

W. S. Blunt. *Proteus: Love-Lyrics, Songs and Sonnets.* 1892. 300 £2 2s. S. 1964 £22; S.1964 £35; S. 1966 £40.

J. Ruskin. *The Nature of Gothic.* [1892]. 500 £1 10s.   S. 1964 £25; H. 1966 £29; H. 1967 £27.

W. Morris. *The Defence of Guenevere...* 1892. 300 £2 2s; 10 on vellum about £12 12s.   S. 1963 £16; S. 1964 £18; S. 1965 1/10 on vellum £65; C. 1966 1/10 on vellum £42; S. 1967 £40.

W. Morris. *A Dream of John Ball...* 1892. 300 £1 10s; 11 on vellum £10 10s.   S. 1963 £18; S. 1964 £17; S. 1964 unopnd. £50; S. 1965 £14; S. 1966 £35.

J. de Voraigne. *The Golden Legend.* 3 vols., 1892. 500 £5 5s.   S. 1964 £42; H. 1965 £44; S. 1966 £40.

R. Lefevre. *The Recuyell of the Hystories of Troye.* 3 vols. in 2 vols., 1892. 300 £9 9s; 5 on vellum £80.   S. 1963 £26; S. 1964 £40; S. 1966 £55.

J. W. Mackail. *Biblia Innocentium.* 1892. 200 £1 1s;   S. 1963 £13; S. 1964 £20.

W. Caxton. *The History of Reynard the Foxe.* 1893. 300 £3 3s; 10 on vellum £15 15s.   S. 1964 £70; S. 1966 unopnd. £75.

W. Shakespeare. *Poems* ed. F. S. Ellis. 1893. 500 £1 5s.; 10 vellum £10 10s.   S. 1964 £28; S. 1964 £42; S. 1967 £60.

W. Morris. *News from Nowhere.* 1893. 300 £2 2s.; 10 on vellum £10 10s. S. 1963 £24; S. 1964 £26; S. 1966 £35; S. 1967 £60.

The Order of Chivalry, transl. W. Caxton. 1893. 225 £1 10s.; 10 on vellum £10 10s. S. 1964 £24;   S. 1964 £32.

G. Cavendish. *The Life of Thomas Wolsey*. 1893. 250 £2 2s.; 6 on vellum £10 10s. S. 1964 £22; S. 1964 £32;   S. 1966 £35; S. 1967 £55.

The History of Godefrey of Boloyne . . . 1893. 300 £6 6s.; 6 on vellum £21. S. 1964 £32; S. 1964 £52; S. 1966 £60; S. 1967 £75.

Sir T. More. *Utopia*. 1893. 300 £1 10s.; 8 on vellum £10 10s. S. 1964 £32; S. 1964 £52.

A. Lord Tennyson. *Maud*. . . 1893. 500 £2 2s.; 5 on vellum n.f.s. S. 1964 £12; S. 1965 £4; S. 1966 £20.

W. Morris. *Gothic Architecture* . . . 1893. 1500 2s 6d.; 45 on vellum 10s and 15s.   C. 1963 £2; H. 1963 £5; S. 1964 £10; S. 1964 1/45 on vellum £32; S. 1965 £3.

W. Meinhold. *Sidonia the Sorceress*. 1893. 300 £4 4s.; 10 on vellum £21. S. 1963 £12; S. 1964 with prospectus £26; S. 1964 £40.

D. G. Rossetti. *Ballads and Narrative Poems*. 1893. 310 £2 2s.; 6 on vellum £10 10s.   S. 1964 £20; S. 1964 £32; S. 1966 £42; S. 1966 £35.

The Tale of King Florus and the Fair Jehane. 1893. 350 7s 6d.; 15 on vellum £1 10s.   S. 1964 £35; H. 1965 £21.

W. Morris. *The Story of the Glittering Plain*. 1894. 250 £5 5s.; 7 on vellum £20.   S. 1963 £58; S. 1964 £45; S. 1966 £65.

Of the Friendship of Amis and Amile. 1894. 500 7s 6d.; 15 on vellum £1 10s.   S. 1962 £4; S. 1963 £12; S. 1964 with prospectus £6; S. 1964 £11; H. 1965 £12 10s.; S. 1967 £10.

D. G. Rossetti. *Sonnets and Lyrical Poems*. 1894. 310 £2 2s.; 6 on vellum £10 10s.   S. 1966 £40; C. 1966 £28.

J. Keats. *Poems*, ed S. F. Ellis. 1894. 300 £1 10s.; 7 on vellum £9 9s. S. 1964 £42; S. 1964 £55; S. 1966 £75; H. 1967 £64.

A. C. Swinburne. *Atalanta in Calydon*. 1894. 250 £2 2s.; 8 on vellum £12 12s. S. 1964 £40.

190

The Tale of the Emperor Coustans and of Over Sea. 1894. 525 7s 6d.; 20 on vellum £2 2s.   S. 1964 £9; H. 1965 £14 10s.; S. 1966 £10.

W. Morris. *The Wood beyond the World.* 1894. 350 £2 2s.; 8 on vellum £10 10s.   S. 1963 £20; S. 1963 £28; S. 1964 £26; S. 1966 £32; S. 1967 £40; S. 1968 1/8 on vellum £600.

The Book of Wisdom and of Lies. 1894. 250 £2 2s.   S. 1964 £30.

P. B. Shelley. *Poetical Works.* Vol. I. 1894. 250 £1 5s.; 6 on vellum £8 8s.

List of Books printed at the Kelmscott Press. 1894.   S. 1964 £10.

Ancoats Brotherhood. 1894-95. 4 pg. lflt., woodcut initals and ornams. S. 1965 £2.

Psalmi Penitentiales... 1894. 300 7s 6d.; 12 on vellum £3 3s. S. 1964 £19.

Savonarola. *Epistola de Contempta Mundi.* 1894. 150, 6 on vellum n.f.s. S. 1964 £24.

The Tale of Beowulf. 1895. 300 £2 2s.; 8 on vellum £10 10s.   S. 1964, 'Note to the Reader' insrtd. £42; S. 1966 £55; S. 1966 £42; S. 1967 £38.

Syr Perecyvelle of Gales. 1895. 350 15s.; 8 on vellum £4 4s.   S. 1964 £13; S. 1966 £24.

W. Morris. *The Life and Death of Jason.* 1895. 200 £5 5s.; 6 on vellum £21.   S. 1964 £48.

W. Morris. *Child Christopher and Goldiland the Fair.* 1895. 600 15s.; 12 on vellum £7 4s.   S. 1962 £13; S. 1964 with prospectus £22; H. 1965 £14 10s.; S. 1966 £12.

P. B. Shelley. *Poetical Works.* 3 vols. 1894-95. 250 £1 5s.; 6 on vellum £8 8s.   S. 1964 3 vols. £110; S. 1966 £85.

D. G. Rossetti. *Hand and Soul.* 1895. For U.S.A. 300; 11 on vellum. For England 225 10s.; 10 on vellum £1 10s.   S. 1966 £22.

Poems Chosen... of Robert Herrick. 1896. 250 £1 10s.; 8 on vellum

£8 8s.   S. 1964 £28; S.1964 £50; S. 1966 £85; S. 1967 £55.

Poems Chosen... of Samuel Taylor Coleridge. 1896. 300 £1 1s.; 8 on vellum £5 5s.   S. 1964 £32; S. 1964 £28; S. 1966 £50.

W. Morris. *The Well at the World's End.* 1896. 350 £5 5s.; 8 on vellum £21.   S. 1964 with prospectus £30; S. 1964 £34; P. 1966 £35; S. 1966 £45.

G. Chaucer. *Works.* [1896]. 425 £20; 13 on vellum £126.   S. 1963 £360; S. 1964 £520; S. 1965 £450; S. 1966 £650; S. 1967 £800.

W. Morris. *The Earthly Paradise.* Vol. I. 1896. 225 10s.; 6 on vellum £7 7s.

Laudes Beatae Mariae Virginis. 1896. 250 10s.; 10 on vellum £2 2s. S. 1963 £8; S. 1964 £17; S. 1964 £20.

W. Morris. *The Earthly Paradise.* Vol. II. 1896. 225 10s.; 6 on vellum £7 7s.

Sir T. Clanvowe. *The Floure and the Leafe...* 1896. 300 10s.; 10 on vellum £2 2s.   S. 1963 £8; S. 1964 £13; S. 1964 £18; S. 1966 £30.

E. Spenser. *The Shepheardes Calender...* 1896. 225 £1 1s.; 6 on vellum £3 3s.   S. 1964 £32.

W. Morris. *The Earthly Paradise.* Vol. III. 1896.
— *Idem.* Vol IV. 1897.
–– *Idem.* Vol. V. 1897.
— *Idem.* Vol. VI. 1897.
— *Idem.* Vol. VII. 1897.
— *Idem.* Vol. VIII. 1897 all 225 10s.; 6 on vellum £7 7s., making 8 vols. 1896-97.   S. 1963 £40; C. 1963 £40; S. 1966 £65.

W. Morris. *The Water of the Wondrous Isles.* 1897. 250 £ 3 3s.; 6 on vellum £12 12s. S. 1964 £18; S. 1964 £26; H. 1966 £43; S. 1966 £60.

Froissart's *Chronicles.* Two trial pages. 1897. 160 on vellum £1 1s.

Sire Degrevaunt. 1897. 350 15s.; 8 on vellum £4 4s.   S. 1964 £12; S. 1965 £16; S. 1966 £17; S. 1966 £10; S. 1966 £13.

Sir Ysambrace. 1897. 350 12s.; 8 on vellum £4 4s.   S. 1964 £14; S. 1966 £8.

S. C. Cockerell. *Some German Woodcuts of the Fifteenth Century.* 1898. 225 £1 10s.; 8 on vellum £5 5s.   S. 1963 £17; S. 1964 £28.

W. Morris. *The Story of Sigurd the Volsung...* 1898. 160 £7 7s.; 6 on vellum £21.   S. 1964 £46.

W. Morris. *Love is Enough...* 1897. 300 £2 2s.; 8 on vellum £10 10s. S. 1964 £30; S. 1966 £50; S. 1967 £65.

A Note by William Morris on his Aims in Founding the Kelmscott Press... 1898. 525 10s.; 12 on vellum £2 2s.   S. 1963 £12; S. 1964 £20; H. 1966 £35.

W. Morris. *The Sundering Flood.* 1898. 300 £2 2s.   S. 1963 £9; S. 1963 £15; C. 1963 £20; S. 1966 £25.

ASHENDENE PRESS

J. Hornby. *Journal.* 1895. 34 n.f.s.   S. 1964 £150.

Dante. *Vita Nuova.* 1895. 50 Japan.; 5 h.m.p.; n.f.s.   S. 1964 £70.

Lay of Bayford Hockey Club. 1895. 38.   H. 1964 £52.

Sette of Odd Volumes. Minutes CLXXVIIth Meeting. 1896.

J. Milton. *Three Poems...* 1896. 50 n.f.s.   C. 1964 £78.

Omar Khayyam. *Rubaiyat.* 1896. 50 n.f.s.   S. 1964 unopnd. £110.
S. 1965 £155.

Marcus Aurelius. *Meditations,* Bk. I. 1897. 30 n.f.s.   S. 1965 £170.

Book of Ecclesiastes, 1897. 27 n.f.s. S. 1965 £170.

F. Bacon. *Of Building and Gardens.* 1897. 16 n.f.s. S. 1965 £240.

Hymns and Prayers... at the Marriage of St. John Hornby and Cicely Barclay. 1898, 154 n.f.s.   C. 1964 £38; S. 1965 £35.

Chaucer. *Prologue... Tales of Canterbury.* 1898. 50 n.f.s.   S. 1965 unopnd £140.

Three Elegies. Lycidas... Adonais... Thyrsis. 1899. 50 n.f.s.   S. 1964 £80; S. 1965 £110.

Aucassin and Nicolette. 1900. 40 £2 2s.   S. 1965 £95.

Revelacion off Sanct Jhon the Devine. 1901. 54 £2 2s.   S. 1965 £70.

St. Francis of Assisi. *I Fioretti.* 1901. 240. S. 1965 £24.

Dante. *Inferno.* 1902. 135 £3 3s.; 14 on vellum £10 10s.

Song of Songs... 1902. 40 on vellum £10 10s.

Horace. *Carmina Alcaica.* 1903. 150 Japan. £2 2s.; 25 on vellum £5 5s.
S. 1964 £30; S. 1965 £35; S. 1966 £28.

Juliana Berners. *Treatyse of Fysshynge...* 1903. 150 £1 11s 6d.; 25 on vellum £5 5s.   S. 1965 £24; S. 1966 £32.

194

Horace. *Carmina Sapphica.* 1903. 150 Japan. £1 11s 6d.; 25 on vellum £5 5s. S. 1965 £55; S. 1967 with 'Carmina Alcaica' £65.

Old Testament. *Songs and Poems.* 1904. 150 £1 5s.; 25 on vellum £4 4s (7 illuminated). S. 1964 £40; S. 1964 1/25 on vellum £90.

S. Francesco di Assisi. *Scelto di Fioretti.* 1904. 125 £2 12s 6d.; 20 on vellum £6 6s. S. 1964 £32; S. 1964 1/25 on vellum £105.

Dante. *Lo Purgatorio.* 1904. 150 £3 3s.; 20 on vellum £10 10s. S. 1964 £42.

Dante. *Lo Paradiso.* 1905. 150 £3 3s.; 20 on vellum £10 10s. S. 1963 *Purgatorio, Paradiso* £75; S. 1965 *Inferno, Purgatoria, Paradiso*; S. 1965 £220.

Sir T. More. *Utopia.* 1906. 100 £1. 11s 6d.; 20 on vellum £10 10s. S. 1963 Stiched sheets in folder £38; S. 1965 £100.

Plutarch. *Two Letters.* 1909. 30 Japan.; 6 on vellum n.f.s. S. 1965 £75.

Story without an End. 1909. 30 Japan.; 6 on vellum n.f.s. S. 1964 £94; S. 1965 £170.

Dante. *Opere.* 1909. 105 oak bds. £10 10s.; 6 on vellum £52 10s. S. 1965 £280.

Virgil. *Opera.* 1910. 40 Japan. £3 3s.; 8 on vellum £15 15s. S. 1964 £135; S. 1965 £220.

Malory. *Morte Darthur.* 1913. 147 paper (incl. 3 Japan.) £12 12s.; 8 on vellum £52 10s. S. 1964 £ 140; S. 1965 £ 170; S. 1967 £240.

B. Hornby. *The Children's Garden.* 1913. 150 paper; 6 on vellum S. 1964 £30; S. 1965 £38.

Lucretius. *De Rerum Natura.* 1913. 80 £2 2s.; 8 on vellum £10 10s. S. 1964 £42; S. 1965 £70; S. 1967 £100.

R. Bridges. *Poems.* 1913. 1914. 85; 6 on vellum n.f.s. S. 1962 (85) pres. copy £34; S. 1965 £65

Plutarch. *Letter to Apollonius.* 1915. 4ll. S. 1965 £38.

H. James. *Refugees in Chelsea.* 1920. 50; 6 on vellum n.f.s.   S. 1964 £55; S. 1965 mor. gt. £90; S. 1966 £75.

Boccaccio. *Il Decameron.* 1920. 105 £12 12s.; 6 on vellum £78 15s. S. 1963 £45; S. 1964 £65; S. 1967 £130.

J. M. Edmonds. *Twelve War Epitaphs* [1920]. Broadside. S. 1965 £20.

U. Verino. *Vita di Santa Chiara.* 1921. 236 £2 12s 6d.; 10 on vellum £10 10s.   S. 1964 £12; S. 1965 £24; H. 1966 £12.

S. Francesco di Assisi. *I Fioretti.* 1922. 240 £4 4s.; 12 on vellum £16 16s.   S. 1963 £22; S. 1965 £24.

E. Spenser. *Faerie Queene.* 1924. 180 £16 16s.; 12 on vellum £110 5s. S. 1963 £85; S. 1964 £100; S. 1965 £120; S. 1967 £160.

Tolstoy. *Where God is Love is.* 1924. 200   C. 1964 £40; S. 1965 £55.

Apuleius. *Golden Asse.* 1924. 165 (incl. 2 Japan.) £5 5s.; 16 on vellum £31 10s.   S. 1964 £34; S.1964 £50; S. 1964 1/3 on Jap. P. £170.

O. Wilde. *Four Tales.* 1924. 65; 7 on vellum n.f.s.   C. 1964 £58; S. 1965 £10; S. 1966 £85.

E. Spenser. *Minor Poems.* 1925. 198 £12 12s.; 15 on vellum £63. S. 1963 £48; S. 1965 £65; S. 1967 £80.

Cervantes. *Don Quixote.* 2 vols., 1927-28. 225 bds. £21, morocco or pigskin £29 8s.; 20 on vellum £157 10s.   S. 1963 pigskin £100; H. 1963 £48; S. 1965 morocco £130; S. 1967 £130.

Hymns and Prayers . . . at the Marriage of M. Hornby and N. Ward. 1928. 250   C. 1964 £12; S. 1965 £6.

Milton. *Hymn on the Morning of Christ's Nativity.* 1928. 220   C. 1964 £18; S. 1965 £25.

Thucydides, transl. by B. Jowett. 1930. 260 paper (240 f.s.) white pigskin £15 15s.; 20 vellum (17 f.s.) in morocco £78 15s.   S. 1964 £95; S. 1965 £105; C. 1966 £75; C. 1967 £110; S. 1965 1/20 on vellum £440.

Hymns and Prayers . . . at the Marriage of R. A. Hornby and V. Blackwood. 1931. C. 1964 £15; S. 1965 £16.

Ecclesiasticus. *The Wisdom of Jesus.* 1932. 328 paper (250 f.s.) £6 6s.; 25 on vellum (20 f.s.) £36 15s.   H. 1963 £39; S. 1964 £50; S. 1965 1/25 on vellum £250.

Daphnis et Chloe. 1933. 290 (250 f.s.) £6 6s.; 20 (17 f.s.) on vellum £42. S. 1963 £28; S. 1964 £25; S. 1965 £28; S. 1966 £28; S. 1965 1/20 on vellum £220.

Roxburghe Club. *Address of Congratulation to Lord Aldenham.* 1935. (39).   S. 1963 £45; S. 1964 £10; S. 1966 £10.

Descriptive Bibliography . . . Ashendene Press. 1895-1935. 390 (340 f.s.) £7 7s.   S. 1963 £55; S. 1964 £62; S. 1966 £90; S. 1966 £110.

Jubilee Celebration 1 Jan. 1943 [1943].   C. 1964 £14.

C. H. St. J. Hornby. *Anthology of Appreciations.* 1946.   C. 1964 £12.

ESSEX HOUSE

Memorandum and Articles of Association of the Guild of Handicraft Ltd. 1898.

B. Cellini. *Treatises on Metal Work and Sculpture.* 1898. 600 £1 15s. S. 1966 £13; C. 1967 £9.

Hymn of Bardaisan. 1899. 300 7s 6d.

J. Bunyan. *Pilgrim's Progress.* 1899. 750 £1 10s.   S. 1966 £7.

Beauty's Awakening... 1899. 25 for the Art Workers' Guild, reprinted by The Studio.

P. B. Shelley. *Adonais.* 1900. 50 on vellum £1 10s.

G. Thomson. *Ruskin and Modern Business.* 1900. 50 n.f.s.

O. C. Hills. *Saint Mary Stratford, Bow.* 1900. 250 12s 6d.

W. Shakespeare. *Poems.* 1900. 450 £2.   S. 1963 £11; S. 1964 £7; S. 1965 £16.

F. W. Bourdillon. *Through the Gateway.* 1900. 50 n.f.s.

J. Keats. *The Eve of St. Agnes.* 1900. 125 on vellum £2 2s.   S. 1966 £18.

The Courtyer of Count Baldessar Castiglione. 1900. 200 £3 3s.   S. 1963 £9.

John Hunter Leaves St. George's Hospital. 1901. A few n.f.s.

T. Gray. *Elegy in a Country Churchyard.* 1901. 125 on vellum £2 2s.

Hymn on the Death of President Lincoln. 1901. 125 on vellum £2 2s.

C. R. Ashbee. *An Endeavour towards the Teaching of John Ruskin.* 1901. 350 £1 1s.

C. R. Ashbee. *A Report...* 1901. 350 (50 on Essex House paper 10s 6d.).

J. Woolman. *Journal...* 1901. 250 £ 2 2s.

Erasmus. *In Praise of Folie*. 1901. 250 £3 3s.

W. Penn. *Some Fruits of Solitude*. 1901. 250 £2 2s.

C. R. Ashbee. *American Sheaves and English Seed Corn*. 1901. 300 £1 10s.

The Psalter. 1901. 250 £4 4s.; 10 on vellum £16 16s.   S. 1963 £14.

E. Spenser. *Epithalamion*. 1901. 150 on vellum £ 2 2s.   S. 1965 £10.

P. B. Shelley. *Letter to T. L. Peacock*. 1901. 45; 5 on vellum n.f.s.

E. Godman. *The Old Palace of Bromley-by-Bow*. 1902. 350 £1 1s.

W. Strang. *The Doings of Death*. 1902. 140 £6 6s.

C. R. Ashbee. *The Masque of the Edwards of England*. 1902. 300 £3 3s.; 20 on vellum £12 12s.   S. 1964 1/20 on vellum £8.

R. L. Stevenson. *Three Letters*. 1902. 54; 6 on vellum n.f.s.

Chaucer. *The Flower and the Leaf*. 1902. 165 on vellum £3 3s. S. 1965 £10.

R. Burns. *Tam o' Shanter*. 1902. 150 on vellum £2 2s.   S. 1964 £7.

J. Milton. *Comus*. 1902. 150 on vellum £3 3s.   S. 1963 £7; S. 1966 £11.

The Snow lay on the Ground. 1902. 400 n.f.s.

The Life and Works of Sir Christopher Wren... 1903. 250 £3 13s. 6d.

Ausgewaehlte Lieder, Heine's ed. by E. Holmes. 1903. 250 £1 1s.; 12 on vellum £2 2s.

Wordsworth's *Ode on the Intimations of Immortality*. 1903. 150 on vellum £2 2s.   S. 1966 £16; S. 1967 £20.

E. Gunn. *The Great House, Leyton*. 1903. 350 £1 1s.

The Prayer Book of King Edward VII. 1903. 400 £12 12s. 9 on vellum £40.   S. 1963 £6; S. 1965 £13.

A Key to the Principal Decorations in the Prayer Book of King Edward VII. 1903. 400, for subscribers.

Supplement showing Variants from the Prayer Book of the Church of England in the Prayer Book of the American Church. 1903. 50, for America.

Coleridge's *Rhyme of the Ancient Mariner.* 1903. 150 on vellum £2 12s 6d.   H. 1963 £6; S. 1966 £15.

T. Hood. *Miss Kilmansegg and her Precious Leg.* 1904. 200 £1 5s.; 4 on vellum £3 3s.

The Essex House Song Book, ed. by Janet E. Ashbee. 1904. Issued in separate sheets, in ten portfolios at 1s per sheet; 5 on vellum at 5s.

Shelley's *Prometheus Unbound.* 1904. 200 £2 2s.; 20 on vellum £7 7s.

F. A. Whiting. *On the Work of the Guild.* 1904. 50 on Essex House Paper 1s.

Report on the Work of the Campden School of Arts and Crafts. 1904.

G. Bishop. *A May-Day Interlude.* 1904.

Bibliography of the Essex House Press, 1898-1904. 1904.

Cicero's *De Amicitia or Book of Friendship.* 1904. 150 £1 15s.; 10 on vellum £6 6s.

C. R. Ashbee. *The Last Records of a Cotswold Community.* 1964. 150 12s 6d.; 75 on Essex House Paper £1 1s.   S. 1962 £3.

Dryden's *Alexander's Feast.* 1904. 140 on vellum £2 2s.

An Address delivered by Lord Redesdale . . . 1904. 50 n.f.s.

Thomas À Kempis. *The Imitation of Christ.* 1904. 100 £5 5s.; 10 on vellum £15 15s.   S. 1965 £11.

Goldsmith's *Deserted Village.* 1904. 150 on vellum £2 12s. 6d.

Caroline Hazard. *The Illuminators.* 1905. 150 n.f.s.

F. A. Hyett. *An Octet of Sonnets.* 1905. 50 n.f.s.

E. Godman. *Norman Architecture in Essex.* 1905. 300 12s and 16s according to binding.

E. Godman. *Mediaeval Architecture in Essex*. 1905. 250 as above.

L. Nightingale. *A Cycle of Sonnets*. 1905. 250 n.f.s.

Report of the Work of the Campden School of Arts and Crafts. 1905. About 100 1s.

Tennyson's *Maud*. 1905. 125 on vellum £3 3s.   S. 1963 £4.

The Second Address of Lord Redesdale   1905.

Browning's *Flight of the Duchess*. 1905. 125 on vellum £2 12s. 6d. S. 1966 £16.

C. R. Ashbee. *Echoes from the City of the Sun*. 1905. 250 12 6d.; 1 on vellum n.f.s.

The Rubaiyat of Omar Khayyam. Printed for the Omar Khayyam Club. 1905. 88 £2 2s.; 17 on vellum £4 4s.

J. Fisher. *A Mornyng Remembraunce*. 1906. 125 £1 1s.; 7 on vellum £3 3s.

Report on the Work of the Campden School. 1905-06. 1906. About 100 1s.

L. Housman. *Mendicant Rhymes*. 1906. 300 12s 6d.

C. R. Ashbee. *A Book of Cottages and Little Houses*. 1906. 200 12s 6d.; 50 on Essex House paper £1 5s.

C. R. Ashbee. *Socialism and Politics*. 1906. About 250 3s 6d.

The Picture of Kebes the Theban, transl. by H. E. Seebohm. 1906. 50 n.f.s.

C. R. Ashbee. *On the Need for the Establishment of Country Schools of Arts and Crafts*. 1906. About 100 n.f.s.   S. 1966 £7.

A. Ramage. *Dr. Johnson: an Essay*. 1906. 100 5s.

Lord Redesdale. *A Tale of Old and New Japan*. 1906. 50 n.f.s.

A. K. Coomaraswamy. *The Deeper Meaning of the Struggle*. 1907. 1000 4d.; 75 h.m.p. 1s.

A. K. Coomaraswamy. *The Aims of Indian Art*. 1908. 225 2s 6d.; 50 on

Essex House paper 5s.; 2 on vellum n.f.s.

C. R. Ashbee. *Conradin: a Philosophical Ballad.* 1908. 250 £1 1s.; 1 on vellum n.f.s.

A. K. Coomaraswamy. *The Two Painters.* 1908. 30 paper and 1 on vellum n.f.s.

A. K. Coomaraswamy. *Mediaeval Sinhalese Art.* 1908. 400 £3 3s.; 25 Essex House paper £5 5s. S. 1964 £5.

A. K. Coomaraswamy. *The Influence of Greek on Indian Art.* July 31. 1908. 75; October 2. 1908. 50, n.f.s.

A. K. Coomaraswamy. *Netra Mangalya.* 1908. 25 n.f.s.

Voluspa. *Done into English...* by A. K. Coomaraswamy. 1909. 100 2s 6d.; 1 on vellum n.f.s.

W. P. D. Stebbing. *The Church of Worth in Sussex* [misdated 1908]. 1909. 88 3s 6d.; 25 Essex House paper 5s.

The Edicts of Asoka, ed. V. A. Smith. 1909. 100 £1 1s.

C. R. Ashbee. *Modern English Silverware.* 1909. 200 £2 2s.

C. R. Ashbee. *The Guild of Handicraft.* 1909. 100 n.f.s.

C. R. Ashbee. *The Private Press: a Study in Idealism.* 1909. 125 £3 3s.; 2 on vellum n.f.s. S. 1965 £16; S. 1966 1/2 on vellum £160.

C. Marlowe and G. Chapman. *Hero and Leander*. 1894. S. 1963 £11;
H. 1966 £13.

J. Milton. *Early Poems*. 1896. 310 £1 10s.   S. 1965 £4; C. 1968 £26.

W. S. Landor. *Epicurus, Leontion, and Ternissa*. 1896. 210 10s. 6d.

Sir J. Suckling. *Poems*. 1896. 310 £1 1s.   S. 1964 £3; S. 1966 £5.

The Passionate Pilgrim and The Songs in Shakespeare's Plays, ed. T. Sturge
Moore. 1896. 310 £1 1s.   S. 1965 £5.

J. Gray. *Spiritual Poems*. 1896. 210 12s.   S. 1964 £22; S. 1966 £4

M. Drayton. *The Nymphidia and The Muses Elizium*. 1896. 210 £1 1s.
H. 1964 £7; S. 1965 £5.

T. Campion. *Fifty Songs*. 1896. 210 15s 6d.

M. Arnold. *Empedocles on Etna*. 1896. 210 10s 6d.   S. 1966 £2.

W. Blake. *The Book of Thel: Songs of Innocence and Songs of Experience*.
1897. 210 10s 6d.

M. Field. *Fair Rosamund*. 1897. 210 12s 6d.

H. Vaughan (Silurist). *Sacred Poems*. 1897. 210 15s.

H. Constable. *Poems and Sonnets*. 1897. 210 £1 1s.   S. 1966 £6.

Apuleius. *Marriage of Cupid and Psyche*. 1897. 210 £1 5s.; 2 on vellum.
H. 1964 £3 15s.; S. 1966 £10.

E. B. Browning. *Sonnets from the Portuguese*. 1897. 300 6s.; 8 on vellum.

Sir P. Sidney. *Sonnets*. 1898. 210 £1 1s.; 8 on vellum.   S. 1966 £6.

C. Ricketts and L. Pissarro. *De la Typographie et de l'Harmonie de la Page
Imprimée...* 1898. 250 10s.; 10 on vellum.

T. Chatterton. *Rowley Poems*. 1898. 210 £1 10s.; 8 on vellum.
S. 1964 £8.

M. Field. *The World at Auction.* 210 15s.; 2 on vellum.

P. B. Shelley. *Lyrical Poems.* 1898. 210 7s.; 8 on vellum. S. 1965 £5.

J. Keats. *Poems.* 1898. 210 £1 16s.; 8 on vellum. S. 1964 £8.

D. G. Rossetti. *The Blessed Damozel.* 1898. 310 6s.; 10 on vellum.

W. Blake. *Poetical Sketches.* 1899. 210 12s. 6d.; 8 on vellum. S. 1964 £8

S. T. Coleridge. *Rime of the Ancient Mariner.* 1899. 210 10s 6d.; 10 on vellum.

D. G. Rossetti. *Hand and Soul.* 1899. 210 6s. 10 on vellum.

C. Ricketts. *Defence of the Revival of Printing.* 1899. 250 6s.; 10 on vellum S. 1966 in bdg. by Sarah T. Prideaux sgd. and dtd '1901' £140.

R. Browning. *Dramatic Romances and Lyrics.* 1899. 210 £1 1s.; 10 on vellum.

W. Shakespeare. *Sonnets.* 1899. 210 £1 1s.

M. de Guérin. *The Centaur and The Bacchante.* 1899. 150 £1 1s.

A. Lord Tennyson. *Poems,* 2 vols. 1900. 320 £2 2s.; 10 on vellum.

Benvenuto Cellini. *Life.* 2 vols. 1900. 300 £4 4s.; 10 on vellum. S. 1964 £8; S. 1965 £7.

M. Field. *The Race of Leaves.* 1901. 280 £1 1s.; 10 on vellum.

Omar Khayyam. *Rubaiyat.* 1901. 310 £1.; 10 on vellum.

Apuleius. *De Cupidinis et Psyches Amoribus.* 1901. 310 £1 10s.

P. B. Shelley. *Poems.* 3 vols. 1901. 310 £1 5s.; 10 on vellum. S. 1964 £22.

Sir. T. Browne. *Religio Medici, Urn Burial . . .* 1901. 310 £2 2s.; 10 on vellum.

Catalogue of Mr. Shannon's Lithographs. 1902 200 12s 6d. 2 on vellum.

W. Wordsworth. *Poems.* 1902. 310 £1 10s.   M. 1963 £1 5s.; S. 1965 £5.

Ecclesiastes; or the Preacher . . . [1902]. 300 £1.; 10 on vellum.
H. 1963 £4 10s.; S. 1964 £4; H. 1966 £6 10s.

W. Meinhold. *The Amber Witch.* 1903. 300 £2 2s.; 10 on vellum.
S. 1966 £5.

Parables from the Gospels. 1903. 310 £1 15s.; 10 on vellum.   S. 1963 £8;
S. 1964 £6.

M. Field. *Julia Domna.* 1903. 240 18s.; 10 on vellum.

King James. *The Kingis Quair.* 1903. 260 £1; 10 on vellum.   M. 1963
£2 2s. S. 1964 1/10 on vellum £32. S. 1967 £7.

T. S. Moore. *Danaë.* 1903. 230 £1; 10 on vellum.

Shakespeare. *Works,* ed. T. Sturge Moore. 39 vols., 1900-03. 310 sets.
S. 1964 £34; S. 1966 £30.

C. Marlowe. *Tragedy of Dr. Faustus.* 1903. 310 £1 5s.

A Bibliography of the Books issued by Hacon and Ricketts. 1896-1903. 1904.
250 15s.; 10 on vellum £3 3s. S. 1966 1/10 on vellum £40.

Margaret Rust. *The Queen of the Fishes*. 1894. 130 £1. C. 1968 in vellum £42.

The Book of Ruth and the Book of Esther. 1896. 155 16s. C. 1968 £14.

J. La Forgue. *Moralites Legendaires*. 2 vols., 1897-8. 220 £1 12s. C. 1968 £24.

C. Perrault. *Deux Contes de ma Mère L'Oye*. 1899. 220 £1; 4 on vellum n.f.s. C. 1968 £24.

G. Flaubert. *La Legende de Saint Julien l'Hospitalier*. 1900. 226 15s. C. 1968 £16.

F. Villon. *Les Ballades*. 1900. 222 £1 5s.; 4 on Japanese h.m.p., n.f.s. C. 1968 £22.

G. Flaubert. *Un Coeur Simple*. 1901. 226 15s. C. 1968 £14.

G. Flaubert. *Herodias*. 1901. 226 15s. C. 1968 £20.

F. Villon. *Autres Poésies...* 1901. 222 £1; 4 Japanese h.m.p. n.f.s. C. 1968 £24.

E. Verhaeren. *Les Petits Vieux*. 1901. 230. C. 1968 £20.

F. Bacon. *Of Gardens*. 1902. 226 16s. S. 1966 mor. gt., g.e. £40. C. 1968 £20.

Ronsard. *Choix de Sonnets*. 1902. 226 £1 10s. C. 1968 £18.

C. Perrault. *Histoire de Peau d'Ane*. 1903. 230 £1 1s. C. 1968 £18.

Ronsard. *Abrégé de l'Art Poetique Français*. 1903. 226 15s. C. 1968 £18.

C'Est d'Aucassin et de Nicolette. 1903. 230 £1 10s. H. 1965 £10 10s; C. 1968 £24.

T. Sturge Moore. *Brief Account of the Origin of the Eragny Press*. 1903. 235 £1 5s.; 6 on vellum £5 5s. C. 1968 £28.

Diana White. *The Descent of Ishtar*. 1903. 226 12s 6d.; 5 on vellum

£3 3s.   C. 1968 £18.

J. Milton. *Areopagitica.* 1904. 200 £1 11s 6d.; 10 on vellum £7 7s.
S. 1963 £8;   C. 1968 with 6 New Yr. Cards by the Pissarros, etc. £32.

R. Browning. *Some Poems.* 1904. 215 £1 10s.; 10 on vellum £7.
C. 1968 £22.

S. T. Coleridge. *Christabel, Kubla Khan...* 1904. 226 £1 1s.; 10 on
vellum £5 5s.   C. 1968 £24.

R. Steele (Ed.). *Some Old French and English Ballads.* 1905. 200 £1 15s.;
10 on vellum £7 7s.   C. 1968 £18.

L. Binyon. *Dream-Come-True.* 1905. 175 12s 6d.; 10 on vellum £3 3s.
C. 1968 £ 20.

T. Sturge Moore. *The Little School...*1905. 175 18s.; 10 on vellum
£4 4s.   C. 1968 £18.

J. Keats. *La Belle Dame sans Merci.* 1906. 200 5s.; 10 on vellum £1 1s.
C. 1968 £32.

B. Jonson. *Songs.* 1906. 175 £2; 10 on vellum £7 7s.   C. 1968 £22.

Christina Rossetti. *Verses.* 1906. 175 £1 1s.; 10 on vellum £5 5s.
C. 1968 £24.

Riquette à la Houppe. 1907. 75 £1 5s.; 8 on vellum £4 4s.   C. 1968 £30.

G. de Nerval. *Histoire de la Reine du Matin...* 1909. 130 for the Société
des Cent Bibliophiles.   C. 1968 £55.

Judith Gautier. *Poèmes Tirés du Livre de Jade.* 1911. 120 £4; 10 on
vellum £8 8s. S. 1965 £24.   C. 1968 £45.

E. Moselly. *La Charrue d'Erable.* 1912. 118 for the Société du Livre
Contemporaine.   C. 1968 £55.

M. Field. *Whym Chow, Flame of Love.* 1914. 27 n.f.s.

CARADOC PRESS

Kalendar: MDCCCC. 1899. 150 5s.

Old Ballad of the Boy and the Mantle. 1900. 300 6s.; 5 on vellum £1 5s.

Kalendar: MDCCCCI. 1900. 300 6s.; 5 on vellum £1 5s.

Collects from... Book of Common Prayer. 1901. 350 7s 6d.; 18 on vellum £1 10s.; 5 on vellum illumintd at prices up to £22.

Kalendar: MDCCCCII. 1901. 350 2s 6d.; 7 on vellum 10s.

Quia Amore Langueo. 1902. 250 7s 6d.; 20 on vellum £1 15s.

W. B. Yeats. *Cathleen ni Hoolihan.* 1902. 300 5s.; 8 on vellum £2 2s. S. 1962 £11; S. 1965 £42.

In Praise of Wisdom: Ecclesiasticus. 1902. 350 4s.; 12 on vellum £2 2s.; 3 'special vellum' illuminted £15.

O. Goldsmith. *Vicar of Wakefield.* 1903. 360 £1 10s.; 14 on vellum £10 10s. S. 1966 £6.

Holy Communion from the Book of Common Prayer. 1904. 350 7s 6d.; 18 on vellum £2 2s.; 5 on 'special vellum' illumintd £20. S. 1963 1/18 on vellum £5.

Proverbys of Saynt Bernarde. 1904. 350 5s.; 12 on vellum £2 2s.; 5 on 'special vellum' illumintd at from £10-£15 15s.

Life of Sir James Falshaw, Bart. 100; 2 on vellum n.f.s.

I. Walton. *Compleat Angler.* 1905. 350 £1 1s.; 14 on vellum £10 10s.

Book of Job. 1905. 20 on vellum (7 only finished) at from £10 10s-£36 15s.

Sir Philip Sidney. *The Defence of Poesie...* 1906. 350 7s 6d.; 14 on vellum £6 6s.

Fulke Greville. *Life of... Sir Philip Sidney.* 1906. 260 10s.; 11 on vellum £6 6s.

James I. *The Kingis Quair.* 1906. 350 7s 6d.; 14 on vellum £2 2s.

Elizabeth Barrett Browning. *Sonnets from the Portuguese.* 1908. 1000 2s 6d.

Historical Paintings... by Frank Brangwyn. 1909. 300 £1 11s 6d.; 25 Japan £5 5s.

Woodcut Borders and Initials, etc., used in Caradoc Press books. 1909. 7 n.f.s.   S. 1964 £26.

Cornelius Tacitus. *De Vita et Moribus*... 1901. 225 £1 5s.; 5 on vellum £5 5s.   S. 1965 £16; S. 1965 £12.

T. J. Cobden-Sanderson. *The Ideal Book*... 1901. 300 12s 6d.; 10 on vellum £3 3s.   S. 1965 £18.

J. W. Mackail. *William Morris*... 1901. 300 15s.; 15 on vellum £3 3s. S. 1965 £6; C. 1966 £10.

A. Lord Tennyson. *Seven Poems*... 1902. 325 £1 5s.; 25 on vellum £6 6s.   S. 1965 £9; H. 1966 £12 10s.

J. Milton. *Paradise Lost*. 1902. 300 £3 3s.; 25 on vellum £15 15s.; (incl. 3 on vellum with gold initials).   S. 1963 £38.

The English Bible. 5 vols. 1903-05. 500 £15 15s.; 2 on vellum n.f.s. S. 1963 £170; S. 1965 £190; C. 1966 £200; S. 1967 £260.

J. Milton. *Paradise Regain'd*. 1905. 300 £3 3s.; 25 on vellum £15 15s (3 with gold initials).   H. 1963 £15 10s.; S. 1965 with Paradise Lost £52; S. 1965 £18; C. 1966 £35.

T. J. Cobden-Sanderson. *London*... 1906. 5 on vellum?   H. 1963 £5; S. 1965 £7; S. 1967 £7.

R. W. Emerson. *Essays*. 1906. 300 £2 2s.; 25 on vellum £10 10s. C. 1964 £22; S. 1965 £18.

Goethe. *Faust*. Erster Theil. 1906. 300 £3 3s.; 25 on vellum £12 12s. (3 with gold initials).   S. 1965 together with 2er Theil £75.

J. Ruskin. *Unto this Last*... 1907. 300 £1 5s.; 12 on vellum £8 8s. H. 1963 £11 10s.; S. 1965 £12; C. 1966 £15.

J. Milton. *Areopagitica*... 1907. 300 £1 5s.; 25 on vellum £3 10s. S. 1965 £20; H. 1966 £25.

T. Carlyle. *Sartor Resartus*. 1907. 300 £2 10s.; 15 on vellum £12. C. 1964 £22; S. 1965 £20; C. 1966 £26; H. 1967 £27.

Catalogue Raisonné... 1908. 300 5s.   S. 1965 £5; S. 1965 £4.

R. Browning. *Men and Women.* 2 vols., 1908. 250 £4 4s.; 12 on vellum £21, some copies flourished.   S. 1964 £45; S. 1965 £20; S. 1965 orig. vellum by Doves bindery and flourished £40; C. 1966 £48.

T. J. Cobden-Sanderson. *Credo. Pleni sunt Coeli...* 1909. 250 £1 1s.; 12 on vellum £3 3s. S. 1965 £15.   C. 1968 £38.

Shakespeare. *Hamlet.* 1909. 250 £2 2s.; 15 on vellum £10 10s. H. 1963 £21; S. 1963 £16; S. 1965 £30; C. 1966 £32.

Shakespeare. *Sonnets.* 1909. 250 £1 10s.; 15 on vellum £7 10s. S. 1963 £19; S. 1965 £24; C. 1965 £28; C. 1966 £24.

G. P. Winship. *William Caxton.* 1909. 300 10s.; 15 on vellum £2 10s. S. 1965 £22.; S. 1967 in morocco by Doves bindery £52.

Goethe. *Faust.* Zweiter Theil. 1910. 250 £3 3s.; 22 on vellum £15 15s.; 3 on vellum with gold illuminated initials £40.

The City Planned. 1910. About 300.

The City Metropolitan. 1910. About 300.

R. Browning. *Dramatis Personae.* 1911. 250 £2 2s.; 15 on vellum £10 10s.   S. 1965 £20.

Pervigilium Veneris. 1911. 150 £1 1s.; 12 on vellum £5.   S. 1963 £11; S. 1965 £5; S. 1967 £9; S. 1967 1/12 on vellum £85; S. 1967 in morocco by Doves bindery £140.

S. Francis of Assisi. *Laudes Creaturarum.* 1911. 250 £1 1s.; 12 on vellum £5.   S. 1965 £20.

Goethe. *Leiden des Jungen Werther.* 1911. 200 £2; 20 on vellum £10; 5 on vellum with illuminated initials in gold £15.   S. 1965 £24.

W. Wordsworth. *A Decade of Years...* 1911. 200 £2 2s.; 12 on vellum £10 10s.   S. 1965 £25; S. 1965 1/12 on vellum £90; S. 1965 £16; C. 1966 £20.

In Principio...1911. 200 £1 1s.; 12 on vellum £3.   S. 1965 £16.

Catalogue Raisonné... 1911. 350 5s.   C. 1965 £8; S. 1965 £6.

Goethe. *Iphigenie auf Tauris*. 1912. 200 £2; 20 on vellum £10; 12 on vellum with illuminated intials in gold £15.

Shakespeare. *Anthony and Cleopatra*. 1912. 200 £2 2s.; 15 on vellum £10 10s. S. 1965 £22; C. 1966 £26.

Shakespeare. *Venus and Adonis*. 1912. 200 £2 2s.; 15 on vellum £5 5s. S. 1965 £22; C. 1966 £28; S. 1967 £24.

Shakespearian Punctuation. 1912. About 300.

Goethe. *Torquato Tasso*... 1913. 200 £2; 15 on vellum £10; 12 on vellum with illuminated initials in gold £15.

Prospice. 1913. About 300.

Shakespeare. *Julius Caesar*. 1913. 200 £2 2s.; 15 on vellum £10 10s. S. 1965 £22; C. 1966 £32.

On a Passage in Julius Caesar. 1913. About 300.

On a Passage in Anthony and Cleopatra. 1913. About 300.

Amantium Irae. Letters... 1914. 150 £2 2s.; 3 on vellum n.f.s.   S. 1963 'Apologia' lf. insrted, £10; S. 1963 Pres. copy. levt. mor. gt-tooled, g.e. £80; S. 1965 £14.

The New Science Museum. 1914. About 300.

Shakespeare. *Coriolanus*. 1914. 200 £2 2s.; 15 on vellum £10 10s. S. 1965 £18.

On a Passage in Shelley's Ode to Liberty. 1914. About 300.

Shelley. *Selected Poems*... 1914. 200 £2 2s.; 12 on vellum £12 12s.

Wordsworth's Cosmic Poetry. 1914. About 300.

Keats. *Selected Poems*... 1915. 200 £2 2s.; 12 on vellum £12 12s. S. 1965 £45.

Shakespeare. *Lucrece*. 1915. 175 £1 5s.; 10 on vellum £5 5s.   S. 1965 £9.

W. Wordsworth. *The Prelude*. 1915. 155 £3 3s.; 10 on vellum £15 15s. C. 1963 £22; S. 1965 £20; C. 1966 £26; S. 1967 1/10 on vellum in morocco by Doves bindery, £300.

Goethe. *Auserlesene Lieder . . .* 1916. 175 £3 3s.; 10 on vellum £15 15s. S. 1965 £26.

Towards an Empire of Science. 1916. About 300.

Literature and Science. 1916. About 300.

Catalogue Raisonné. 1916. 150 £2 2s.; 10 on vellum £10 10s. S. 1965 £30; S. 1965 £35.

G. Herbert. *Poems.* 1923. 300 (250) h.m.p. 10s 6d.; 25 morocco £1 11s 6d. S. 1963 £12; H. 1964 £10; S. 1967 1/43 in morocco £60.

H. Vaughan. *Poems.* 1924. 500 (450) h.m.p. £1 11s 6d.; 25 morocco £3 3s. S. 1963 £13; S. 1963 £11; S. 1967 1/30 in morocco £75.

J. C. Hughes. *Caneuon Céiriog: Poems in Welsh.* 1925. 400 (350) h.m.p. £1 1s.; 25 morocco £3 13s 6d. S. 1963 £6; H. 1966 £7; S. 1967 1/30 in morocco £70.

T. G. Jones. *Detholiad o Ganiadau. Collected Poems.* 1926. 450 15s.; 25 morocco £2 12s 6d. S. 1963 £7; S. 1965 £7; S. 1963 1/26 mor. gt. £46; S. 1967 1/26 in morocco £80.

E. Thomas. *Chosen Essays.* 1926. 250 £1 5s.; 50 h.m.p., morocco £4 14s 6d. S. 1963 £9; S. 1964 £10; C. 1966 £2; S. 1967 1/33 in morocco £90.

E. Thomas. *Selected Poems.* 1927. 250 £1 5s.; 25 morocco £7 7s. S. 1963 £10; S. 1964 £12; H. 1966 £7; S. 1966 £14; S. 1967 1/25 in morocco £80.

Life of Saint David. ed. E. Rhys. 1927. 150 h.m.p. £5 5s.; 25 morocco £12 10s 6d. S. 1963 vell. £40; S. 1967 1/25 in morocco £120.

Llyfr y Pregethwr: The Book of Ecclesiastes in Welsh. 1927. 225 h.m.p. 12s 6d.; 25 morocco £4 14s 6d. S. 1963 £8; S. 1967 1/25 in morocco £75.

Lord Herbert of Cherbury. *Autobiography.* 1928. 275 h.m.p. £4 4s. 25 morocco £11 11s. S. 1963 £15; S. 1964 1/25 mor. £70; S. 1967 1/25 in morocco £110.

W. H. Davies. *Selected Poems.* 1928. 310 S. 1963 £11; H. 1963 £7; H. 1966 £8; S. 1967 1/25 in morocco £100.

R. Davies. *An Account of the Convincement...* 1928. 150 h.m.p. £2 2s.; 25 morocco. S. 1963 £5; S. 1964 levt. mor., t.e.g. £26; S. 1967 1/25 in morocco £55.

Penillion Omar Khayyam... by Sir J. M. Jones. 1928. 285 h.m.p. 15s.; 25 morocco. S. 1963 £8; S. 1967 1/25 in morocco £65.

T. L. Peacock. *Misfortunes of Elphin.* 1929. 175 h.m.c. £2 2s.; 25 morocco. S. 1963 £12; S. 1966 £12; H. 1967 £13; S. 1967 1/25 in morocco £90.

W. H. Davies. *Selected Poems.* 1929. 285 bds. £1 11s 6d.; 25 morocco. H. 1964 £6 5s; S. 1967 1/25 in morocco £100.

Psalmau Dafydd: The Book of Psalms in Welsh... 1929. 175 h.m.p. £5 5s.; 25 morocco. S. 1963 mor.-bkd. bds. £18; S. 1964 £26; S. 1967 1/25 in morocco £75.

Christina Rossetti. *Poems*, chosen by W. de la Mare... 1930. 275 marbled paper bds. £2 12s 6d.; 25 morocco £8 18s 6d. S. 1962 £8; S. 1963 £18; S. 1963 £15; H. 1966 £10; S. 1967 1/25 in morocco £140.

Abu Obeyd. *The Stealing of the Mare.* Trans. Lady Anne Blunt... 1930. 250 Japan. vellum £4 4s.; 25 morocco £8 8s. S. 1963 £18; S. 1963 £17; P. 1964 £17; S. 1966 £22; S. 1967 1/25 in morocco £110.

League of Nations Union-Welsh National Council Advisory Education Committee, Order of Service. 5 vols. 1930-36 S. 1965 £9.

C. Lamb. *Elia and the Last Essays of Elia.* 2 vols. 1931. 260 buckram £5 5s.; 25 morocco £10 10s. S. 1962 £16; S. 1963 £18; S. 1963 £22; S. 1967 1/25 in morocco £75.

Euripides. *Eight Plays* trans. G. Murray. 2 vols. 1931. 475 h.m.p. £12 12s.; 25 morocco £21. S. 1963 £24; S. 1964 £28; S. 1966 £26; S. 1967 2 vols. in 1, 1/25 in morocco £210.

J. Milton. *Comus.* 1931. 225 bds. £1 15s.; 25 morocco £8 8s. S. 1963 £17; S. 1967 £16; S. 1967 1/25 in morocco £120.

The Fables of Aesop trans. W. Caxton. 1931. 225 h.m.p. £5 5s.; 25 morocco £12.12s. S. 1963 £38; S. 1964 £48; H. 1966 £22. C. 1967 1/25 morocco £45; S. 1967 1/25 in morocco £170.

W. J. Gruffyd. *Caniadau.* 1932. 375. h.m.p. £1 1s.; 25 morocco £6 6s.

S. 1963 £10; S. 1967 1/25 in morocco £100.

R. Vansittart. *The Singing Caravan*. 1932. 225 h.m.p. £2 2s.; 25 morocco £10 10s.   S. 1966 £22; S. 1967 1/25 in morocco £130.

S. Butler. *Erewhon*. 1932. 275 Japan. vellum £3 3s.; 25 morocco £8 8s. S. 1963 £13; S. 1967 £28; S. 1967 1/25 in morocco £150.

The Revelation of St. John the Divine. 1932. 246 red cf. £6 6s.; nos. 1-15, 102, 242, 243 morocco £12 12s.   S. 1963 £26; S. 1963 £18; S. 1965 £25; S. 1967 1/18 in morocco £210.

O. Edwards. *Clych Atgof*. 1933. 385 h.m.p. £1 1s.; 15 morocco £5 5s. S. 1964 £10; S. 1967 1/15 in morocco £65.

J. Milton. *Four Poems*... 1933. 235 calf £2 2s.; 15 morocco £7 7s. S. 1963 £20; S. 1967 1/14 in morocco £100.

XXI Welsh Gypsy Folk-Tales. Collected by J. Sampson. 1933. 235 sheepskin £3 3s.; 15 morocco £8 8s.   S. 1963 £12; S. 1963 £16; S. 1967 1/15 in morocco £170.

T. Jones. *Theme with Variations*. 1933. 175.   S. 1963 £5; S. 1964 £7.

The Lamentations of Jeremiah. 1933. (250), nos. 16-129 and 240-250 in calf, 130-239 in blue goatskin £5 5s.; 15 black morocco £12 12s. S. 1963 £22; S. 1964 £22; S. 1967 1/15 in morocco £200.

W. H. Davies. *The Lovers' Song-Book*. 1933. 232 marbled bds.; nos. 1-15, £1 1s.; 202, 226, 227 morocco £6 6s.   S. 1963 £11; S. 1963 £7; S. 1967 1/19 in morocco £100.

S. de Madariaga. *Don Quixote: An Introductory Essay in Psychology*. 1934. 235 bds. £2 2s.; 15 morocco £6 6s.   S. 1963 £15; P. 1964 £8; S. 1967 1/15 in morocco £85.

L. Haberly. *Anne Boleyn and other Poems*. 1934. 285 morocco £1 1s.; nos. 1-15 polished morocco £4 4s.   S. 1963 unpold. mor. gt. £20; H. 1964 £21; S. 1965 £18; S. 1965 £9; S. 1967 £20; S. 1967 1/15 in elaborate morocco £75.

Lope de Vega. *The Star of Seville*. 1935. 160 black morocco £3 3s.; 15
216

purple morocco £8 8s. S. 1963 mor. gt. and blind tooled, t.e.g. £30; S. 1963 £20; S. 1966 £22; S. 1967 1/16 in maroon morocco £120.

R. Bridges. *Eros and Psyche*. 1935. 285 pigskin £5 5s.; 15 green morocco £12 12s. S. 1963 £20; H. 1963 £16; S. 1964 £26; S. 1964 £15; S. 1967 1/15 in green morocco £150.

Xenophon's *Cyropaedia*... 1936. 135 green morocco £6 6s.; nos. 1-15 brown morocco £15 15s. S. 1963 mor. gt., t.e.g. £66; S. 1963 £42; S. 1967 1/15 in brown morocco £380.

J. W. Fortescue. *The Story of a Red Deer*. 1936. 235 cloth £1 5s.; 15 morocco £7 7s. S. 1963 £11; S. 1964 £14; S. 1965 £10; S. 1967 1/15 in morocco £130.

Distressed Areas of South Wales – Conference on Social Reconstruction, Order of Service. 4 vols. 1934-36. S. 1965 £8.

Fulke Greville, Lord Brooke. *Caelica* ed. Una Ellis-Fermor. 1937 210 pattern paper bds. £1. 15s.; 15 morocco £8. 8s. S. 1967 1/15 in morocco £120.

South Wales Girls' Camp – Order of Service. 6 vols., 1932-37. S. 1965 £9.

The History of Saint Louis by John, Lord of Joinville. 1937. 185 maroon morocco £6. 6s.; 15 blue morocco £14. 14s. S. 1933 mor. gt., t.e.g. £65; S. 1964 mor. gt. t.e.g. £50; S. 1967 1/15 in blue morocco £290.

J. E. Hartzenbusch. *The Lovers of Teruel*. 1938. 146 red goatskin £2. 2s.; 29 green morocco £9. 9s. S. 1964 niger goat, t.e.g. £38; S. 1966 orig. morocco, t.e.g. £32; S. 1967 1/20 in green morocco £110.

A. de Guavara. *The Praise and Happinesse of the Countrie-Life*. 1938. 380 bds. 10s. 6d.; 20 morocco £2. 12s. 6d. S. 1964 £16; S. 1967 1/20 in morocco £55.

National Council of Music – Annual Conference, Order of Service. July 1932, October 1936, 1937 and Sept. 1938. 4 vols. S. 1965 £6.

G. B. Shaw. *Shaw Gives Himself Away: An Autobiographical Miscellany*.

1938. 277 green morocco with orange inlays £3 3s.; 3-15, 18-25, 1-2, 16-17 in dark green morocco £9 9s.   S. 1963 mor. £30; S. 1965 orig. mor. with orange inlays £70; H. 1966 £43; S. 1966 £35; S. 1967 1/21 dark green morocco £170.

E. Wynne. *Gweledigaetheu y Bardd Cwsc (Visions of the Sleeping Bard)* trans. T. G. Jones. 1940. 155 cloth £1 5s.; 20 morocco £9 9s.
S. 1963 £24; S. 1967 1/20 in morocco £130.

Lascelles Abercrombie. *Lyrics and Unpublished Poems.* 1940. 155 marbled bds. £1 5s.; 20 morocco £10 10s. S. 1963 £13; S. 1967 1/20 in morocco £110.

A. E. Coppard. *Adam and Eve, and Pinch Me.* 340 bds. 4s 6d.; 160 canvas or buckram 6s.; 2nd edn. July 1921 500 bds. 6s.; 3rd edn. Dec. 1921 (1000) 100 bds. 900 Jonathan Cape 7s 6d.
S. 1962 £6; S. 1965 £13.

H. T. Wade Gery. *Terpischore and other Poems.* 1921. (350) 3s 6d.; 2nd. edn. (350) 4s 6d.; 20 h.m.p. 7s 6d.

J. D. Beresford. *Signs and Wonders.* 1921. (1500) bds. 5s.; buckram 6s 6d.

A. E. Coppard. *Clorinda Walks in Heaven.* 1922. (1200) bds. 6s 6d.; 430 Jonathan Cape 7s 6d.; 25 h.m.p. 15s.

Havelock Ellis. *Kanga Creek.* 1922. 1375 bds. 4s 6d.; 25 h.m.p. (?) 15s.

M. Armstrong. *The Puppet Show.* 1922. 1200 bds. 6s 6d.; 25 h.m.p. 15s 6d.; 2nd edn. 1923 (1500) 6s 6d. S. 1962 Sigd.-cl.-bkd. bds. £7.

A. E. Coppard. *Hips and Haws.* 1922. 480 bds. 6s 6d.; 25 h.m.p. 15s 6d.; 2nd edn. 1923 (1500) 6s 6d.

R. Hughes. *Gipsy Night...* 1922. (750) 4s 6d.

P. Quennell. *Masques and Poems.* 1922. (375) 7s 6d.; (500) paper 2s 6d.; 35 signed £3 3s.

Sir T. Browne. *Hydrotaphia.* 1923. (115) £1 1s.

— *The Garden of Cyrus.* 1923. (115) £1 1s.

— *Religio Medici.* 1923. (115) £1 11s 6d.

— *Letter to a Friend...* 1923. (115) £1 11s 6d.   S. 1964 £7

E. Spenser. *Wedding Songs.* 1923. 350 bds. 7s 6d.; 25 Japanese vellum numbered £1 1s.

[Apuleius]... *Golden Asse.* 1923. 450 bds. £1 16s.   P. 1967 £6.

J. Taylor. *Selection*, ed. M. Armstrong. 1923. (350) £1 11s 6d.

Longus. *Daphnis and Chloe*, trans. G. Thornley. 1923. (450) 18s 6d. [1930 (97 illus.) J. E. Laboureur £3 3s.] S. 1966 £5.

Brantome. *Lives of Gallant Ladies*. 2 vols. 1924. 625 £3 3s.; 75 qtr. parchment, signed £6 6s.; 18 h.m.p., qtr. leather £18 18s.
S. 1962 £11; S. 1965 £18; S. 1965 £14; P. 1965 £8 10s.; S. 1966 £16.

Rochefoucault. *Moral Maxims*. 1924. (325) 13s.

H. Carey. *Songs and Poems*. 1924. 350 qtr. parchment 18s 6d.; 30 vellum £2 2s.   H. 1966 £5 10s.; S. 1966 £7.

H. Thoreau. *Where I Lived...* 1924. 350 qtr. parchment 8s 6d.; 30 morocco £1 15s.

Henry VIII. *Miscellaneous Writings*, ed. F. Macnamara. 1924. 300 qtr. parchment £1 16s.; 35 h.m.p. £3 3s.

J. Swift. *Directions to Servants*. 1925. 350 qtr. parchment 18s 6d.; 30 vellum £2 2s.   C. 1968 £9.

Havelock Ellis. *Sonnets... from the Spanish*. 1925. (500) 12s 6d.

Enid Clay. *Sonnets and Verses*. 1925. (450) 15s.   S. 1962 £2; S. 1966 £6; S. 1966 £8; C. 1968 £4.

R. Browning. *Pictor Ignotus...* 1925. (360) 17s 6d.   S. 1965 £6.

J. Swift. *Selected Essays*, ed. R. E. Roberts. 1925. (450) 18s 6d.

R. Burns. *Songs*. 1925. (450) 16s.   S. 1967 £3.

C. Cibber. *Apology for the Life of —* 2 vols., 1925 (450) £1 16s.

Samson and Delilah. 1925. (325) 18s 6d.   S. 1965 limp morocco gt., t.e.g. £7; C. 1968 £8.

Song of Songs. 1925. 720 buckram £1 1s.; 30 illus. hand col'd £5 5s. S. 1963 £10; S. 1964 £12; S. 1965 £14; S. 1965 £16; S. 1966 £20; S. 1966 £12; S. 1966 £16; C. 1968 1/30 £45; C. 1968 £16.

The Nativity. 1925. (370) 17s 6d.

J. Swift. *Gulliver's Travels*. 2 vols., 1925. 450 £3 3s. 30 h.m.p. signed
220

£6 6s.   S. 1963 £1.

E. P. Mathers. *Red Wise.* (500) 17s 6d.

The Passion... 1926. (250) £1 5s.   S. 1965 £11; S. 1965 £16; C. 1968 £16.

H. Fielding. *Apology for the Life of Mrs. Shamela Andrews*, ed. R. B. Johnson. 1926. (450) 15s.

E. P. Mathers. *Procreant Hymn.* 1926. (200) £2 2s.   S. 1962 £12; C. 1968 £16.

E. Sharpham. *Cupid's Whirligig.* 1926. (550) 15s.

L. Carlell. *Osmond the Great Turk.* 1926. 15s.

Book of Jonah. 1926. (175) £1 5s.   S. 1964 £20; C. 1968 £24.

Chamfort. *Maxims and Considerations.* 2 vols. 1926. (550) £1 10s.

L. Carlell. *The Fool would be a Favorit.* 1926. (550) 15s.

A. E. Coppard. *Pelegea...* 1926. (425) 15s.

F. Coventry. *Pompey the Little.* 1926. (400) 18s 6d.

E. Gill. *Id Quod Visum Placet.* 1926. 150.   S. 1967 £16.

Aesop. *Fables*, trans. R. L'Estrange. 1926. (350) 17s 6d.

J. Marston. *Metamorphosis of Pigmalion's Image.* 1926. (325). 12s 6d.

T. Carew. *A Rapture.* 1927. (375) 12s 6d.

W. Shenstone. *Men and Manners.* 1927 (500) 15s.

Sir J. Suckling. *Ballad Upon a Wedding.* 1927. (375) 12s 6d.

G. Chaucer. *Troilus and Criseyde.* 1927. 218 £10 10s.; 6 on vellum £42. S. 1964 £80; S. 1966 £75; S. 1967 1/6 on vellum £850; C. 1968 £160.

E. Gill. *Art and Love.* 1927.   S. 1962 1/35 in vellum £20; S. 1966 1/35 in vellum £42; C. 1968 1/260 £10.

N. Breton. *The Twelve Moneths.* 1927 (500) 17s 6d.

Chester Play of the Deluge. 1927. (275) £1 10s. S. 1962 £4; S. 1967 £12;
C. 1968 £20.

Lucian. *The True Historie.* 1927. (275) £3 3s.   S. 1962 £10; S. 1966 £18;
S. 1967 £28; C. 1968 £35.

Psalms of David. 1928. (500) 16s. S. 1966 £6.

J. Earle. *Micro-Cosmographie.* 1928. (400) £1 5s.

Ladie's Handbook of Etiquette. 1928. (500) 15s.

A. E. Coppard. *Count Stefan.* 1928. (600) 16s.

J. Swift. *Miscellaneous Poems.* 1928. (375). 18s 6d.

L. Sterne. *Sentimental Journey.* 1928. (50). £1 1s.

J. Tellier. *Abd-er-Rhaman in Paradise.* 1928. (500) 16s.

E. Gill. *Art and Prudence.* 1928. (500) 17s 6d. C. 1968 £6.

J. Keats. *Lamia...* 1928. 485 £3 3s.; 15 on vellum £37 16s.
S. 1963 £11; S. 1965 £16; S. 1966 £15; C. 1968 £22.

G. Chaucer. *Canterbury Tales.* 4 vols., 1929. 485 £6 6s.; 15 on vellum
£30 5s.   S. 1963 £78; S. 1963 £80; S. 1965 £115; 1966 £95; S. 1966
£140; S. 1967 1/15 on vellum £1900; C. 1968 £190.

Circle of the Seasons. 1929. (500) £1 10s.

Sir T. More. *Utopia.* 1929. (500) £1 16s.   S. 1963 £13; S. 1965 £11.

L. Sterne. *Tristram Shandy.* 3 vols., 1929-30. (500) £2 2s.
H. 1963 £7 10s.

L. Andreyev. *Abyss.* 1929 (500) 12s 6d.

A. Smith. *Atrocities of the Pirates.* 1929. (500) 15s.

Plato. *Phaedo* trans. B. Jowett. 1930. (500) £1 16s.   S. 1963 £8;
C. 1968 £10.

Lucina sine Concubitu. 1930. (500) 15s.

222

S. Gantillon. *Maya*. 1930. (500) £1 15s.

R. Gibbings. *The Seventh Man*. 1930. (500) 12s 6d.

H. Fielding. *Journey from this World . . .* 1930 (500) £1 10s.

A. E. Coppard. *Hundredth Story*. 1931. (1000) £1 1s. S. 1962 £2.

E. Gill. *Clothing without Cloth*. 1931. (500) 16s.
S. 1966 £7; S. 1966 £11; S. 1967 £8; C. 1968 £12.

T. F. Powys. *When Thou wast Naked*. 1931. (500) £1 1s.

G. Flaubert. *Salambo*. 1931. (500) £3 3s.

The Four Gospels. 1931. 488 £8 8s.; 12 on vellum £84.
S. 1963 £75, £80; S. 1965 £125; S. 1966 £ 120; S. 1967 £170.

Initiation. 1932. (325) 12s 6d. C. 1968 £6.

Ovid. *Amores*. 1932. (350) £2 2s. C. 1964 £12; S. 1965 £8; S. 1965
£10; S. 1967 £14.

H. E. Bates. *A German Idyll*. 1932. (307) 17s 6d. S. 1965 £6; S. 1966 £5.

W. Shakespeare. *Twelfth Night*. 1932. (275) £3 3s. S. 1963 £11;
C. 1968 £18.

H. Fielding. *Life of Mr. Jonathan Wild . . .* 1932. (350) £1 10s.

A. E. Coppard. *Crotty Shinkwin*. 1932. (500) £1 1s. S. 1966 £4.

Consequences . . . 1932. 1000 6s.; 200 numbered, signed £2 2s.

Rummy . . . 1932. 1000 6s.; 250 numbered, signed £1 1s.

R. Davies. *Daisy Matthews . . .* 1932. (325) £1 1s.

H. Walpole. *The Apple Trees*. 1932. (500) £1 1s.

Lord Dunsany. *Lord Adrian*. 1933. (325) £1 1s.

H. E. Bates. *The House with the Apricot*. 1933. (300) £1 1s.

L. Powys. *Glory of Life*. 1934. 275 £3 3s.; 2 on vellum £31 10s. C. 1968
£38.

E. Gill. *The Lord's Song*. 1934. (500) 12s. 6d.   C. 1965 £6; C. 1967 £9.

Apuleius. *Cupid and Psyche*, trans. W. Adlington. 1934. (150) 16s.

Sermons by Artists. 1934. (300) £1 1s.

W. Bligh and J. Fryer. *Harriet and Mary*. 1934. C. 1965 1/50 morocco
£20.

Voyage of the Bounty's Launch ... 1934. (300) £2 2s.   S. 1962 £17.

R. H. Mottram. *Strawberry Time*. 1934. (250) £1 1s.

Book of Ecclesiastes. 1934. 247 £3 3s.; 3 on vellum £31 10s.

Cosmetics for My Lady. 1934. (300) 10s. 6d.

A. Calder-Marshall. *A Crime against Cania*. 1934. (250) £1 1s.

F. Toussaint. *The Garden of Caresses*. 1934. 275 £1 4s. Full vellum with
additional engrs. £5 5s.

E. Clay. *The Constant Mistress*. 1934. 200 15s.; 50 morocco with
addit'n'l set engrs. £2 2s.   S. 1964 1/50 morocco £16; S. 1967 £4;
C. 1968 1/50 in morocco £10.

J. Morrison. *Journal*. 1935. (325) £3 3s.   S. 1965 £32; S. 1966 £24;
C. 1968 £35.

J. Lindsay. *Storm at Sea*. 1935. (250) £1 1s.

Mr. Glasspoole and the Chinese Pirates. 1935. (315) 18s.   H. 1965 £5.

L. A. G. Strong. *The Hansom Cab and the Pigeons*. 1935. (200) 6s.

H. E. Bates. *Flowers and Faces*. 1935. 259 £2 2s. 60 h.m.p. £5 5s.; 6 on
vellum £15 15s.

Evadne Lascaris. *The Golden Bed of Kydno*. 1935. 140 £3 3s.; 60 morocco £5 5s.

Grammont. *Heartsease and Honesty*. 1935. 275 12s. 6d. 25 h.m.p.
£1 11s. 6d.

O. Chase, T. Chappel and G. Pollard. *Wreck of the Whale-Ship Essex* ...

1935. (275) £2 2s.   S. 1962 £13; S. 1965 £24.

The Song of Songs. 1936. 135 £4 4s.; 65 h.m.p. £8 8s.; 4 on vellum £52 10s.

P. Miller. *The Green Ship.* 1936. 134 £2 2s.; 62 morocco £5 5s. 4 on vellum £52 10s.   S. 1962 1/62 £14; S. 1967 £9; S. 1966 1/62 morocco £16.

T. E. Lawrence. *Crusader Castles.* 2 vols., 1936. (1000) £5 5s.
C. 1962 £28; S. 1964 £36; S. 1964 £48; S. 1966 £60; S. 1967 £90; S. 1967 £95.

E. P. Mathers. *Love Night.* 1936. 120 £2 2s.; 75 bnd. vellum £6 6s.; 5 on vellum £52 10s.   S. 1963 £5; S. 1966 £12; S. 1967 1/75 orig. vellum £24.

Nancy Quennell. *The Epicures Anthology.* 1936. 7s 6d.; 150 calf £2 2s.

A. S. Pushkin. *Tale of the Golden Cockerel.* 1936. 3s 6d.; 100 numbered £1 11s. 6d.

Chanticleer, a Bibliography... 1936. 2s 6d. 300 numbered £1 1s. S. 1966 £4.

W. Bligh. *The Log of the Bounty.* 2 vols., 1937. (300) £6 6s.
S. 1965 £42; S. 1965 £50; S. 1966 £50.

L. Powys. *The Book of Days.* 1937. 245 £4 4s.; 50 morocco £7 7s.; 5 on vellum £52. 10s.   H. 1963 £5 5s.; C. 1965 1/50 morocco £22; H. 1966 1/50 morocco £32.

J. Milton. *Paradise Lost.* 1937. 196 £10 10s.; 4 on vellum £105.

Bligh's Voyage in the Resource. 1937. (350) £3 3s.   S. 1965 £24.

A Croppe of Kisses... Ben Jonson. 1937. 200 £2 2s.; 50 morocco £5 5s. S. 1962 £13; S. 1964 £12; S. 1966 1/50 morocco £18.

P. Miller. *Ana the Runner.* 1937. 8s 6d.; 150 numbered £1 10s. S. 1966 1/150 h.m.p. £12.

The First Fleet... 1937. 370 £3 3s.; 5 morocco £12 12s.   S. 1962 £9.

Joan Rutter. *Here's Flowers*. 1937. 8s 6d.; 200 numbered £2 2s.

C. Whitfield. *Mr. Chambers and Persephone*. 1937. 8s 6d.; 150 numbered £1 10s.

Elisabeth Geddes. *Animal Antics*. 1937. 3s. 6d.

Roses of Sharon. 1937. 115 £2 2s.; 10 pigskin £5 5s.

T. F. Powys. *Goat Green*... 1937. 8s 6d.; 150 h.m.p. £1 10s.

Golden Cockerel *Greek Anthology*. 1937. 126 £5 5s.; 74 hf. pigskin £12 12s.; 6 on vellum £78 15s. H. 1963 £6; S. 1965 £12; S. 1967 hf. morocco £26; S. 1966 1/74 h m.p., orig. cl. gt. £18.

Lacombe. *Compendium of the East*. 1937. 290 £3 3s.; 10 morocco £15 15s.

T. Gautier. *Mademoiselle de Maupin*. 1938. 450 £3 3s.; 50 vellum £8 8s. H. 1962 £4 15s.; S. 1964 £6; S. 1965 1/50 orig. vellum £15; S. 1966 £18; S. 1967 1/50 orig. vellum £30.

V. G. Calderon. *The White Llama*. 1938. 8s 6d.; 75 h.m.p. £1 10s.

L. Cranmer-Byng. *Tomorrow's Star*. 1938. 7s 6d.

H. Swire. *The Voyage of the Challenger*. 2 vols., 1938. (300) £8 8s. S. 1964 £30.

Nancy Quennell. *A Lover's Progress*. 1938. 190 £3 3s.; 25 morocco £6 6s. S. 1962 £7; H. 1966 £10 10s.; S. 1966 £8.

De Brebeuf. *Travels and Sufferings of—*. 1938. (300) £3 3s. S. 1962 £11; C. 1965 £15.

A. E. Coppard. *Tapster's Tapestry*. 1938. 8s 6d. 75 morocco £1 10s.

Golden Cockerel *Rubaiyat*... 1938. 270 £3 3s.; 30 white morocco, signed £15 15s. S. 1963 £15; S. 1963 orig. qtr. morocco £17; C. 1965 £18; S. 1965 £24; S. 1966 £32.

L. Binyon. *Brief Candles*. 1938. 3s. 6d.; 100 h.m.p. £1 11s 6d. S. 1966 1/100 £15.

T. Besterman. *The Pilgrim Fathers*... 1939. (300) £2 2s. C. 1965 £6.
226

The Vigil of Venus, trans. F. L. Lucas. 1939 (100) £10 10s. S. 1962 £17.

H. G. Wells. *The Country of the Blind*. 1939. 250 £2 2s.; 30 vellum £5 5s.

C. Whitfield. *Lady from Yesterday*. 1939. 8s. 6d.; 50 h.m.p. £1 10s.

The Wisdom of the Cymry, trans. Winifred Faraday. 1939. 5s.; 60 h.m.p. £2 2s.

T. E. Lawrence. *Secret Despatches from Arabia*. 1939. 970 £3 3s.; 30 pigskin £15 15s.

John Fryer of the Bounty... 1939. (300) £2 2s.   H. 1962 £8 15s.; C. 1965 £11.

Gertrude Bell. *The Arab War*. 1940. 470 £2 2s.; 30 morocco £10 10s. S. 1962 £7; S. 1964 £4; S. 1965 1/30 morocco £14; S. 1966 £7.

T. E. Lawrence. *Men in Print*. 1940. 470 £2 2s.; 30 morocco £10 10s. S. 1966 £22.

Glue and Lacquer... 1941. 320 £2 2s.; 30 morocco £10 10s.
S. 1964 £13; H. 1964 £9 10s.; S. 1966 £10; H. 1966 £4 5s.; C. 1967 1/30 morocco £32.

W. H. Hudson. *Letters to R. B. Cunninghame Graham*... 1941. (250) £1 10s.

Shaw-Ede. *T. E. Lawrence's Letters to H. S. Ede*. 1942. 470 £2 12s 6d.; 30 morocco £10 10s.   C. 1965 £11; S. 1966 £13.

A. C. Swinburne. *Lucretia Borgia*... 1942. 320 £4 4s.; 30 morocco £15 15s.   S. 1965 1/30 morocco £16; S. 1965 1/30 morocco £32; S. 1966 £8; P. 1967 £15.

The Tenbury Letters. 1943 (300) £2 2s.

H. St. J. B. Philby. *A Pilgrim in Arabia*. 1943. 320 £3 3s.; 30 morocco £10 10s.

S. de Chair. *The Golden Carpet*. 1943. 470 £3 3s.; 30 morocco £10 10s.

Pertelote. 1943. 2s 6d.; qtr. morocco £1 11s 6d.

S. de Chair. *The Silver Crescent*. 1943. 470 £3 3s.; 30 morocco £10 10s.
S. 1962 £5.

T. J. Hogg. *The Athenians*... 1943. 300 £3 3s.; 50 morocco £10 10s.
C. 1965 1/50 morocco £18.

A. C. Swinburne. *Hymn to Proserpine*. 1944. 300 15s.; 50 morocco
£5 5s.

The Ninety-First Psalm. 1944. 300 12s.; 50 morocco £4 4s.

Harriet and Mary. 1944. 450 £3 3s.; 50 morocco £10 10s.
C. 1965 1/50 morocco £20.

A. Sparrman. *A Voyage Round the World*... 1944. 300 £4 4s.; 50
morocco £15 15s.   H. 1965 £26; C. 1968 £38.

Shelley at Oxford... 1944. 450 £3 3s.; 50 morocco £10 10s.
C. 1965 £22.

V. G. Calderon. *The Lottery Ticket*. 1945. 300 15s.; 100 qtr. morocco
£1 10s.

C. Whitfield. *Together and Alone*. 1945. 400 £1 1s.; 100 qtr. morocco
£2 2s.

Napoleon. *Supper at Beaucaire*. 1945. 400 7s 6d.; 100 in vellum £3 3s.

Napoleon. *Memoirs*. 2 vols., 1945. 450 £6 6s.; 50 morocco £31 10s.

The First Crusade. 1945. 400 £5 5s.; 100 in vellum £21.   H. 1962 £5;
S. 1962 in vellum £12; S. 1964 in vellum £18 S. 1966 £10.

G. Jones. *The Green Island*. 1946. 400 £2 2s.; 100 morocco £4 4s.

Matthew Flinders' *Voyage in Schooner 'Francis'*... 1946. 650 £4 4s.;
100 morocco £21.   S. 1964 1/100 mor. £24; H. 1966 1/100 mor. £28;

H. 1966 £7 10s. S. 1967 1/100 morocco £48.

O. Rutter. *We Happy Few*. 1946. 650 £1 10s.; 100 morocco £5 5s.

228

T. Gray. *Elegy written in a Country Churchyard.* 1946. 670 £1 5s.; 80 morocco £4 4s.

P. de Heriz. *La Belle O' Morphi.* 1947. 650 £1 10s.; 100 hf. morocco £4 4s.

P. Miller. *Woman in Detail.* 1947. 430 £1 10s.; 100 qtr. morocco £4 4s.

J. Keats. *Endymion.* 1947. 400 £7 7s.; 100 in vellum £21.   S. 1964 1/100 in vellum £26; C. 1965 £11; H. 1966 £13 10s.; S. 1966 £32; S. 1966 £22; S. 1967 £16.

Mabinogion. 1948. 475 £10 10s.; 75 morocco £31 10s.   H. 1962 £19 10s.; S. 1965 £30; P. 1966 £18; H. 1966 1/75 morocco £38.

Homeric Hymn to Aphrodite. 1948. 650 £4 4s.; 100 morocco £12 12s. H. 1962 £5 5s.; C. 1964 £8; C. 1965 £6; S. 1963 1/100 morocco £24; S. 1966 £4; S. 1967 1/100 morocco £30.

A. C. Swinburne. *Laus Veneris.* 1948. 650 £1 11s. 6d.; 100 morocco £6 6s.   S. 1964 1/100 morocco £16; S. 1967 1/100 morocco £24.

S. Johnson. *The New London Letter-Writer . . .* 1948. 400 £1 10s.; 100 qtr. morocco £4 4s.

F. L. Lucas. *Gilgamesh, King of Erech.* 1948. 440 £1 11s 6d.; 60 hf. morocco £6 6s.

I. Bannet. *The Amazons.* 1948. 420 £5 5s.; 80 morocco £15 15s. H. 1962 £2 15s.; S. 1964 £4; S. 1964 £6.

J. B. Cabell. *Jurgen.* 1949. 400 qtr. cf. £5 10s.; 100 morocco, signed £15 15s.   S. 1962 £5; S. 1962 1/100 morocco £19.

Musaeus. Hero and Leander, transl. F. L. Lucas. 1949. 400 buckram £3 3s.; 100 vellum, signed £7 7s. S. 1967 £8; S. 1967 1/100 vellum £22.

Cockalorum. Bibliography of the Golden Cockerel Press. 1943-1948. 1949. Unlimited cl. 10s 6d.; 250 qtr. morocco £3 3s.

A. C. Swinburne. *Pasiphaë.* 1950. 400 buckram £2 12s 6d.; 100 vellum £6 16s 6d.   S. 1963 1/100 vellum £10; S. 1967 1/100 vellum £26.

J. A. Komensky. *The Labyrinth of the World*... transl. Count Lutzow. 1951. 300 canvas £7 10s.; 70 morocco £17 17s.

Caesar's Commentaries, transl. Somerset de Chair. 1951. 250 buckram £12 12s; 70 morocco £26 5s.   S. 1963 £3.

Salmacis and Hermaphroditus, transcribed Gwyn Jones. 1951. Paper wrpprs. £2 2s.; 300 blue fabric £7 7s.; 50 hf. morocco £12 12s.; 30 morocco £18 18s.; C. 1968 £12.

Sir Gawain and the Green Knight, transl. Gwyn Jones. 1951. Paper wrpprs. £2 2s.; green and pink fabrics £8 8s.; 60 morocco £21. S. 1963, orig. cl. £10; H. 1966 £5 10s.

Phyllis Hartnoll. *The Grecian Enchanted*. 1952. 300 in fabrics £7 7s.; 60 morocco £21.   S. 1963 1/60 morocco £22; S. 1967 £12.

Nelson's Letters... ed. G. Rawson. 1953. Paper wrpprs. £2 2s.; in fabrics £7 7s.; 60 morocco £21.   S. 1963 cl. gt. £7; H. 1966 £8.

Against Women... transl. Gwyn Williams. 1953. 250 fabric £5 5s.; 100 Indian lizard £14 14s.

Letters of Maria Edgeworth and Anna Laetitia Barbould... ed. W. S. Scott. 1953. 240 in fabrics £4 4s.; 60 qtr. white sheepskin £8 8s. S. 1966 1/60 £9.

Wm. Browne of Tavistock. *Circe and Ulysses*. 1954. 200 qtr. buckram £4 4s.; 100 morocco £12 12s.

Somerset de Chair. *The Story of a Lifetime*.1954. 100 sheepskin £29 8s (10 copies I-X ex editio).

J. Barclay. *Euphormio's Satyricon*, transl. P. Turner. 1954. Paper wrpprs. £2 2s.; qtr. canvas £7 7s.; 60 morocco £21.

Eurof Walters. *The Serpent's Presence*. 1954. Paper wrpprs. £1 11s 6d.; in fabrics £4 4s.; 60 hf. morocco £8 8s.

C. Stewart. *Topiary*... 1954. 300 hf. buckram £3 3s.; 100 hf. morocco £5 5s.   S. 1963 1/100 hf. morocco £2.

R. Herrick. *One Hundred and Eleven Poems*. 1955. 445 qtr. parchment £10 10s.; 105 sheepskin £21. S. 1963 1/105 £30; H. 1966 £18; P. 1967 1/105 £46.

The Saga of Llywarch the Old, reconstruction by Glyn Jones. 1955. 140 qtr. morocco £4 4s.; 60 morocco £ 8 8s.

P. B. Shelley. *Zastrozzi*... 1955. 140 qtr. morocco £5 5s.; 60 morocco £12 12s.

W. Russell Flint. *Minxes Admonished*... 1955. 400 qtr. morocco £10 10s.; 150 morocco £21. S. 1963 1/150 morocco £15.

Appollonius of Tyre, transl. P. Turner. 1956. 225 qtr. morocco £4 4s. 75 morocco £12 12s.

S. Mallarmé. *L'Apres-Midi d'un Faune*, transl. Aldous Huxley. 1956. Paper wrpprs. £1 11s 6d.; qtr. morocco £4 4s.; 100 morocco £10 10s.

Grimms' Other Tales... 1957. 425 fabric £5 5s.; 75 morocco £10 10s.

J. Dryden. *Songs and Poems*. 1957. 400 qtr. morocco £12 12s.; 100 morocco £25 4s. S. 1963 £5; P. 1964 £7.

Xenophon. *The Ephesian Story*, transl. P. Turner. 1957. 225 qtr. morocco £5 5s.; 75 morocco £12 12s.

Omar Khayyam. *Rubaiyat*, transl. E. Fitzgerald. 1958. 125 canvas £4 4s.; 75 morocco £8 8s. S. 1963 1/75 morocco £17.

Ovid. *Metamorphoses*... 1959. 125 canvas £8 8s.; 75 morocco £15 15s. S. 1963 1/75 morocco £26.

Wm. Cynwal. *In Defense of Women*, transl. Gwyn Williams. 1960. 400 fabric £5 5s.; 100 morocco £10 10s.

Shakespeare. *Poems and Sonnets*. 1960. 370 buckram £5 5s.; 100 morocco £10 10s.

W. Shakespeare. *Works*. Stratford Town Edn. Ed. A. H. Bullen. 10 vols. 1904-07. (1000) £10 10s.; (12 on vellum). C. 1964 £20; H. 1965 £28; C. 1966 cont. vellum gt. unc. £52.

W. Shakespeare. *Sonnets*. 1905. 7s 6d.

W. Shakespeare. *Venus and Adonis*, and *Songs*. 1905. 3s 6d.

Catullus. *Carmina recens*. S. G. Owen. 1906. 6s.

Anacreon, transl. T. Stanley. 1906. 6s.; (4 on vellum).

W. Drummond. *A Cypress Grove*. 1907. 2s 6d.

W. B. Yeats. *Collected Works*. 8 vols. 1908. S. 1963 £46; H. 1964 £60; P. 1966 qtr. vellum gt., g.t. £135.

The Italian Poets... transls. by D. G. Rossetti. 1908. 7s 6d.

W. B. Yeats. *Poems*. 2nd ser. 1910. 6s.

W. B. Yeats. *Deirdre*. 1911. S. 1964 £3 5s.

W. Shakespeare. *Sonnets*. 1912.

W. J. Lawrence. *The Elizabethan Playhouse*... 1st ser. 1912. 12s 6d.

— *Idem*. 2nd ser. 1913. 12s 6d. S. 1962 ex lib.-Peter Murray Hill. 2 vols. £17.

G. Harvey. *Marginalia*, ed. G. C. Moore-Smith. 1913. (780) 16s.

G. Villiers, D. of Buckingham. *The Rehearsal*, ed. M. Summers. 1914. 7s 6d. Also 510 10s 6d.

Mrs. Aphra Behn. *Works*. ed. M. Summers. 6 vols. 1915. $ 25.00; edn. de luxe $ 50.00. C. 1963 £22; S. 1964 Hf. mor. gt., g.t. £46; S. 1965 1/50 h.m.p. £70.

H. Dugdale Sykes. *Sidelights on Shakespeare*... 1919. 7s 6d.

W. Shakespeare. *Twenty-five Sonnets*. 1921. 2s 6d.; 325 on h.m.p.

10s 6d.

M. Drayton. *Nimphidia*... Publ. A. H. Bullen. 1921. 5s.

W. Shakespeare. *Sonnets*. 1921. 10s 6d.

W. Shakespeare. *Songs from*. 1921. 1s 6d.

P. B. Shelley. *Epipsychidion*. 1921. (500).

R. Hughes. *The Sisters' Tragedy*... 1922. 2s.

Horace. *Carminum*... ed. D. Godley. 1922. (150 l.p.c.).

W. Hemminge. *Elegy on Randolph's Finger*. [ed.] G. C. Moore-Smith. 1923. 3s 6d.

F. S. Boas. *Shakespeare and the Universities*... 1923. 12s 6d.

A. Tatius. *Loves of Clitophon and Leucippe*, transl. W. Burton... ed. S. Gaselee and H. F. B. Brett Smith. 1923. 494 (or 498) on h.m.p. £3 3s.; 2 (or 5) on vellum £31 10s. S. 1963 £2; C. 1966 1/5 vellum £48.

W. Shakespeare. *The Players' Shakespeare*.. introd. by Granville Barker. 7 vols. 1923-25. 450 rag paper £4 4s each; 100 h.m.p. £12 12s each.

Ernest Gimson, His Life and Work by W. R. Lethaby, A. H. Powell and F. L. Griggs. 1924. (550) £4 4s. S. 1967 mor. gt. £12; S. 1963 £12.

Ovid. *Hys Booke of Metamorphose*... ed. S. Gaselee and H. F. B. Brett-Smith. 1924. 375 h.m.p. £3 3s; 3 vellum £31 10s.

The Nutbrown Maid. 1925. 2s 6d; 55 h.m.p. £1 1s.

M. Drayton. *Nimphidia*... 1925. 2s 6d.

England's Helicon... ed. H. Macdonald, publ. Etchells & Macdonald. 1925. 900 £1 1s.; 59 h.m.p. £2 2s.

T. Smollett. *Novels*. 11 vols. 1925-26. £4 2s 6d. Also l.p.lib'y.edn 500 1926. S. 1963 £26; C. 1963 £18; H. 1965 £38.

Aucassin and Nicolette... trans. L. Housman. 1925. 5s.; 160 h.m.p. £1 1s.

M. Drayton. *Endimion and Phoebe* . . . ed. J. W. Hebel. 1925-26. 7s 6d.; 50 edn. de luxe numb. £1 5s.

W. Morris. *Defence of Guenevere.* 2s 6d. wrpprs.; 4s 6d bds. 55 h.m.p. £1 1s.

M. Drayton. *Ballad of Agincourt* . . . 1926. 2s 6d. Also 2s. 6d. wrpprs.; 4s 6d. bds.; 30 h.m.p.

H. Fielding. *Novels.* 10 vols. 1926. 800 cl. £3 15s.; 200 hf. leather £7 7s. 520 l.p.lib'y edn.   S. 1965 £38.

G. Gascoigne. *Hundreth Sundrie Flowers,* ed. B. M. Ward. Publ. Etchells & Macdonald. 1926. 400 £1 1s.; 50 h.m.p. £2 2s.

E. Hamilton Moore. *Fifteen Roses* . . . 1926-27. 250 7s 6d.; 100 h.m.p. £1 1s.

Omar Khayyam. *Rubaiyat.,* trans. E. Fitzgerald. 1926. 2s 6d. wrpprs.; 4s 6d bds.; 55 h.m.p. 1927 £1 1s.; re-issue leather bdg. 1928. 3s 6d.

The Phoenix Nest . . . ed. H. Macdonald. Publ. Etchells & Macdonald 1926. 500 bds. 18s.; 50 h.m.p. £2 2s.

S. Sitwell. *Doctor Donne and Gargantua* . . . Privately printed 1926. (65) Canto the Third S. 1964 £4.

L. Sterne. *Works.* 7 vols. 1926-27. (500) £2 12s. 6d.
H. 1963 £15 10s.; C. 1963 £24; H. 1965 £34; H. 1966 £29.

E. Coplestone. *Advice to a Young Reviewer.* 1927. 3s 6d.

Sir G. Etherege. *Works,* ed. H. F. B. Brett-Smith [2 vols. Plays]. 1927. 15s.; 3rd vol. *Poems and Letters.* 1930. 15s.

D. Defoe. *Novels* . . . etc. . . . 14 vols. 1927-28. £5 5s.; 500 l.p. lib'y edn. S. 1964 hf. cf. gt., g.t. £65; H. 1965 buckram £78.

F. L. Griggs. *The Campden Alphabet* . . . 1927. 100 £2 12s 6d.

H. D. Thoreau. *The Moon.* 1927. (500 for U.S.A.).

Froissart's *Cronycles of Englande, Fraunce, Spayne* . . . trans. Lord Berners. 8 vols. 1927-28. 350 (320) £26 5s.; 7 Jap. vellum and 7 vellum. S. 1964 £55; S. 1964 £60; S. 1964 unopnd £90; C. 1967 £95; S. 1967 1/7 Jap. vell. £280.

F. Bacon. *Essayes or Counsels Civill and Morall* . . . Publ. Cresset Press. 1928. 250 h.m.p. £10 10s.; 8 vellum £105. C. 1963 £6; C. 1966 £7; S. 1966 £8; S. 1967 £35; S. 1967 £22.

Plutarch. *Lives of the Noble Grecians and Romanes* . . . trans. Sir T. North. 8 vols. 1928. 500 £5. 500 $ 10 a vol., or in 3/4 levant $ 20 a vol. 100 h.m.p. numb'd. S. 1964 £30; S. 1964 hf. mor. gt., g.t. £55; S. 1964 1/100 h.m.p. £60; H. 1966 £34; C. 1967 £40.

G. Bret Harte. *The Villas of Pliny* . . . Houghton Mifflin Co. 1928. $ 7.50.

J. Bunyan. *Pilgrim's Progress* . . . 2vols. Cresset Press. 1928. 195 h.m.p. £17 6s 6d.; 10 vellum £157 10s. S. 1962 £9; S. 1967 £48.

The Collects . . . trans. by R. W. Macan. 1928. 250 h.m.p. £1 1s.

Pindar's *Odes of Victory: Olympian and Pythian Odes*, trans. C. J. Billson. 1930. 250 h.m.p. £3 13s 6d.

Pindar's *Odes of Victory: Nemean and Isthmian Odes*, trans. C. J. Billson. 1930. 250 h.m.p. £3 13s 6d.

G. Chaucer. *Works*, ed. A. W. Pollard. 8 vols. 1928-29. 375 (350) h.m.p. £26 5s.; 11 vellum. S. 1963 £60; S. 1965 unopnd. £68; C. 1967 £90.

M. Besley. *The Second Minuet* . . . 1929. bds. 5s.; 50 numb'd, signed 10s. 6d.

A. Trollope. *The Barchester Novels*, ed. M. Sadleir. 14 vols. 1929 £8 15s.; 500 l.p. lib'y edn. S. 1963 £60; H. 1964 £68; H. 1964 £78; P. 1965 £60; C. 1966 Hf. mor. gt., g.e. £170; S. 1966 £65.

Venerable Bede. *History of the Churche of Englande*, trans. T. Stapleton. 1929. Either 2 vols. bds. or 1 vol. leather spine. 450 h.m.p. £5 5s.; 10

vellum.   H. 1962 1 vol. £16 10s.; C. 1964 2 vols. £20; H. 1964 1 vol. £19; S. 1965 2 vols. £25; H. 1965 1 vol. £26; H. 1967 1 vol. £10; H. 1967 £5 15s.; S. 1967 2 vols. unopnd. £28.

S. Richardson. *Novels.* 21 vols. 1929-32. 600 £7 17s 6d.; l.p. lib'y edn. 100 £17 17s. S. 1962 1/100 £60; H. 1965 £52.

R. B. Sheridan. *The School for Scandal*, introd. R. Crompton Rhodes. 1930. h.m.p. 475 (450) £3 3s.

W. Shakespeare. *Twenty-five Sonnets.* 1930. (350) 2s 6d.

E. Spenser. *Works*, ed. W. L. Renwick. 8 vols. 1930. h.m.p. 350 £31 10s, 11 vellum.   S. 1963 £29; C. 1964 £32; H. 1964 £36; H. 1964 £38; H. 1965 £42; S. 1966 £44; C. 1967 £38.

A. Bierce. *Battle Sketches.* 1930 h.m.p. 350 £2 10s. Publ. First Ed'n Club £1 15s.

T. De Quincey. *Confessions of an English Opium Eater.* h.m.p. 1500. Publ. Ltd. Ed'ns Club $ 10.00.

Homer. *Whole Works*, trans. G. Chapman. 5 vols. 1931. h.m.p. 500 £15 15s. 10 vellum.   S. 1963 £30; H. 1964 £38; S. 1967 unopnd. £45.

M. Drayton. *Works*, ed. J. W. Hebel. 5 vols. 1931-32. £7 17s. 6d.

F. Faust. *Dionysus in Hades.* 1932. 4s 6d.

Brontës. *The S. H. P. Brönte*, ed. T. J. Wise and J. A. Symington. 19 vols. 1932-34. £12 12s.   C. 1963 £160; H. 1964 17 vols. (ex. 19) £125; H. 1965 £165.

Sir W. Scott. *Some Unpublished Letters*, arrang. J. A. Symington. 1932. (1000) 10s 6d.

Sir W. Scott. *New Love Poems.* 1932.

E. B. Browning. *Sonnets from the Portuguese.* 1933. wrpprs. 2s 6d. Cr. 4to. 18s.

Le Morte Darthur, ed. A. H. Bullen. 2 vols. 1933. Hf. leather £19; full leather.

W. Shakespeare. *Works*, S.H.P. 1 vol. edn., 1934. 1000; 10 vellum; trade edn. (cl.) 6s. Hf. leather 10s 6d. American reprint (1289 pp.) publ. O.U.P., N.Y.   Publ. Odhams Press. 1944.

May Morris. *William Morris*... 2 vols. 1934. (750) £2 12s 6d.

May Morris. *William Morris*... 2 vols. 1936. (750) £2 12s 6d.

R. H. Clapperton. *Paper: An Historical Account*... 1935. (60) £6 6s. S. 1963 £26.

J. Hernandez. *The Gaucho Martin Fierro*... 1935. 400 £1 12s.; h.m.p. 50 £5 5s.

The Decameron... 2 vols. 1935. (300) £12 12s. C. 1964 hf. morocco £26; S. 1965 orig. morocco £55; C. 1966 £30.

B. Jonson. *Poems*, ed. B. H. Newdigate. 1936. (750) £1 11s 6d.

A. Pope. *Prose Works*, ed. N. Ault. Vol. 1. 1936. (750) £1 10s.

The Phoenix and Turtle. S.H.Q. 1937.

L. Haberly. *Mediaeval English Pavingtiles*. 1937. (425) £4 4s.

J. Swift. *Works*, ed. H. Davis. 14 vols. 1939-68.   H. 1962 vols. 1-4 & 6-13 £11 10s.; S. 1966 vols. 1-13 £38.

Campden: XXIV engrav. after... F. L. Griggs. 1940.. £2 12s 6d.

S. A. Courtauld (Ed.). *Some Silver Wrought by the Courtauld Family*... privately printed. 1940. (100).

B. H. Newdigate. *Michael Drayton and his Circle*. 1941. 15s.

INDEX